Sustainable Development

T0300156

This groundbreaking new work establishes links between sustainable development, needs, well-being and the capabilities approach that is central to human development and the United Nations Development Programme. By challenging the role of people in sustainability policy, this collection's argument refocuses sustainable development on needs and makes it easier for people to relate positively to its core values. This exciting new book incites a whole new way of looking at sustainable development.

Even though the word 'needs' is central to the most popular definition of sustainable development, the concepts of needs and capabilities remain within the debate on human development, without going further into intergenerational justice or environmental protection. The discussion of needs reaches non-academics in a more direct way than talking about abstract thresholds, substitutability and other issues dear to academic debate on sustainability. This collection links the questions of intra- and intergenerational justice with issues of quality of life, life courses and well-being. Dealing with needs entails dealing with deeper layers of consciousness, revealing emotions and questioning habits and values. In this way, the collection presents an opportunity for substantial social change as well as a challenge for research and policymaking.

This thought-provoking collection asks its readers to reconsider the role of needs based on the philosophical arguments presented, to understand how sustainability can become a part of the capability approach, to better consider the dependency of life chances on birth contingencies, and to see the relationship between capabilities, needs and well-being in a different light. The editors finish by clarifying the possibilities and challenges of a needs-based sustainability policy for policymakers, and explain the role of deeply held values. This book should be of interest to postgraduates and researchers in Environmental and Ecological Economics, as well as many other disciplines including Political Economics, Social Ecology, Human Ecology, Sustainability Science and Developmental Politics.

Felix Rauschmayer is a senior research fellow at the Helmholtz-Centre for Environmental Research, Leipzig, Germany. **Ines Omann** is a senior researcher at the Sustainable Europe Research Institute, Austria. She is also a lecturer in ecological economics and sustainability at the University of Graz and the University of Natural Resources and Applied Life Sciences, Austria. **Johannes Frühmann** is a researcher at the Sustainable Europe Research Institute, Austria.

Routledge studies in ecological economics

Sustainable Development

Capabilities, needs, and well-being

**Edited by Felix Rauschmayer,
Ines Omann and Johannes Frühmann**

LONDON AND NEW YORK

First published 2011
by Routledge
2 Park Square, Milton Park, Abingdon, Oxon OX14 4RN

Simultaneously published in the USA and Canada
by Routledge
711 Third Avenue, New York, NY 10017

Routledge is an imprint of the Taylor & Francis Group, an informa business

First issued in paperback 2011

Typeset in Times by Wearset Ltd, Boldon, Tyne and Wear

British Library Cataloguing in Publication Data
A catalogue record for this book is available from the British Library

Library of Congress Cataloging in Publication Data
Sustainable development: capabilities, needs, and well-being/edited by
Felix Rauschmayer, Ines Omann, and Johannes Frühmann.
p. cm.
Includes bibliographical references and index.
1. Sustainable development. I. Rauschmayer, Felix, 1967– II. Omann,
Ines. III. Frühmann, Johannes.
HC79.E5S86476 2010
338.9'27–dc22   2010018692

ISBN: 978-0-415-58652-8 (hbk)
ISBN: 978-0-415-51681-5 (pbk)
ISBN: 978-0-203-83974-4 (ebk)

Contents

Illustrations

Figures

Tables

Boxes

Contributors

Paul-Marie Boulanger, Director, Institut pour un Développement Durable, Ottignies, Belgium.

Ivonne Cruz, Postdoctoral Research Associate, Harte Research Institute for Gulf of Mexico Studies, Corpus Christi, United States.

Johannes Frühmann, Researcher, SERI – Sustainable Europe Research Institute, Vienna, Austria.

Ortrud Leßmann, Research Fellow, Helmut-Schmidt University. Faculty of Economics and Social Science, Hamburg, Germany.

Manfred Max-Neef, Director Economics Institute, Universidad Austral de Chile, Valdivia, Chile.

Tell Muenzing, Senior Advisor, SustainAbility Ltd., London, UK.

Ines Omann, Scientific Team Leader, SERI – Sustainable Europe Research Institute, Vienna, Austria.

John O'Neill, Professor of Political Economy, University of Manchester, UK.

Luc Van Ootegem, Affiliated Researcher, Higher Institute of Labour Studies (HIVA, KULeuven), Leuven, Belgium; Professor, University College Ghent (Hogeschool Gent), Ghent, Belgium.

Felix Rauschmayer, Senior Researcher, Department of Environmental Politics, UFZ – Helmholtz-Centre for Environmental Research, Leipzig, Germany.

Sophie Spillemaeckers, Senior Research Associate, Higher Institute of Labour Studies, Leuven, Belgium.

Gerben J. Westerhof, Associate Professor, University of Twente, Psychology and Communication of Health and Risk, Enschede, the Netherlands.

Foreword and acknowledgements

In finishing this book, we are filled with joy that we started, continued, and completed this project. Writing, discussing, refining, reading, refereeing, editing etc. was a challenging, exciting and stimulating journey towards our central aim: Make sustainable development alive so that all people, now and in future, can lead a more flourishing life.

The journey included retreats in Vienna and in the Swiss Jura Mountains. Academic discussions as well a systemic constellations, self-inquiry into emotions, values, and needs as well as reflections on logical consistency were some of the travel ingredients.

We are grateful to Rob Langham, Louisa Earls, and their colleagues from Routledge for their encouragement and support, to two anonymous reviewers of the book concept, to Maria Pircher, Anne Wessner and Franziska Dombrowski for their technical support during the editing of the book, and to the general support of our institutes, the UFZ – Helmholtz-Centre for Environmental Research and SERI, Sustainable Europe Research Institute, respectively.

Executive summary

*Felix Rauschmayer, Ines Omann and
Johannes Frühmann**

> Sustainable development is a development that meets the needs of the
> present without compromising the ability of future generations to meet their
> own needs.
>
> (WCED 1987)[1]

Sustainable development (SD) is most prominently defined with respect to the
needs of current and future generations. Political and scientific discussion,
though, refrains from this concept, even though much can be gained by referring
to needs. This book brings together chapters that clarify the concept of needs
directly or relate it to other scientific approaches. On the one hand, there is the
capability approach which is widely used by human development studies and
politics and can thus be utilized for bringing the Brundtland definition of SD into
practice. On the other hand, meeting needs is intrinsically linked to well-being
which is the main driver for human action.

This edited volume takes a new look at the links between needs, capabilities,
well-being and SD. Its *conceptual aim* is to propose and critically discuss these
links from different disciplinary backgrounds (economics, philosophy, sociology, and psychology). Its *political aim* is to restimulate the discussion about
sustainable development.

It is our impression that the discussion about SD does not touch citizens
and decision makers (anymore?). The discretionary use of the term 'sustainable development' or 'sustainability' by politicians and lobby groups discredit
the political aim; very technical scientific discussions (e.g. about substitutability of natural capital) remove the conceptual discussion on SD from its central
goal and from implementation problems alike. In his preface, Max-Neef
pleads for reshaping economics training and research away from questions of
'how to maximize utility' towards the Aristotelian origin of economics, i.e.
oikonomia as the art of living and living well, herewith embracing values,
ethics, and aesthetics. The discussions in this book can be understood in this
perspective.

This book links current attempts that all aim at orienting policy more towards
what really matters:

- Needs approaches take universal human needs as the central criterion f
  human flourishing (Chapters 1, 2, 6);
- The capability approach accentuates human agency freedom for develo]
  mental policy (Chapters 3 and 4);
- Research on well-being and life courses aims at a better and fuller unde
  standing of the relationship between SD and human well-being and li
  course (Chapters 4 and 5).

These approaches are presented together with proposed links on their capacity
address the central societal challenge of sustainable development: intra- ar
intergenerational justice. Whereas more emotions-considering approaches (we]
being/happiness and needs) have the potential to touch and appeal to citizens ar
decision makers, their focus on individuals pose challenges for societal decisio1
making, necessarily involving institutions and organizations. These challeng(
might require more integrative institutions and forms of science and of scientif
policy advice (Chapters 6–8).

The first chapter of this book opens the discussion and proposes an overarcl
ing framework for the concepts dealt with in the subsequent chapters. The:
discuss the different approaches more in detail (Chapters 2–5) and move the di
cussion towards policy or research implications (Chapters 6–8). Chronologicall
the first chapter (written by the three editors) was the starting point for the boo]
Chapters 2–7 have been written following the editors' invitation, and Chapter
is – at least for two of the editors – the end of a first learning experience, havin
read and refereed all earlier chapters.[2] We hope that our work stimulates critiqu
and discussion and that you, the reader, will therefore support us in movin
further in the direction of conceptual clarity and progress towards SD and huma
flourishing.

The following gives brief summaries of all eight chapters.

Needs, capabilities and quality of life: refocusing sustainable development

Felix Rauschmayer, Ines Omann and Johannes Frühmann

This chapter explains why refocusing on needs, capabilities, and quality of li]
can make SD more appealing to politicians, scholars and citizens alike. Th
authors develop a framework, according to which capabilities are crucial t
meeting needs, which in turn triggers well-being. Capabilities and well-being ar
the main constituents of quality of life. The framework links the main topics c
the book and is the starting point for the journey of linking sustainable develop
ment, capabilities, needs, well-being and quality of life. Human flourishin
emerges by an ongoing process, focusing more on the eudaimonic aspects c
well-being than its hedonic components.

SD policy is reformulated as an expression of particular values aimed ¿
encouraging people and societies to develop specific capabilities. Those wi

enable people to select certain strategies over others for meeting their needs so that *all* people – both those living now and in the future – can have a decent quality of life. Conception of SD policy should be based on capabilities, needs and quality of life rather than on the frameworks currently used, which usually relate to the three dimensions environment, economy and society. This provides important points of reference for the methods used in designing and evaluating SD policies. Refocusing SD policies on needs comes closer to what really matters to people and can even be a starting point on how to approach intergenerational justice.

The overshadowing of needs

John O'Neill

Discussions of sustainability in economics have shifted from the needs-based formulation of the concept in the Brundtland report to the preference-based formulation that is standard in welfare economics. This chapter contrasts the logical features of the concepts of need and preference and suggests that the characterization of the concept of sustainability in terms of needs has both theoretical and practical virtues which disappear in the shift to the language of preferences. A needs-based approach captures the plurality of different constituents of well-being, and the limits to the substitutability between different kinds of goods that the current generation must pass on to future generations if human welfare is to be maintained. It offers a better account of the nature and seriousness of the ethical obligations that are owed both to the poor in current generations and to future generations. It provides a more adequate starting point for the acknowledgement of forms of human dependence and vulnerability that informs basic concerns with sustainability. In developing these arguments this chapter also addresses the questions of the relative merits of needs-based and capabilities-based approaches to welfare and sustainability, and examine how far they can be reconciled.

Sustainability as a challenge to the capability approach

Ortrud Leßmann

The capability approach (CA) was developed by Amartya Sen and Martha Nussbaum as an approach to the evaluation of individual well-being and social welfare. The chapter shows some difficulties of conceptualizing SD in the CA which has not been a priority for CA scholars so far. It does so in three steps.

The chapter first outlines the basic concepts employed by the CA which defines a person's well-being in terms of the beings and doings (the functionings) a person achieves and her capability to choose among different combinations of such functionings. Capability reflects the freedom to lead one way of life or the other and achieve well-being whereas the achievements are represented by the functionings attained. Since people may have objectives other than personal well-being, the CA distinguishes between well-being goals and agency goals.

The chapter then hints at some problems for conceptualizing sustainability within the CA. First, the CA is not opposed to the understanding of well-being in terms of needs, but capabilities provide an understanding that goes further in important ways. Second, the CA focuses on intragenerational justice and has to be augmented with a longer time horizon in order to analyse intergenerational justice. Third, the CA has not taken up the discussion on ecosystem services yet, nor outlined the process of how functionings are produced in much detail.

Finally, sustainability is defined on the social level and demands immediate political action, whereas the CA provides foremost a measure for the evaluation of well-being on the individual level. This part of the chapter argues that since the CA conceives of individuals as social beings it has the potential to overcome these contrasts and meet the challenge of SD.

The last part concludes by summarizing which questions are the most pressing when striving for a conception of SD within the CA.

From individual well-being to sustainable development: a path where psychologists and economists meet

Sophie Spillemaeckers, Luc Van Ootegem and Gerben J. Westerhof

SD aims at meeting the needs of current and future generations. Although there is an international consensus that well-being is a right for all and that future generations are to be considered, many see SD as too complex, or too threatening for their own well-being. In this chapter economic and psychological theories are brought together to unveil some of this complexity and to find some explanations for this recalcitrance.

To analyse the well-being of a population indicators are needed. This chapter addresses the shortcomings of utilitarian indicators, such as those based on income, resources or happiness, describes alternatives proposed by economic and psychological sciences, and discusses where these converge.

From an economic perspective, a *capabilities model of well-being* was developed making use of the capabilities approach and current research on basic needs. The challenge remains to use and adapt this model such that it can be used for those aspects of SD that go beyond individual well-being.

From a psychological perspective, the *eudaimonic approach* of flourishing is promising. It also goes beyond the hedonic fixation on happiness and takes into account the individual's self-realization as well as social integration in defining a good life. The challenge remains to integrate this psychological perspective into the capabilities and SD approaches.

The life-chances concept: a sociological perspective in equity and sustainable development

Paul-Marie Boulanger

This chapter is mainly devoted to the exploration and discussion of the encompassing concept of life chances as a more sociological way to look at well-being, justice and SD. The dominant discourses on well-being in terms of welfare, capability or needs generally adopt a somewhat individualistic and static perspective, probably because of the influence exerted by economists in the public and political debate. It is argued that *life-chances* and *life-course* approaches bring additional information with respect to what both the capability-functioning and the needs-satisfaction perspectives carry. In particular, they draw our attention to the impact of the totally contingent circumstances of birth on individual prospects in terms of longevity, health, career opportunities, income, wealth, power, autonomy, etc. Indeed, the life-chances and life-course approaches insist on two fundamental interdependent characteristics of human life: its social structural embedding and its sequencing in well-differentiated periods correspond to different roles and status and therefore to different needs and capabilities.

SD is then looked at in a life-chances perspective and presented as a global justice endeavour aiming at guaranteeing sufficient life chances to all, irrespective of the contingent spatial-temporal circumstances of birth. The notion of sufficient life chances is interpreted in a twofold way: as a minimum set of options and opportunities in terms of livelihoods, and as options and opportunities guaranteeing the satisfaction of an extended Rawlsian set of basic needs.

Human needs frameworks and their contribution as analytical instruments in sustainable development policymaking

Ivonne Cruz

The conclusions and recommendations of the Brundtland report (WCED 1987) gained broad acceptance as it described the urgent need for humanity to make development sustainable ensuring that it meets the needs of the present without compromising the ability of future generations to meet their own needs. Meeting essential human needs however requires not only political systems aiming to promote participation in decision making but the acknowledgement of people's values in the building of a new society coherent with its aspirations.

This chapter presents some of the challenges faced in SD policymaking processes as to how they include different valuable aspects of natural and human systems. The *Human-Scale Development approach* is proposed as a resourceful framework to incorporate human needs debates in sustainable policymaking. Due to the particular way this approach defines well-being dimensions and how needs and satisfiers interrelate with each other, it provides a holistic setting and therefore a proposal for SD policy consideration. The chapter describes a methodology to guide policy processes pursuing holistic sustainability outcomes, herewith developing an innovative feature to guide integrated SD policy for present and future generations.

A plea for the self-aware sustainability researcher: learning from business transformation processes for transitions to sustainable development

Felix Rauschmayer, Tell Muenzing and Johannes Frühmann

This chapter looks at transition processes towards SD from the perspective of the researcher. It relies on experiences in business and distinguishes the internal context of the individual (such as knowledge, beliefs, values, priorities, and needs) from the external context (such as resources, regulation, infrastructure or culture). Both, the deeper internal *roots* of behaviour and their *interplay* with the external context should be more considered in designing and implementing transition processes towards SD.

In order to analyse behaviour and its contextual factors in more detail the chapter introduces a 4-quadrant model differentiating between two complementary dimensions: inside/outside and individual/collective. If behaviour transformation is meant to be sustainable, change has to happen in the internal-individual perspective – as deep-seated needs and values are the main motivational factors for human behaviour and the working material for behavioural transformation.

With an example from the business sector the chapter shows how behavioural transformation can be achieved and sustained and how the new emerging (and more sustainable) system can be aligned better through such a multiperspective approach. Furthermore, the example highlights which capabilities and skills are necessary for the facilitator to work with concepts such as needs and values in the process. The facilitator (often replaced by the researcher in cases of SD transition processes) has to be able to access and focus on the deeper layers of consciousness, and s/he needs high levels of emotional intelligence, deep listening skills, and to be able to work with empathy. Transformation does not come from intellect.

In order to develop research methods further, researchers will therefore have to gain the experience of personal transformation processes and ability to understand, lead, and facilitate such processes. This requires new forms of training and personal engagement.

Transition towards sustainable development: which tensions emerge? How do we deal with them?

Ines Omann and Felix Rauschmayer

'I want to bring my children (aged six and ten) safely to school. It is raining outside, we are late. They could go there by public transport, which means a walk of five minutes, a tram for ten minutes and a bus for eight minutes. There is the car, today I have got time, because I am not working in the morning. What shall I – as a person who wants to live a sustainable lifestyle and be a role model for my kids – do?'

The case just described shows a typical situation in our Western societies faced by people, who see sustainable development as an important value. The current chapter describes three possible classes of such tensions: (1) intra-individual, (2) intra-societal and (3) intergenerational. They only arise if a transition towards SD is wanted. The authors explain in the beginning of the chapter why they want such a transition. Reasons are found in culture, socialization, belief systems, values and emotions.

The next section goes deeper into the three classes of tensions and brings real life examples of those. The reasons behind action (beliefs, values, needs) are usually not seen; only the behaviour is obvious. We therefore suggest dealing with these tensions by looking exactly to the issues that are not easily seen.

This can be done in a four-step process, which starts by recognizing the tension(s), followed by a reflection upon the possible reasons for these tensions (beliefs, values, needs). The result of this reflection can be communicated and discussed between the persons concerned or with the public. These steps prepare for the last step, the creativity process for finding solutions.

In the last section we refer to the framework of the first chapter of this book and show where the tensions can be placed and which leverage points are given for measures and activities to overcome these tensions.

Notes

* With contributions from John O'Neill, Ortrud Leßmann, Sophie Spillemaeckers, Luc Van Ootegem, Gerben J. Westerhof, Paul-Marie Boulanger, Ivonne Cruz, Tell Muenzing and Manfred Max-Neef.
1 WCED (United Nations World Commission on Environment and Development) (1987) *Our Common Future*, online, available at: www.un-documents.net/wced-ocf.htm [accessed 3 April 2010].
2 Each chapter has been refereed by at least two peers.

Preface

The death and rebirth of economics

Manfred Max-Neef

The increasing concern about sustainability and its different approaches, interpretations, indicators and strategies, is the result of the way in which economics has evolved as a discipline. There is a direct correlation between sustainability as a preoccupation and the imposition of the neoliberal ideology as the dominant economic model. Before 1970 sustainability had not even emerged as a concept. Economics has, obviously, not always been the same. Its development has been a succession of bifurcations between alternative visions, with a clear tendency of that alternative which best favours wealth and power always becoming dominant. Neoliberalism is not only the culmination of such a tendency, but it also represents, as we shall see, the death of true economics.

Aristotle, in the introductory chapters of his *Politics*, made a clear distinction between what he called *oikonomia*, meaning the management of the household, and *krematistike*, meaning the art of acquisition. Aristotle's *oikonomia* concerned domains related to the production, and reproduction, of use-values such as agriculture, crafts, hunting and gathering, mining and even warfare. *Oikonomia* embraced values, ethics and aesthetics as fundamental conditions for the attainment of its final goal which is, 'the art of living and living well'. Commerce (chrematistics) being concerned with the art of money-making – accumulation of exchange-values through trade – was considered by the philosopher as secondary from logical and historical points of view. Exchange-value had to logically be subordinate to use-value. What we have today is exactly the opposite. What we call economics in our present world is in reality not economics, but chrematistics. Economics no longer exists!!

The chapters contained in this book are all contributions for the reconstruction of economics. Human needs, quality of life, values, well-being and sustainability are, of course, inseparable parts of 'the art of living and living well'. Certainly none of these have any relation to the neoliberal ideology, concerned exclusively with growth and accumulation in monetary terms.

The reconstruction of economics is a colossal change from what we have. Now, if we want to change something, we must first understand the origins of that which we want to change. Neoliberalism, the late offspring of neoclassical economics, has become the political ideology that dominates almost all economics departments in our universities. In fact it has been the universities that gave rise to neoliberalism, and continue to be its enthusiastic promoters as the only definitive and respectable school of economic thought. I am, therefore, convinced that no significant changes can be expected unless the teaching of economics undergoes a deep transformation.

Where does neoliberalism come from? The story begins almost a century and a half ago, in 1870, when economists made a case to demonstrate that economics was a science just as much as Newtonian physics. The most important economists of the time, Stanley Jevons and Leon Walras, were simply fascinated with classical mechanics. Hence, they had to develop a model that had similar properties with the model of the universe designed by Newton. Just as Newtonian physics proposed gravitation as a universal law describing the behaviour of the universe, neoclassical economists had to devise a similar universal law capable of describing the behaviour of human beings. Such a universal law turned out to be 'utility'; meaning that every human being always behaves and acts in such a way as to maximize his/her utility.

Walras in his *Elements of Pure Economics* (1877) declares that 'this pure theory of economics is a science which resembles the physico-mathematical sciences in every respect'. The way of demonstrating this 'every respect' was achieved through the imposition of fanatical mathematical formalisms that have no relation whatsoever with real-life economics.

The neoclassical fabrication was successful enough as to be accepted as legitimate by the academic community. However, it coexisted with other visions which were considered as legitimate, like the institutional economics proposed by Veblen and others. During the 1930s, without disappearing, it was off-sided by Keynesianism, yet continued to coexist with it as well as with other approaches like those proposed by the Marxians. Other schools like Post-Keynesians, Austrian, Behaviourist and Feminist added their own contributions up to the late 1960s. Up to then students like me had the choice of multiple perspectives when analysing economic problems, and courses such as Economic History and History of Economic Thought (now completely vanished from the curricula) were fundamental in every department of economics.

The extraordinary thing about nineteenth century neoclassical economics, in its neoliberal version, is that it has achieved its final triumph in the late twentieth century. This is amazing indeed. In fact, we no longer have a physics of the nineteenth century, nor do we have nineteenth century biology or astronomy or geology or engineering any more. All sciences have shown a permanent evolution. Economics is the only exception where problems of the twenty-first century are supposed to be interpreted, analysed and understood using nineteenth century theories. In a necrological impulse, 'mainstream' economists of today look for guidance and inspiration in a cemetery of 150 years ago, as if nothing had happened ever since. This is preposterous, to say the least, and the fact that universities go along with it is an epistemological scandal of immense proportions.

The conspicuous facts that during 2008 and 2009 have shown that the neoliberal doctrine is not only wrong, but poisonous, seem not to disturb the 'mainstream' economists that still control the immense majority of the economics departments. If those economists, in the wake of the present global disaster, would at least slightly resemble the attitude of natural scientists, they would recognize and confess the inadequacy of their theories, and proclaim the urgent need for designing or accepting new ones. Nothing of the sort is happening, and we still have, instead of economic education, economic indoctrination.

From the point of view of a 'normal' academic mind, it is really difficult to understand how such an unreal, simplistic and dogmatic intellectual construction has managed to seduce and even to convince academia, politicians and the general public that the fantasy world from which its conclusions are drawn, is actually the real world. Edward Fullbrook illustrates this well:[1]

> In the neoclassical make-believe world everything, like in a fairytale, works wondrously well. There is never any unemployment, markets of all kinds always clear instantly; everyone gets exactly what they deserve; market outcomes are invariably 'optimal'; everyone maximizes their potential; and all citizens possess a crystal ball that infallibly foresees the future. In this axiomatic paradise (without messy things like social beings, institutions, history, culture, ethics, religion, human development and the indeterminacy that always accompanies freedom) there is no government ownership, no regulation, no corporate accountability, no building codes, no health and safety laws, no collective bargaining rights, no food standards, no controls on oligopoly and monopoly, no welfare, no public health departments, etc. etc. Instead there are just 'markets'. Markets, markets, markets. For those who take the model literally, the solution to all human problems is to make the real world more like the neoclassical make-believe world. All you need are markets. If you can't yet get rid of something that is not a market, then make it look like a market. That is the central idea of neoliberalism. Simpleminded? Of course. Deluded? Totally. But … it can be applied to virtually everything.

This must come to an end, because economists trained according to these fantasies, end up being like idiot savants. Geniuses when playing with mathematical symbols, but total ignoramuses about the real world in which they live.

To continue promoting a poisonous ideology disguised as science is suicidal. The cure is certainly not easy, but is has begun. This book is a clear demonstration of such an effort. The next step should be the awakening of economics departments and their willingness to offer, as in the 1950s and 1960s, the multiplicity of economic visions, so that students can make their choices based on all the accumulated knowledge contained in the development of their discipline. The necessary creativity to understand the realities of our new century can only occur in the realm of intellectual plurality and freedom.

> What we have now, are two parallel worlds. One 'mainstream' still anchored in the economics departments, immune to all messages and evidences that might bring about any change, and the 'alternatives' (like those in this book)

dispersed all over the place, perceived by the 'mainstream' as subversive agents, still incapable of bringing about the fall of the neoliberal wall. Sooner or later, however, the wall will collapse. We are in the situation so lucidly described by the great Max Planck over one hundred years ago, when he was faced with the orthodoxy of the Maxwellian physicists: 'A new scientific truth does not triumph by convincing its opponents and making them see the light, but rather because its opponents eventually die, and a new generation grows up that is familiar with it'.[2]

The situation in which we are now is precisely that of a growing new generation waiting to attend the funeral of the 'official' holders of the truth.

The contributors of this book are members of that new generation. The fact that human needs, well-being and quality of life are to become again the fundamental aim of sustainable development is encouraging indeed. It was in 1986 that colleagues and I proposed the principles of Human Scale Development and its human needs theory that were published by the Dag Hammarskjöld Foundation of Sweden, in Spanish first, and two years later in English. It generated almost immediate interest and enthusiasm not only among alternative groups but, surprisingly, among many peasant communities in South America. We were really astonished when we realized that the original Spanish version became in those days the most photocopied document on the continent. We used to arrive in Andean communities to be approached by local leaders with a photocopy of a photocopy of a photocopy, almost unreadable, ready to discuss whether their interpretation was correct and whether their projects satisfied the philosophy of Human Scale Development. It was moving to witness how such marginal communities adopted the principles and designed development projects that conventional experts would have been unable to conceive. Some of these projects have survived and flourished successfully until today. A conspicuous case is the Asociación de Desarrollo Campesino (Peasant Development Association) in the South of Colombia that even organizes, every few years, an international symposium with distinguished guests who spend three days discussing development with the peasants and with their children, as equals, in fascinating round tables. In fact the next symposium has taken place in July 2010.

The first lesson that we learned from those experiences, was that the language of Human Scale Development and its needs theory can easily be understood by simple people who lack any formal education, apart from a few years in primary school. The second lesson learned was that no true development can succeed without the understanding, participation and creativity of the people themselves. The third lesson was that which mobilizes the common people does not necessarily mobilize academics. In fact what took the peasants almost no time to understand, took about 15 years to generate interest in Human Scale Development at academic levels. Now it is finally in, and its human needs theory is recognized as one of the most important contributions in the field.

Human needs, capabilities, quality of life and well-being is what people understand. Not the abstraction of macroeconomic indicators that have nothing to do with real life. Development is about people and not about objects. The fact that once again, as this book shows, we are willing to rediscover and respect human feelings and the value of all manifestations of life, means that a better world is possible. In a way it feels like a fascinating voyage back to the origins.

So, why not finish this Preface with a little Aristotelian dream? Let us imagine that economics becomes again the manner of managing the household in order to achieve *the art of living and living well*, respecting the right of all others to achieve the same, and within the limits of the carrying capacity of our planet.

To all the contributors of this book: Strength, Determination and Good Luck!

Notes

1 Edward Fullbrook, 'Economics and neoliberalism', in G. Hassan (ed.), *After Blair: Politics After the New Labour Decade*, 2007, London: Lawrence and Wishart.
2 Philip Smith and Manfred Max-Neef, *Unmasked Economics*, to be published by Green Books, UK, in October 2010.

1 Needs, capabilities and quality of life

Refocusing sustainable development

Felix Rauschmayer, Ines Omann and Johannes Frühmann

Introduction: back to the sources of sustainable development

> Sustainable development is a development that meets the needs of the present without compromising the ability of future generations to meet their own needs.
>
> (WCED 1987)

While many scientific and policy papers state that the concept of needs is central to the Brundtland definition of sustainable development (SD), it is usually absent from subsequent discussion (Boulanger 2008; Jackson *et al.* 2004; Mebratu 1998). Instead, these papers go on to discuss goods and services, poverty, natural capital, decision making structures, approaches, concepts, strategies, models and so on. It may be appropriate not to discuss needs explicitly if the issues discussed instead (such as natural capital) are closely linked to needs. This is rarely the case, however. Apart from a recent paper by Cruz *et al.* (2009), we have found no discussion of this issue in the literature, meaning that there has been no exploration of the reasons why this concept, which is central to the original definition of SD, so quickly disappears off the radar in the SD debate.

We suggest three possible explanations for this omission. (1) Needs are often understood (as in the Brundtland report) in terms of basic material necessities such as food, water and shelter, and are therefore readily associated with the issue of more economic growth and – to a lesser extent – a more equitable distribution of resources in the present and the maintenance of natural capital to secure ecosystem services in the longer term. (2) As a scientific concept, needs – as we understand them here – are usually linked to psychology and thus to decisions made by individuals in their everyday lives. Sustainable development, by contrast, is generally understood as a societal issue related to policy decisions. Only a few publications exist that link SD and personal decision making. These include an early study on a sustainable Germany (BUND and Misereor 1996) and the RESOLVE project (University of Surrey, UK). (3) Making needs a key concept requires a thoroughgoing conceptual shift in core elements of economic, sociological, philosophical and environmentalist paradigms. Referring to the philosophical debate, Wiggins (2005) has the impression that many people shy

away from such profound change. In the following sections of this chapter, v
hope to provide good reasons for explanations (2) and (3).

Current ways of rendering SD operational (e.g. via material flows and oth
ecological criteria, the triangle of sustainability, triple bottom lines, or utili
accounting such as happiness economics) have not had the desired effect of ge
erating a paradigm of a different understanding of development on which pol
ical decisions can be based. And although the concept of SD has been use
increasingly in policy rhetoric and the media over the last 20 years, a genuin
transition towards SD has not yet begun.

In this chapter, which comes from a perspective of researchers working
industrialized countries, we argue that a broader understanding of needs
required that goes beyond the notion of basic material necessities and opens ι
new avenues for refocusing SD and putting it into practice. Reframing SD
line with a broader understanding of needs would impact on personal ar
policy-related decisions alike and can be achieved by further elaborating tl
capability approach (see below, section on the capability approach, as well ;
Leßmann, Chapter 3, and Spillemaeckers *et al.*, Chapter 4). Our argume
draws on ideas found in economic, philosophical, psychological and sociolog
cal literature (cf. Alkire 2002). In the following, we define needs as the mo
fundamental dimensions of human flourishing. Actions intended to meet the;
needs require no further explanation or justification, and a heightened awar
ness of needs being met is accompanied by positive emotions (and a decrease
negative emotions).

It is not clear, though, how the terms 'capabilities', 'resources', 'income' ar
'needs' are related to one other and to the idea of 'meeting the needs of prese
and future generations'. Which concept of needs lies behind the Brundtland def
nition? Is there a clear link between needs, sustainable development and quali
of life, a term increasingly used in research and policy? And what is the link ι
Sen's and/or Nussbaum's capability approach?[1]

The aim of our chapter is, first and foremost, to contribute towards clarifyir
these links. Our hope is that such clarification may revive debate about tr
objectives of sustainable development, taking it beyond the commonly use
approach 'balancing' environmental, economic and social concerns and tr
rather jaded debate about weak and strong sustainability, which is linked to tr
question of the substitutability of different kinds of capital. In addition, we hop
to build a foundation on which policy decisions related to SD can be based. Ou
second major aim is to make the concept of SD[2] more appealing by creatin
robust links to the notion of quality of life and human well-being (cf. Costan;
et al. 2007; Dodds 1997).

The chapter is structured as follows.

First, we clarify the meaning of the different concepts – 'needs', 'strategies
'values', 'capabilities', 'well-being' and 'quality of life' – addressed in th
chapter. Our approach is based on an integrated model of quality of life. It relate
to both objective conditions (reflected and valued by capabilities) and subjectiv
perceptions (well-being). These two are linked in turn by the dual concepts c

strategies and needs, which occupy a central position in the model we propose. As we will show, distinguishing between needs and strategies is crucial to making meaningful use of the needs concept in (SD) policy processes. In the third section we explain the link between our approach and SD. First, we explain how the way we understand SD changes when the needs concept is refined and redeployed. Needs-based SD policies generate a new kind of dynamics and to some extent require different methods from the ones currently used for decision support. We demonstrate this by discussing the German 'cash for old bangers' programme. In our concluding section, we outline the future prospects and open questions emerging from a refocusing of SD.

It is clear to us that some of our concepts remain rather vague and leave quite a few issues unaddressed. Quite a few of these will be taken up by the subsequent chapters of this book. Chapter 8 (Rauschmayer and Omann) will address the tensions that arise when one decides to undertake a transition to sustainable development. We hope that by elaborating our refocusing and its implications for SD policy and research, we will stimulate a fresh debate that links SD in a tangible way to meeting the needs of those who are currently underprivileged and of future generations. Ultimately our hope is that an improved quality of life for all will be made possible.

Needs, capabilities and quality of life

Needs

According to Gasper (1996), the term 'needs' has three generic meanings which feed into three types of analysis respectively: (a) descriptive analysis: needs are understood as positive entities related to some form of want or desire; (b) instrumental analysis: needs are understood as requisites for meeting a given end; (c) normative analysis: needs are understood as justified or priority requisites. Many studies rely on all three meanings at the same time and, for example, try to draw normative legitimacy from an empirically observed importance of instrumental needs.

In the following, based on (b) above, we take human flourishing in its fullest sense (Alkire 2002) as the given end[3] and understand needs as final requisites for achieving this end. While in everyday language goods or services that satisfy a specific need are themselves called 'needs' (e.g. 'I need a beer'), we will restrict usage of the term 'need' to the level immediately preceding the ultimate aim of human flourishing. In the context of an action-oriented framework, one might use the definition offered by the philosopher Finnis: we call needs such reasons for action that require no further reason (Grisez *et al.* 1987: 103); if a person is asked why she does something, she cannot reasonably refer to any other end than that of her good life.

By restricting the use of the word 'need' in this way, our aim is to achieve greater clarity with respect to the different levels of argument about why a person desires a particular good or service (see O'Neill, Chapter 2 in this book, for a wider discussion on needs). Does this good or service contribute to meeting a specific need? Is this need a constitutive aspect of full human flourishing?

There are many different lists of needs in circulation. In this chapter, rather than debating the relative preferability of one list or the other, we draw on the work of Sabina Alkire. Alkire (2002) compared lists of basic dimensions of human well-being deriving from the fields of moral philosophy, psychology, economics and development studies. She found few basic differences between them. Here, for pragmatic reasons, we base our discussion on Max-Neef's list of needs, which seems to be most relevant to the topic of our chapter, in that it is oriented not towards ideas about individual well-being or individual poverty but towards projects aimed at societal development. Max-Neef and his collaborators (Max-Neef *et al.* 1991) proposed a list of nine needs:[4] SUBSISTENCE, PROTECTION, AFFECTION, UNDERSTANDING, PARTICIPATION, IDLENESS, CREATION, IDENTITY, FREEDOM, to which (following Costanza *et al.* 2007) we add TRANSCENDENCE, as suggested by Max-Neef and colleagues (Max-Neef *et al.* 1991: 27).

The idea that these needs can be subsumed under a single rubric (such as utility) is neither convincing nor especially conducive to the aim of achieving full human flourishing. By contrast, multi-dimensional frameworks make it possible to evaluate pros and cons and to explicate dilemmas within a societal decision-making process; they also help to reveal any unintended side effects of decisions (cf. O'Neill *et al.* 2008: Chapter 5).

The categorization of needs into various irreducible, non-hierarchical and incommensurable dimensions, or categories, which are nonetheless interrelated and interactive, has been found by several studies to be helpful (see Alkire 2002; Max-Neef 1991). Several authors claim these needs are universal (e.g. Max-Neef *et al.* 1991; Rosenberg 2001; Nussbaum 2000; in a weaker sense also Alkire 2002), whereas opinions differ with regard to the finiteness of the categories. To our way of thinking, the question of the finiteness of the dimensions is not significant in terms of developing the conceptualization of quality of life further or even for rendering it operational. In a concrete context of implementation participants might agree to add another need, split one category in two or three, or to neglect one category. This does not endanger the project of defining local quality of life and the links of SD with it. The idea of universal needs, though, becomes important when decisions are being made on behalf of people who are not present, as well as for the social dynamics involved in devising common strategies. This idea has a philosophical and anthropological foundation that can be debated – leading this discussion is not the focus of this chapter, though.

Needs and strategies

Max-Neef and his collaborators developed a matrix of needs and axiological categories (Table 1.1) largely on the basis of small-scale workshops held in small communities in Latin America (Max-Neef *et al.* 1991). Table 1.1 builds on Max-Neef's list of fundamental human needs. Divided into four existential categories – being, having, doing and interacting – the matrix lists examples of strategies

Table 1.1 Matrix of needs including examples of corresponding strategies in four categories (adapted from Max-Neef et al. 1991: 32–33)

Existential categories/ fundamental human needs	Being (qualities)	Having (things)	Doing (actions)	Interacting (settings)
SUBSISTENCE	physical and mental health	food, shelter, work	feed, clothe, rest, work	living environment, social setting
PROTECTION	care, adaptability, autonomy	social security, health systems, work	cooperate, plan, take care of, help	social environment, dwelling
AFFECTION	respect, sense of humour, generosity, sensuality	friendships, family, relationships with nature	share, take care of, make love, express emotions	privacy, intimate spaces of togetherness
UNDERSTANDING	critical capacity, curiosity, intuition	literature, teachers, policies, educational	analyse, study, meditate, investigate	schools, families, universities, communities
PARTICIPATION	receptiveness, dedication, sense of humour	responsibilities, duties, work, rights	cooperate, dissent, express opinions	associations, parties, churches, neighbourhoods
IDLENESS	imagination, tranquillity, spontaneity	games, parties, peace of mind	day-dream, remember, relax, have fun	landscapes, intimate spaces, places to be alone
CREATION	imagination, boldness, inventiveness, curiosity	abilities, skills, work, techniques	invent, build, design, work, compose, interpret	spaces for expression, workshops, audiences
IDENTITY	sense of belonging, self-esteem, consistency	language, religions, work, customs, values, norms	get to know oneself, grow, commit oneself	places one belongs to, everyday settings
FREEDOM	autonomy, passion, self-esteem, open-mindedness	equal rights	dissent, choose, run risks, develop awareness	anywhere
TRANSCENDENCE	inner centeredness, presence	religions, rites	pray, meditate, develop awareness	places for worship

(or 'satisfiers' as Max-Neef calls them) to meet these needs. The 'being' column lists personal or collective attributes (expressed as nouns). The 'having' column lists institutions, norms, mechanisms, tools (not in a material sense), laws, etc. The 'doing' column lists personal or collective actions (expressed as verbs). The 'interacting' column lists locations and milieus. We understand these categories more in an instrumental than in a fundamental way: they remind the participants that 'having' is not the only way of meeting one's need for IDLENESS, for example. Particularly for rich countries with a high degree of materialization, moving away from 'having' towards other ways of meeting one's needs is certainly a significant way to reduce resource consumption and protect natural resources. It is important to note that the needs are abstract; they are neither substitutes for one another, nor do they conflict with one other. Conflicts arise only at the level of specific negotiable strategies.

Such a matrix can be used (and developed further) to take stock of existing goods and services and to highlight the ways in which they (or the social or natural systems providing these goods and services) contribute to or inhibit the fulfilment of needs (Pick and Poortinga 2005). While some goods and services can be seen clearly in some situations as strategies to meet one specific need, they very often meet or fail to meet several other needs at the same time. For example, at an individual level, having a car (strategy) may meet a person's needs for AFFECTION, IDLENESS and FREEDOM, but it may also inhibit their FREEDOM in the sense that after having bought a car, the person has less money available for buying goods and services to meet other needs. It is important to note that a clear link between the effects of a strategy and the needs met by this strategy can only be drawn by the subjects impacted by the strategy. Observers might guess – but cannot ultimately be sure of – the needs-related reasons a person has for buying a car; this guess is informed by knowledge about the social, environmental and psychological structure within which the decision to buy a car is embedded. At a societal level, the deforestation of a watershed might endanger long-term PROTECTION, AFFECTION (relation with nature), TRANSCENDENCE, IDENTITY and SUBSISTENCE, while increasing PROTECTION and SUBSISTENCE in the short term.

The dynamic results of such needs-based approaches, which unify social and personal development (e.g. Rosenberg 2001), are similar: focusing on needs and linking strategies to needs 'allow[s] for the discovery of unexpected facets of a problem, thus increasing awareness about what [is] relevant' (Max-Neef *et al.* 1991: 43). A clear dynamic evolves in the process of clarifying the relationship between strategies and needs: clarifying the reasons why I might want to buy a car (i.e. the needs I want to meet with it) and the reasons that inhibit me from doing so (i.e. my unmet needs) enables me to consider whether other strategies might not be better suited to meeting my needs; and it enables me to consider whether some of the original needs I had now seem less important in the light of newly emerging ones, for example. The relationship between strategies and needs also shifts over time. For example, smoking may contribute to AFFECTION in the short term, but this might change over time or in different social and cultural settings; smoking may also compromise or destroy a longer term human need for SUBSISTENCE: health.

The capability approach

The capability approach (CA) 'is a broad normative framework for the evaluation of individual well-being and social arrangements, the design of policies and proposals about social change in society' (Robeyns 2003: 5). It was developed by economist Amartya Sen and philosopher Martha Nussbaum and evaluates human well-being according to capabilities, meaning what people do or are and what they are able to do or to be. Capabilities are oriented towards the kind of life that people, upon reflection, find valuable. This aim, as well as the capabilities themselves, depends on the cultural context and on the capital (human, produced, natural, financial, social) available to the individual. By realizing capabilities through the implementation of strategies (or by turning capabilities into achieved functionings, to use Sen's language), needs get met and well-being arises.

A major feature of the CA is the importance of FREEDOM: it is not only the functionings, or the resulting well-being that counts, but the FREEDOM for each and every one to lead a life they judge to be valuable, i.e. the set of capabilities available to them. It therefore takes a liberal perspective on quality of life. It differs from mere resource-oriented approaches by acknowledging the cultural and contextual contingency of capabilities. Sen defines agency freedom as the 'freedom to achieve whatever the person, as a responsible person, decides he or she should achieve' (Sen 1985). So agency relates directly to FREEDOM but can also be expressed on a social level through participation (Alkire 2005). Whereas Sen distinguishes between the well-being and the agency aspect of a person – the former relating to his or her personal advantage, the latter to everything that might matter for this person (Sen 1987: Chapter 3) – we use well-being differently (see next but one section).

From capabilities to needs

We can distinguish between different levels of strategies. For example:

- income is a strategy to buy a book;
- a book is a strategy to get information;
- information is a strategy to acquire the knowledge necessary to take part in a discussion;
- taking part is a strategy to meet one's need for PARTICIPATION, AFFECTION and UNDERSTANDING.

Each strategy on each level is a part of the capability set. For example, I need certain resources to buy a book (e.g. income, bookseller, a shared understanding of what it means 'to buy') and the actual agency to buy a specific kind of book (something that was very limited in Maoist China, for example) which will help me to gain the knowledge to enable me to take part in a discussion which, finally, meets my needs. Strictly speaking, only the 'taking part' level can be called a capability. 'However, both in reality and in Sen's more applied work, these distinctions often blur' (Robeyns 2003: 6).

Preferences, wants or desires, as understood by mainstream economics, usually relate to market goods or services. Other types of goods and services such as many ecosystem goods and services have been integrated as well into economic reasoning (Millennium Ecosystem Assessment 2005; Stern *et al.* 2006; European Communities 2008). Even rather abstract capabilities have been reclassified as quasi-market goods, e.g. in contingent valuation studies on the beauty of landscapes or other economic valuation studies on the economic value of education.

In a few rare cases, specific goods approximate closely to abstract needs (e.g. water for SUBSISTENCE), but in most cases, the functional relations are more complicated – function and meaning often vary within different contexts. A specific food, for example, has certain nutritional, cultural and social characteristics which enable or inhibit us with regard to possessing specific capabilities to meet specific needs (e.g. a bowl of rice meets different needs for a starving person than for a well-fed person; it meets different needs in Asia than it does in Argentina, or in a Buddhist temple than in a sushi restaurant).

Needs, as we understand them, are abstract, universal and fundamental for human flourishing; the strategies chosen to meet needs, however, are specific and negotiable. This distinction is crucial in the way it impacts on the process of negotiation leading to public decisions and policies – any participant can acknowledge (and connect with) the needs of any other participant without necessarily accepting the strategies the other has chosen to meet this need. While the FREEDOM, say, of each participant is not subject to negotiation, the strategies motivated by this need (such as extensive car travel) may be questioned and negotiated. This distinction highlights the role of culture, of course of life (see Boulanger, Chapter 5 of this book) and of resource availability in the selection of different strategies (or capabilities).

Distinguishing between needs and different levels of strategies can also be used as a means of conceptualizing the story lines which, according to O'Neill, Holland and Light, are necessary for decision making related to sustainable development (O'Neill *et al.* 2008, Chapter 11); it is also a means of identifying the level of capabilities to be influenced by a particular public policy.

From needs to well-being to quality of life

Of the many definitions of well-being that exist (e.g. Dodds 1997), we focus on enduring, overall life satisfaction, as this seems to be the most salient aim of policy (Veenhofen 2000). Following the psychological literature (Westerhof and Keyes 2008: Chapter 4), we differentiate between hedonic and eudaimonic well-being (Samman 2007). Hedonic well-being is a multidimensional concept which includes cognitive evaluations of life in general (i.e. life satisfaction) as well as positive and negative affects (Diener 1984; Diener *et al.* 1999). This is the kind of well-being that most economists refer to when they measure happiness. The second concept of well-being, eudaimonic well-being, dates back to Aristotle, for whom the actualization of virtues was the way to live a good or meaningful life.[5] Current literature subdivides eudaimonic well-being into psychological and social well-being. The psychologist Ryff found six elements of positive functioning that comprise what she calls psychological well-being: self-acceptance, personal growth, purpose in life, environmental mastery, autonomy and positive relations with others (Ryff 1989; Ryff and Keyes 1995). Keyes (1998) added five dimensions of social well-being: social acceptance, social actualization, social contribution, social coherence and social integration (see Spillemaeckers *et al.*, Chapter 4 of this book).

Keyes (2005) describes flourishing as a state in which individuals combine a high level of emotional well-being with an optimum level of psychological and social functioning. Similarly, languishing refers to a state in which low levels of hedonic well-being are combined with low levels of psychological and social well-being. Mental health is described by the World Health Organization (2004: 12) as 'a state of well-being in which the individual realizes his or her own abilities, can cope with the normal stresses of life, can work productively and fruitfully, and is able to make a contribution to his or her community'. The three core elements in this definition of mental health are (1) well being and (2) effective functioning for an individual, and (3) effective functioning for a community (World Health Organization 2004).

Of course, there are links between both types of well-being and between each need and the different subcategories of well-being, but research has not advanced sufficiently to establish these links clearly or provide explanations for them (Westerhof and Keyes 2008). Our understanding is that well-being arises when a person is conscious of the needs they have that are currently being met. This is clearly a very subjective aspect of quality of life. Many needs might point instead to eudaimonic well-being which, up until now, has not been the focus of interest in measuring happiness. Including needs and eudaimonic well-being in the analysis may shed new light on the relationship between resources, agency and hedonic well-being, but this requires further research.

The concept of quality of life (QOL) in its modern manifestation gained currency in the 1960s and 1970s in the USA and Europe. However, the concept can also be found in the welfare economics of the period between the two wars (e.g. Arthur C. Pigou *Economics of Welfare* 1920). The revival of the concept in the USA and Europe in the second half of the last century is probably due to the mounting evidence that material wealth does not guarantee a high QOL. The political debate about QOL was interrupted again by the growth crisis of the 1970s. After that, two important traditions of empirical observation and analysis of well-being and QOL emerged: the Scandinavian tradition of prosperity research and the American quality of life research. The Scandinavian school sees the citizen as an active, creative being, and the autonomous definer of his own goals. Resources are merely means to achieve the latter (Tåhlin 1990). The indicators used to measure QOL are objective ones only; similarities exist here to Sen's concept of capabilities.

The American school is strongly influenced by social psychology and mental health research, which emphasize subjective experience. Hedonic well-being is the principal benchmark against which state actions and societal development are to be measured. As QOL is experienced directly by humans (Campbell 1972), they are the best experts to judge their individual QOL. This school uses subjective indicators such as happiness or life satisfaction to measure QOL.

In recent years attempts to combine both approaches have led to concepts that define QOL through an objective component on the one hand, such as available resources, income and the capacities to meet needs with these resources, and a subjective component on the other, related to a person's subjective well-being or perception of his/her life (Zapf 1984). Objective conditions are generally seen as being constitutive of subjective perceptions. This integrated concept of QOL facilitates a holistic and comprehensive approach to the observation of material and non-material values.

In this chapter we use the holistic approach in which QOL consists of both objective and subjective components. Box 1.1 contains the definitions of the main components, and Figure 1.1 shows our conceptualization of quality of life related to SD.

Box 1.1 Definition of key concepts used in this chapter

- **NEEDS** are the most fundamental dimensions of human flourishing. We call needs those reasons for action that require no further explanation or justification.

- **STRATEGIES** are instrumental means to fulfill needs. Typically, strategies relate positively and/or negatively to more than one need.

- **VALUE** is the attribution of a specific degree of importance to a need or strategy or to a set thereof. In this regard, sustainable development is a value as it confers high importance to specific strategies to particularly meet the needs of PROTECTION and AFFECTION.

- **CAPABILITIES** determine the objective conditions, i.e. resources in human, social and material capital, and the freedom to choose which needs are to be fulfilled and how.

- **WELL-BEING** refers to emotional states and reflections of meaning in life based on the subjective experience of one's fulfillment of needs. Its hedonic part reflects the pleasure experienced and is linked to emotional well-being, its eudaimonic part reflects the striving to realize one's personal and social potential.

- **QUALITY OF LIFE** is related to individuals and has two components: capabilities and well-being.

While it would go beyond the bounds of this chapter to explain the figure fully, we list here the most relevant features with regard to the topic of this chapter:

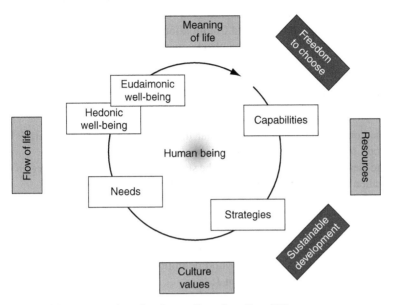

Figure 1.1 A process-based understanding of quality of life.

- Quality of life is generated in a circular, dynamic process that links capabilities to well-being through strategies and needs;
- Capabilities require FREEDOM and resources;
- Strategies are selected within a capability set based on values that are linked to the cultural background of an individual;
- SD is a value related to meaning of life and – again, dependent on the culture in which it is formulated – is translated into policies that focus on

    - the use and distribution of material resources,
    - the wider availability of capabilities,
    - the selection of strategies;

- The meeting of needs per se does not necessarily result in a high level of well-being – for this, it is necessary to be aware of needs being fulfilled;
- Eudaimonic well-being (linked to meaning of life) creates the link back to capabilities; taking only hedonic well-being into account leads to the symptom of the 'hedonic treadmill' (Binswanger 2006).

Reflection on SD policy processes

SD as a value

Let us now bring SD into the focus of the discussion. Sustainable development is a concept that relates to societal development and, in particular, to society's capacity to meet individual needs both now and in the future. The first politically relevant definition of SD – and still the one most widely referred to – was set out in 1987 in the report of the UN World Commission on Environment and Development (WCED) *Our Common Future*, also known as the Brundtland report:

> Sustainable development is development that meets the needs of the present without compromising the ability of future generations to meet their own needs. It contains within it two key concepts:
>
> •   the concept of 'needs', in particular the essential needs of the world's poor, to which overriding priority should be given; and
> •   the idea of limitations imposed by the state of technology and social organization on the environment's ability to meet present and future needs.
>
> (WCED 1987)

From the beginning sustainable development was defined in relation to society's capacity to meet human needs. However, the concept of needs remained quite unclear because the report offered no valid definition of needs. It merely gives some examples, as in Chapter 6, Section 1:

> The essential needs of vast numbers of people in developing countries for *food, clothing, shelter, jobs* – are not being met, and beyond their basic needs these people have legitimate aspirations for an improved quality of life.

The only other set of examples it provides is similar and is found in Chapter 6, Section 3:

> Critical objectives for environment and development policies that follow from the concept of sustainable development include: …meeting essential needs for *jobs, food, energy, water, and sanitation*;…

These extracts suggest that the needs concept within the Brundtland definition is focused on basic physical needs, which in Max-Neef's scheme are covered by the concept of SUBSISTENCE (see Table 1.1). The other fundamental human needs contained in Max-Neef's scheme are not addressed directly by the Brundtland definition. Perhaps they are hinted at with the phrase 'improved quality of life', but the report offers no clear definition of this term either. The Brundtland report's global perspective – with its limited concept of needs – is simply not precise enough to conceptualize SD (Boulanger 2008).

Our concept makes it possible to see SD clearly as a value, i.e. as the attribution of importance to specific needs or strategies or to a particular set thereof. Values provide orientation in our life and are a way of giving meaning to it. Caring for ourselves and others (those living now as well as future generations) is the most basic motivation for adopting SD among one's values. Pursuing SD is a strategy that enables us to meet our need for PROTECTION by caring for ourselves and other people. We also express AFFECTION when we pursue SD. Furthermore, in most forms of SD, we encourage PARTICIPATION, safeguard SUBSISTENCE and CREATE new lifestyles.[6] SD translates into numerous strategies at various levels, governmental, economic and individual. At the same time, when different values are given priority, SD strategies are often (perceived as) an obstacle to FREEDOM, to PROTECTING one's own immediate interests (if one is well-off), and to IDENTITY. SD provides opportunities to meet everybody's needs, now and in the future; in doing so, as shown above, it places particular emphasis on a specific set of needs, namely PROTECTION, AFFECTION, PARTICIPATION and SUBSISTENCE.

The specific set of strategies which is appropriate to use for SD is disputed. The many and varied interpretations of SD highlight different aspects of needs and strategies. SD attributes importance to community-oriented needs and is therefore not as attractive for people motivated more by meeting their agency-oriented needs, which are given considerable emphasis in western cultures today (Wilber 1995). Linking SD strategies back to needs instead of presenting them as technocratic, quasi-mathematical restrictions on FREEDOM provides an opportunity to lower many people's resistance to SD strategies, particularly if the need for FREEDOM on the part of the opponents of SD is acknowledged and addressed. This does not necessarily involve accepting their strategies to meet this need, as, probably, there are still better strategies to live a life of FREEDOM.

Sustainable development policies

We are now in a position to propose the following redefinition: SD policy is a specific expression of values aimed at encouraging people to cherish and develop specific capabilities and to choose certain strategies over others, so that all people, both those living in the present and in the future, can have a decent quality of life. This means that the aim of SD is to increase the quality of life for current and future generations, i.e. to generate increasing well-being and more capability sets for current and future generations, at least above a certain level.[7]

The concept of needs is at the heart of the Brundtland definition of sustainable development. Nevertheless, abstract needs are not suited to being the point of leverage for government intervention. In addition, focusing only on specific strategies (enabling or prohibiting) might be perceived as an illegitimate restriction on FREEDOM. By increasing people's capability sets, governments respect this need for FREEDOM; at the same time, however, the risk arises that this space might be used for unsustainable actions, i.e. for actions that prevent others from meeting their needs. Therefore, not all policies that increase people's capability sets contribute to SD, only a subset of such policies. Restrictions on the complete set arise through

1 knowledge about human dependency on natural and social resources for some need fulfilment, combined with

2 the values of intra- and intergenerational justice and the corresponding policy measures implied by SD.

These restrictions translate into SD-oriented policies directed at strategies, values, agency and resources. Not all needs require natural resources. The need for SUBSISTENCE seems to be the one with the strongest links to material resources. While there might be some yogis who apparently live without food or warmth, such an achievement cannot be generalized (and again: a policy prescribing this specific strategy for meeting the need for SUBSISTENCE denies the need for FREEDOM). All other needs can, in principle, be met with less material input than currently used in Western countries. And, as can be deduced from the debate about the so-called Easterlin Paradox (Easterlin 1974), the use of material resources above a certain threshold is apparently not generally conducive to well-being.

To be implemented successfully in a democracy, SD should not lower the quality of life of (a substantial proportion of) current voters. Furthermore, SD policies, like all policies, demand legitimacy. The requirements of legitimacy increase with the moral distance of the beneficiaries of the policy: for example, helping German workers not to lose their jobs is considered legitimate for a German government; actions trying to avoid flooding in Bangladesh in 50 years do not have the same legitimacy. As SD policies are typically intended to improve the QOL of people not involved in formulating and implementing them, sources for legitimacy must be sought. In addition to improving input, through-put and output legitimacy (Scharpf 1998; Engelen *et al.* 2008), the concept of needs offers the possibility of linking SD to the concept of an ethically good life or a meaningful life. The form and substance of this link, of course, depends on the cultural context concerned.

The essential moral imperative behind the concept of SD (and thus its main source for political legitimacy) is intra- and intergenerational justice. The Welsh assembly defines social justice as follows: 'Social Justice is about every one of us having the chances and opportunities to make the most of our lives and use our talents to the full' (Welsh Assembly 2010). This definition focuses on the input required for meeting one's needs – that is, on capabilities – and not on the outcome of this process, i.e. well-being. A just distribution of income and material resources may be one condition for social justice which is relatively easy to measure and monitor, but it is neither a sufficient nor a necessary one. Whereas it might also be possible to conceptualize and render operational intragenerational justice in terms of capabilities with regard to other issues (such as education, juridical equity, access to positions of social and political responsibility or to those on the Nussbaum list (Nussbaum 2000)), this is much more difficult in questions of intergenerational justice (cf. Robeyns and Van der Veen 2007). Nonetheless, the difficulty of this task is not a good reason for not dealing with it; indeed it is a normative challenge that calls for action. Societal triple bottom lines are indirect attempts to do so, albeit indirectly, as the link to the object of intergenerational justice (e.g. capabilities) is generally rather weak. In this chapter, we can only acknowledge the necessity of dealing with these issues; we are not yet able to offer a way through this most difficult conceptual issue in SD (Leßmann, Chapter 3).

In more practical terms, policy processes that demonstrate an explicit link to the needs they are designed to meet thus relate strategies to what really matters (i.e. needs) and, in doing so, generate fresh and dynamic debate in society by establishing a clear separation between (commonly acknowledged and shared) needs and (negotiable) strategies. This differentiation stimulates creativity and results in greater FREEDOM, as needs-oriented negotiations about strategies prompt ideas about better ways of meeting the needs in question than the proposed (and contested) strategy. Referring to needs triggers emotions, and policy processes must be able to include these in a constructive and productive way. Up until now, such processes have been rare.

Needs-based policy processes provide a means of addressing SD in a more encompassing way than processes that structure knowledge according to substitutability or a segregation into three or more dimensions; they thus offer a promising approach for realizing SD as a set of values. Methods that could be used for such processes include, for example, needs-based multi-criteria analysis (Cruz *et al.* 2009; Rauschmayer 2005), participatory scenario workshops, systemic constellations (Sparrer 2007), and other types of process work (Mindell 1995). What these have in common is a commitment on the part of SD scholars as process managers to explicitly incorporate (the expression of) emotions (see Rauschmayer *et al.*, Chapter 7 in this book, on the resulting challenges for the researcher).

Illustrative example: the 'cash for old bangers' premium

In the face of the 2008/09 financial crisis, the German government decided to launch a new policy called the 'environmental premium'. This policy stated that anyone who traded in their old banger and bought a new car would receive €2,500. The first tranche of money available was initially restricted to €1.5 billion; this was increased in April 2009 to €5 billion. The official aim is twofold: to improve air quality by the use of newer cars which at least fulfil the emissions norm EU 4, and to stimulate new demand for the (German) car industry, thereby securing German jobs. An important additional aim was to generate confidence in the government's capacity to act, partly in view of the upcoming general elections in October 2009, and partly because of the enormous economic and political importance of public trust generally.

It is not our aim here to discuss whether this policy achieved its aims or whether the aims set were appropriate.[8] Instead, our aim is to analyse the main features of this policy with respect to QOL in terms of capabilities, needs and well-being.

The policy extended the capability set of people living in Germany,

a   who were considering replacing their old car with a new one in 2009 and who had enough resources to do so;
b   who would otherwise lose their job in the car industry (and upstream industries);
c   who suffer low air quality due to the emissions from old cars.

The needs we see touched upon here are shown in Table 1.2.

How does this translate into hedonic and eudaimonic well-being? Perhaps the greatest effect for car buyers was an increase in hedonic well-being; for the other two groups, it is difficult to say. Being employed is – in contemporary German culture – so important that it contributes to fulfilling nearly all needs and thus different kinds of well-being. Being in basic good health might also contribute to meeting all other needs.

One could look at this table and ask: would there have been other, more effective strategies (than the 'environmental premium') to meet these needs? Could the needs have been met more effectively, and could more needs have been met? For example, a specific CO_2 or particulate matter component could conceivably have been included in the premium. More pertinent in a context of sustainable development, though, is the aim of extending the range of people taken into account to include all people, both those alive now and future generations, living in Germany and elsewhere.

As a first and rather trivial step, we might extend (b) above quite easily to include employees in the car industry elsewhere, as it was Hyundai, Suzuki and Fiat that profited most from the premium.[9]

Other impacts of this policy that were foreseeable from the beginning[10] are the following:

d   Using personal income to buy a new car takes money away from other potential uses and may trigger personal insolvency.
e   Car manufacturing and car repair services will have severe problems starting in 2010.
f   Scrapping cars that still work restricts the capability set of people (e.g. in Africa or Eastern Europe) who usually buy used cars from the German market.

Table 1.2 Effects of old banger premium on three target groups

Addressees of policy/ FUNDAMENTAL HUMAN NEEDS	(a) car buyer	(b) car industry employee	(c) person suffering from air pollution
SUBSISTENCE	+ In rare cases	+	+
PROTECTION	+ (better safety in new cars)	+	+
AFFECTION	?	+	?
UNDERSTANDING	?	?	?
PARTICIPATION	?	+	?
IDLENESS	?	?/+	?
CREATION	?	?/+	?
IDENTITY	+	+	?
FREEDOM	+	+	+
TRANSCENDENCE	?	?	?

g   Car production leaves a very large environmental footprint in terms of raw material, energy consumption and emissions. The resources used for the car production generated by the premium are not available elsewhere or at another time; the emissions contribute to climate change and health problems. The capability sets of current and future generations are restricted.

One might leave the direct effects of (d) aside as being the responsibility of those people (in (a)) who profit from the premium; indirect effects, e.g. on the tourism industry, are relevant, though. It may well be that the effects of (e) counterbalance (b) – here, we encounter a problem of political economy: Germany faced general elections in October 2009. Apparently, the effects of (f) and, above all, of (g) have not been considered seriously in German policymaking.

Considering the needs affected by this 'cash for old bangers' strategy prompts a number of questions. Are there more effective strategies for generating confidence in government and meeting the needs of the beneficiaries of the policy (mainly car industry employees, as these were considered the main losers of the financial crisis) without indirectly preventing other people from meeting their needs? For example, what would have been the impact on everyone's needs of going a step further towards introducing a general and unconditional basic income, in other words, by using the €5 billion in a different way? Such a strategy would not have supported the car-oriented culture in Germany (a culture that is detrimental to the German economy in the medium term and to all people in the medium and long term due to its contribution to climate change); however, it could have been implemented in a policy that involved less consumption of energy and raw materials (these are two major causes of a reduction in capability sets elsewhere and in the future). From the point of view of well-being, this means moving away from the aim of increasing or maintaining a certain level of (short-lived) hedonic well-being towards eudaimonic well-being (with a positive feedback loop to capabilities). In general, investing in increases in those capability sets that are likely to support the meeting of needs in a way that results in an increase in eudaimonic well-being, can therefore be considered to be more sustainable.

One of the authors conducted a role play on how to decide in the situation of the German government during winter 2008/2009. During a workshop on Nonviolent Communication (Rosenberg 2001), five participants took the roles of different ministers and checked which feelings arose due to the 'cash for old bangers' proposal and which of their needs and which needs of the German population should be better met (using the needs list of Rosenberg 2001, which is longer than the one used by Max-Neef). The role players then came up with new strategies. The following needs were mentioned several times (in parentheses are some strategies for achieving them): (1) for the German population: security/stability/order (economic growth), meaning (i.e. responsibility for the environment and for future generations under the condition that the economy is not endangered by strategies focusing on such responsibility), and trust (quick and effective decisions by politicians); (2) for themselves as politicians: recognition/

authenticity, security (improve chance of re-election by showing action), effectiveness (use money in an industry that reacts quickly), and creativity (look for more complex solutions than the proposed premium). The issue of intragenerational justice was only referred to with regard to the German society; being just beyond Germany or beyond the current generation (i.e. the value base of sustainable development) was mentioned by one player, but not taken up by the others who could not see how strategies developed in the light of SD could meet their needs for security and effectiveness.

The council of ministers then looked for a consent decision, i.e. a proposal that would not encounter major opposition. In the discussion, the (supposed) needs of the population played an important role, and here particularly the need for security that was supposed to be endangered by the economic crisis. From the politicians' needs, authenticity and effectiveness were the most mentioned. The decision adopted was a split 'cash for old bangers' premium: the full premium for car-sharing organisations and half of the premium for individuals. The issue of justice between people living in cities and in the countryside was seen as relevant and still to be integrated in this proposal.

Being in a role play, the question of trust in the council of ministers was not that relevant as in real life, and it was rather easy for the participants to reveal their emotions and needs (see Rauschmayer *et al.*, Chapter 7 in this book). Nevertheless, the value of SD was not relevant in this role play (like, apparently, in the real decision process), and this even though the participants certainly were 'greener' in their ideological positions than the then conservative-social democrat government. In consequence, there is one major issue that we learnt from this role play: appealing to needs does not lead per se to more sustainable outcomes. Therefore, for SD policy the challenge remains that values which are not part of one's identity will not play a role in autonomous decisions. We have the impression that SD still is a value with weak influence on decisions. We suspect the greatness of the moral challenge of global intra- and intergenerational justice of being the reason for this weakness. In order to strengthen a value that has been adopted, but which still is very weak, individuals might wish to opt for strengthening it on a metalevel, e.g. by introducing a compulsory sustainability assessment.

We highlight in the following some differences of the approach just described to a more classical cost-benefit analysis, as the most common economic decision support instrument. Instead of dealing with preferences expressed in monetary terms, this process deals with strategies aiming at meeting needs. This implies the following main differences that are interrelated: a setting of personal inquiry instead of a market setting, multidimensionality instead of monodimensionality, subjectivity instead of quasi-objectivity, a necessarily participatory process instead of desk studies, and a dynamic process involving individual and social learning instead of a static approach, a strong focus on processes instead of outcomes (cf. Rauschmayer *et al.* 2009). Particularly interesting in this is the dynamic aspect of relating strategies to needs, of checking whether the needs focused on – and the trade-offs between prospective beneficiaries and non-beneficiaries of a specific strategy – are in accordance with the decision maker's values (SD and others), and of adjusting the strategy accordingly. Whenever this is done in an open, transparent way, an increase in trust and legitimacy can be expected (Varga von Kibèd *et al.* 2008).

Needs-based approaches to policy allow the clarification of the extent to which we consider – or fail to consider – the needs (and not the preferences) of currently deprived or future generations. Furthermore, in appropriately designed policy processes, distinguishing between needs and the strategies available to meet these needs, between well-being resulting from conscious needs fulfilment and the capability set relevant to this fulfilment, and thus highlighting the connection between the resources necessary to achieve current well-being and the resources needed by future generations may lead to a conscious choice regarding the particular aspects of sustainability a policy should aim to achieve. Currently, '[a]lmost any policy ... can be claimed to be consistent with sustainability, since the definition has been stretched by government to be sufficiently wide to be practically almost meaningless' (Helm 1998: 17).

Conclusion

Our refocusing of SD leads us to identify the following promising aspects:

1   From a research point of view, this re-focusing enables the research fields of SD, capabilities, well-being, and QOL to be linked in a meaningful way. There have been several recent papers that have attempted to link several of these fields, but – apart from grey literature from the Belgian WellBebe-project (e.g. Boulanger 2008, cf. also Chapter 5 in this book) – we have not come across any encompassing concepts (e.g. Costanza *et al.* 2007 cite Nussbaum but do not mention capabilities).

2   From a disciplinary point of view, it shows how different disciplines can work together in sustainability science: economics, psychology, sociology, political sciences, environmental sciences and philosophy. This promising development has to be qualified, of course, by noting the relative loss in importance of scientific disciplines in mode-2 knowledge production (Nowotny *et al.* 2003) and when dealing with challenges requiring post-normal science (Funtowicz and Ravetz 1993).

3   From a societal point of view, it promotes a dynamic and explicit process of searching for strategies that better meet the needs of current generations of humans. This was demonstrated in Max-Neef's studies and is an extrapolation of one-to-one or small-group settings (Rosenberg 2001). It has yet to be shown how this can work in large communities or even at national or international level.

4   From a SD point of view, linking SD to quality of life offers a concrete and positive approach. It enables issues of intra- and intergenerational justice, which form the basis of SD, to be integrated into the process. The age-old moral challenge of 'how to live a good life and live according to my values'

has the potential to create more positive motivation for actors dealing with SD (Luks and Siemer 2007).

5   From a policy point of view, state interventions towards achieving social justice require directing specifically at guaranteeing minimum capabilities, improving the effectiveness of capabilities, and improving the effectiveness with which needs are met. This capability-orientation is gaining influence in development policy and has something to offer SD policy as well. It is not clear, though, how intergenerational justice can be conceptualized and rendered operational in a capability approach.

Linked to these promising aspects, we also see additional challenges on the way ahead:

- How can a social policy based on a rather individualized concept of needs best be developed?
- How can we better acknowledge the importance of caring about future generation's needs and how can these needs be integrated systematically in decision processes? (See Boulanger, Chapter 5 in this book.)
- How can participatory decision-making processes based on this concept be organized in such a way that emotions are included as a matter of course? For example, how can the anger of participants, who do not share the values of SD, be addressed?
- What place should be given to individual, intrasocietal and intergenerational tensions that will inevitably arise? (Again, see Boulanger, Chapter 5 in this volume.)
- How can appropriate research be designed?

We are convinced that policies based on this approach have the potential to motivate people far more than policies based on concepts such as strong or weak sustainability or three or more dimensions. The benefits of the approach are several: quality of life is generally accepted as an overarching aim for policy and individual decision making; capabilities address the culturally important need for FREEDOM; the distinction between capabilities, strategies and needs opens up new spaces for negotiation; needs are an intuitively appealing concept, being linked to what is essential in life; and, finally, the distinction between eudaimonic and hedonic well-being enables us to escape from the hedonic treadmill and to create a positive feedback loop to capabilities.

Acknowledgements

We are grateful for comments from Oliver Zwirner, Ortrud Leßmann, /Cathleen Cross and Peter Söderbaum, as well as from further people in- and outside academia to whom we presented these ideas. We are grateful to the German ministry for research end education which supports the research project GeNECA (2010–2013) where we continue to work on these questions.

Notes

1 Of the publications listed in the bibliography on the homepage of the Human Development and Capability Approach Association (724 documents as of July 2008), none uses the keyword sustainability or sustainable development (www.capabilityapproach.com).
2 We continue to use the term 'sustainable development', and not 'sustainability', for two reasons: first, we are conscious that our societies need further development to meet the needs of present and future generations (not necessarily an economic development in the sense of GDP growth), and, second, we see parallels between such societal and individual human development to meet one's own needs. Both reasons appeal to the dynamics expressed by SD in contrast to the static term sustainability.
3 We are aware that consensus on the meaning of such criteria will often be too little. 'Needs ethics should not try to cover all of life, but limit themselves to providing a basis and complement to other ethics' (Gasper 1996: 12).
4 In the following, the ten needs are printed in capital letters in order to highlight the importance they have in our concept.
5 Links exist between Sen's understanding of well-being and agency on the one hand and hedonic and eudaimonic well-being on the other:

> The standard of living is 'personal well-being related to one's own life.' If we add the outcomes resulting from sympathies (i.e. from helping another person and thereby feeling oneself better off), we measure well-being. If well-being is supplemented with commitments (i.e. an action which is not beneficial to the agent herself), then we are focusing on overall agency (Sen 1987).
>
> (Robeyns 2003: 15)

6 We doubt that the lifestyles currently pursued in Western societies would resist a thorough analysis of their needs-meeting capacity.
7 The minimum level of quality of life or capability set, respectively, has to be determined in a political decision process, mainly contingent on availability of resources and culture.
8 A study made for the German government states that people bought smaller, less emitting and less noisy cars than the ones they had before (Höpfner *et al.* 2009). While the government, based on this static comparative study, claims a positive environmental effect, a dynamic study, including a wider set of strategies (car-sharing, public transport instead of private cars, less mobility), would probably give different results.
9 However, the political legitimacy of measures advantaging foreign workers in foreign countries is not very high.
10 Of course, neither of these lists is complete.

References

Alkire, S. (2002), Dimensions of human development, *World Development*, 30(2): 181–205.
—— (2005), Needs and capabilities, in S. Reader (ed.), *The Philosophy of Need*, Cambridge University Press: Cambridge, pp. 229–251.
Binswanger, M. (2006), *Die Tretmühlen des Glücks: Wir haben immer mehr und werden nicht glücklicher. Was können wir tun?* Herder: Freiburg.
Boulanger, P.-M. (2008), *Substantive conceptions of well-being and quality of life: needs and stress theories*, Working Paper for WellBeBe. Ottignies: Institut pour un Développement Durable: 54pp., online, available at: www.wellbebe.be/ Mydocs/Needs&Stress. pdf [accessed 27 April 2010].

—— (2011), The life-chances concept: a sociological perspective in equity and sustainable development, Chapter 5, this volume.

BUND and Misereor (1996), *Zukunftsfähiges Deutschland*, Birkhäuser: Basel.

Campbell, A. (1972), Aspiration, satisfaction and fulfilment, in A. Campbell and P. Converse (eds), *The Human Meaning of Social Change*, Russell Sage Foundation: New York, pp. 441–446.

Costanza, R., Fisher, B., Ali, S., Beer, C., Bond, L., Boumans, R., Danigelis, N.L., Dickinson, J., Elliott, C., Farley, J., Gayer, D.E., MacDonald Glenn, L., Hudspeth, T., Mahoney, M., McCahill, L., McIntosh, B., Reed, B., Turab Rizvi, S.A., Rizzo, D.M., Simpatico, T.M. and Snapp, R. (2007), Quality of life: an approach integrating opportunities, human needs, and subjective well-being, *Ecological Economics*, 61(2–3): 267–276.

Cruz, I. (2011), Human needs frameworks and their contribution as analytical instruments in sutainable development policymaking, Chapter 6, this volume.

Cruz, I., Stahel, A. and Max-Neef M.A. (2009), Towards a systemic development approach: building on the Human-Scale Development paradigm, *Ecological Economics*, 68(7): 2021–2030.

Diener, E. (1984), Subjective well-being, *Psychological Bulletin*, 95(3): 542–575, cited in Westerhof and Keyes (2008).

Diener, E., Suh, E.M., Lucas, R. and Smith, H. (1999), Subjective well-being: three decades of progress, *Psychological Bulletin*, 125(2): 276–302, cited in Westerhof and Keyes (2008).

Dodds, S. (1997), Towards a 'science of sustainability': Improving the way ecological economics understands human well-being, *Ecological Economics*, 23(2): 95–111.

Easterlin, R. (1974), Does economic growth improve the human lot? Some empirical evidence, in R. David and R. Reder (eds), *Nations and Households in Economic Growth: Essays in Honor of Moses Abramovitz*, Academic Press: New York.

Engelen, E.J., Keulartz, F.W.J. and Leistra, G. (2008), European nature conservation policymaking: from substantive to procedural sources of legitimacy, in E.J. Keulartz and G. Leistra (eds), *Legitimacy in European Nature Conservation Policy: Case Studies in Multilevel Governance*, Springer: Wageningen, pp. 3–21.

European Communities (2008), *The Economics of Ecosystems and Biodiversity*, European Communities: Cambridge.

Funtowicz, S. and Ravetz, J. (1993), Science for the Post-Normal Age, *Futures*, 25(7): 739–755.

Gasper, D. (1996), *Needs and Basic Needs: A Clarification of Meanings, Levels and Different Streams of Work*, Working Paper No. 210 of the Institute of Social Studies, online, available at: http://ideas.repec.org/p/iss/wpaper/210.html.

Grisez, G., Boyle, J. and Finnes, J. (1987), Practical principles, moral truth and ultimate ends, *American Journal of Jurisprudence*, 32: 99–151.

Helm, D. (1998), The assessment: environmental policy – objectives, instruments, andi nstitutions. *Oxford Review of Economic Policy*, 14(4): 1–19.

Höpfner, U., Hanusch, J. and Lambrecht, U. (2009), *Abwrackprämie und Umwelt – eine erste Bilanz*, Heidelberg, IFEU – Institut für Energie und Umweltforschung, online, available at: www.bmu.de/verkehr/downloads/doc/44905.php [accessed 24 September 2009].

Jackson, T., Pager, W. and Stagl, S. (2004), *Beyond Insatiability: Needs Theory, Consumption and Sustainability*. Working Paper Series No. 2004/2, Centre for Environmental Strategy, University of Surrey: Guildford, online, available at: http://portal. surrey.ac.uk/pls/portal/docs/PAGE/ENG/RESEARCH/CES/CESRESEARCH/ ECOLOGICAL-ECONOMICS/PROJECTS/FBN/ BEYONDINSATIABILITY.PDF

Keyes, C.L.M. (1998), Social well–being, *Social Psychology Quarterly*, 61(2): 121–140, cited in Westerhof and Keyes (2008).

—— (2005), Mental illness and/or mental health? Investigating axioms of the complete state model of health, *Journal of Consulting and Clinical Psychology*, 73(3): 539–548, cited in: Westerhof and Keyes (2008).

Leßmann, O. (2011), Sustainability as a challenge to the capability approach, Chapter 3, this volume.

Luks, F. and Siemer, S.H. (2007), Whither sustainable development? A plea for humility, *GAIA – Ecological Perspectives for Science and Society* 16(3): 187–192.

Max-Neef, M.A. (ed.) (1991), *Human Scale Development: Conception, Application and Further Reflections*, The Apex Press: New York.

Max-Neef, M.A., Elizalde, A. and Hopenhayn, M. (1991), Development and human needs, in Max-Neef (1991), pp. 13–54.

Mebratu, D. (1998), Sustainability and sustainable development: historical and review, *Environmental Impact Assessment Review*, 18: 493–520.

Millenium Ecosystem Assessment (2005), *Ecosystems and Human Well-being: Synthesis*, online, available at: www.millenniumassessment.org/documents/ document.356.aspx.pdf

Mindell, A. (1995), *Sitting in the Fire: Large Group Transformation using Conflict and Diversity*, Lao Tse Press: Portland, OR.

Nowotny, H., Scott, P. and Gibbons, M. (2003), 'Mode 2' Revisited: The New Production of Knowledge, *Minerva* 41(3): 179–194.

Nussbaum, M.C. (2000), *Women and Human Development: The Capabilities Approach*, Cambridge University Press: Cambridge.

O'Neill, J. (2011), The overshadowing of needs, Chapter 2, this volume.

O'Neill, J., Holland, A. and Light, A. (2008), *Environmental Values*, Routledge: Abingdon/New York.

Pick, S. and Poortinga, Y.H. (2005), Conceptual framework and strategies for the design and instrumentation of development programs: a scientific, political and psychosocial view, *Revista Latinoamericana de Psicologia* 37(3): 445–459.

Pigou, A.C. (1920), *Economics of Welfare*, Macmillan: London.

Rauschmayer, F. (2005), Linking emotions to needs. A comment to Fred Wenstøp's article 'Mindsets, rationality and emotion in multi-criteria decision analysis', *Journal of Multi-Criteria Decision Analysis*, 13(4): 187–190.

Rauschmayer, F. and Omann, O. (2011), Transition towards SD. Which tensions emerge? How do we deal with them? Chapter 8, this volume.

Rauschmayer, F., Muenzing T. and Frühmann J. (2011), A plea for the self-aware sustainability researcher. Learning from business transformation processes for transitions to sustainable development, Chapter 7, this volume.

Rauschmayer, F., Berghöfer, A., Omann, I. and Zikos, D. (2009), Examining processes or outcomes? Evaluation concepts in European governance of natural resources, *Environmental Policy and Governance* 19(3): 159–173.

Robeyns, I. (2003), *The Capability Approach – An Interdisciplinary Introduction*, online, available at: www.ingridrobeyns.nl/Downloads/CAtraining20031209.pdf.

Robeyns, I. and Van der Veen, R.J. (2007), *Sustainable quality of life – Conceptual analysis for a policy-relevant empirical specification*, Netherlands Environmental Assessment Agency (MNP): Bilthoven.

Rosenberg, M. (2001), *Nonviolent Communication: A Language of Life*, Puddle Dancer Press: Encinitas, CA

Ryff, C.D. (1989) Happiness is everything, or is it? Explorations on the meaning of psychological well-being, *Journal of Personality and Social Psychology*, 57(6): 1069–1081, cited in Westerhof and Keyes (2008).

Ryff, C.D. and Keyes, C.L.M. (1995), The structure of psychological well-being revisited, *Journal of Personality and Social Psychology*, 69(4): 719–727, cited in Westerhof and Keyes (2008).

Samman, E. (2007), Psychological and Subjective Wellbeing: A Proposal for Internationally Comparable Indicators, *Oxford Development Studies*, 35(4): 459–486.

Scharpf, F.W. (1998), *Interdependence and Democratic Legitimation*, MPI für Gesellschaftsforschung: Köln.

Sen, A.K. (1985), Well-being agency and freedom: The Dewey Lectures 1984, *Journal of Philosophy*, 82(4): 169–221.

—— (1987), *On Ethics and Economics*, Blackwell: Oxford.

Sparrer, I. (2007), *Miracle, Solution and System – Solution-focused Systemic Structural Constellations for Therapy and Organisational Change*, SolutionsBooks: Cheltenham.

Spillemaeckers, S., Van Ootegem, L. and Westerhof, G.J. (2011), From individual well-being to sustainable development – a path where psychologists and economists meet, Chapter 4, this volume.

Stern, N., Peters, S., Bakhshi, V., Bowen, A., Cameron, C., Catovsky, S., Crane, D., Cruickshank, S., Dietz, S., Edmonson, N., Garbett, S.L., Hamid, L., Hoffman, G., Ingram, D., Jones, B., Patmore, N., Radcliffe, H., Sathiyarajah, R., Stock, M., Taylor, C., Vernon, T., Wanjie, H. and Zenghelis, D. (2006), *Stern Review: The Economics of Climate Change*, HM Treasury: London.

Tåhlin, M. (1990), Politics, dynamics and individualism – the Swedish approach to level of living research, *Social Indicators Research* 22(2): 155–180.

Varga von Kibéd, M., Sparrer, I. and Ritter, M. (2008), Allparteilichkeit, Anerkennung und Ausgleich: Die systemische Dreiheit für mehr Gerechtigkeit. Grundlagen für eine faire Weltwirtschaft, in C. Eigner and P. Weibel (eds), *UN/Fair Trade*. Springer: Vienna/New York, pp. 84–91.

Veenhoven, R. (2000), The four qualities of life – ordering concepts and measures of the good life, *Journal of Happiness Studies*, 1: 1–39.

WCED (United Nations World Commission on Environment and Development) (1987), *Our Common Future*, online, available at: www.un-documents.net/wced-ocf.htm [accessed 12 April 2010].

Welsh Assembly (2010), *Social justice*, online, available at: www.wales.gov.uk/topics/socialjustice/?lang=en [accessed 22 February 2010].

Westerhof, G.J. and Keyes, C.L.M. (2008), *Positive Mental Health: From Happiness to Fulfillment of Potentials. Happiness and Capability: Measurement, Theory and Policy*, Radboud University Nijmegen: Ravenstein.

Wiggins, D. (2005), An idea we cannot do without: what difference will it make (eg. to moral, political and environmental philosophy) to recognize and put to use a subsantial conception of need? in S. Reader (ed.), *The Philosophy of Need*, Cambridge University Press: Cambridge, pp. 25–50.

Wilber, K. (1995), *Sex, Ecology, Spirituality: The Spirit of Evolution*, Shambhala: Boston, MA.

World Health Organization (2004), *Promoting mental health: Concepts, emerging evidence, practice (Summary report)*, WHO: Geneva.

Zapf, W. (1984). Individuelle Wohlfahrt. Lebensbedingungen und wahrgenommene Lebensqualität, in: W. Glatzer and W. Zapf (eds), *Lebensqualität in der Bundesrepublik*, Campus: Frankfurt am Main, pp. 13–26.

2 The overshadowing of needs

John O'Neill

> We must shift America from a needs- to a desires-culture. People must be trained
> to desire, to want new things, even before the old have been entirely consumed. We
> must shape a new mentality in America. Man's desires must overshadow his needs.
> (Paul Mazer, a banker working for Lehman Brothers, quoted in *The Century of
> Self* BBC 2002, www.archive.org/details/the.century.of.the.self)

1 Needs, preferences and sustainability

The concept of need was central to the influential 'Brundtland' characterisation
of sustainable development, in the 1987 report of the World Commission on
Environment and Development.

> Sustainable development is development that meets the needs of the present
> without compromising the ability of future generations to meet their own
> needs. It contains within it two key concepts:
>
> - the concept of *needs*, in particular the essential needs of the world's poor,
>   to which overriding priority should be given; and
> - the idea of *limitations* imposed by the state of technology and social organ-
>   ization on the environment's ability to meet present and future needs.
>
> (WECD 1987)

Subsequent discussions of sustainability have shifted from a language of needs
to the language of preferences that has been central to modern welfare economics. Sustainable development is to be understood as economic and social
development that maintains or improves human welfare. David Pearce is typical
in offering the following characterisation of sustainability:

> 'Sustainability' therefore implies something about maintaining the level of
> human well-being so that it might improve but at least never decline (or, not
> more than temporarily, anyway). Interpreted this way, sustainable develop-
> ment becomes equivalent to some requirement that well-being does not
> decline through time.
>
> (Pearce 1993: 48)

The concept of welfare that is employed here is understood in terms of preference satisfaction. As Pearce put it in a more recent co-authored paper on discounting: 'the entire body of "welfare economics" centres round the formal identity of the statement "X prefers A to B" and the statement "X has higher welfare in A rather than B"' (Pearce *et al.* 2003: 121).

Part of my purpose in this chapter is analytical, to trace out a series of logical features of the concept of need and the way it contrasts with that of preference. I outline these features in the next section. My central purpose is more substantive – to bring out what is at stake in this shift from the language of needs to the language of preferences in the characterisation of sustainability. The Brundtland formulation of the concept of sustainability has both theoretical and practical virtues which are lost with the shift to the language of preferences.

In developing this argument I will also address supplementary questions that are central to a number of the contributions to this book. The language of needs is not of course the only alternative to that of preference in the characterisation of the concepts of welfare and sustainability. Another welfare concept that belongs to a similar conceptual space as that of needs is that of capabilities.*

Defenders of the capabilities approach have suggested that there are good reasons for preferring a language of capabilities to that of needs (Alkire 2005; Sen 1984). The supplementary questions I address are the following: Should the concept of need employed in the Brundtland formulation be replaced or supplemented with that of capabilities? How far can needs-based and capabilities-based approaches to welfare and sustainability be reconciled?

2   The concepts of need and preference

I start with the analytical distinctions that will be central to this chapter.[1] Before turning to the contrast between needs and preferences, it will be useful to make some distinctions between different uses of the concept of need itself. First there is a distinction to be drawn between instrumental and absolute or categorical uses of the concept of need (Wiggins 1998). Some needs-claims specify needs that are instrumental to the realisation of an end that is itself optional. If I am to have a luxury cruise in the Caribbean, then I need £4,000. However, a person might respond by asking if I really need that luxury cruise. Other needs claims are not instrumental in that sense. They are absolute or categorical in that the ends themselves are not optional in this sense. The ends are 'unforsakeable'. They are a condition of living a minimal level of human flourishing at all, such that a person can be said to be harmed if they are not met. The concept is usefully characterised thus by David Wiggins:

I need [absolutely] to have x
if and only if
I need [instrumentally] to have x if I am to avoid being harmed
if and only if
It is necessary, things being what they actually are, that if I avoid being harmed then I have x.

(Wiggins 1998: 10)

Wiggins usefully draws attention to a number of dimensions of absolute or categorical needs which are important in considering the demands they make both on moral agents and public policy: their gravity – how bad the harm involved is; their urgency – how rapidly action must be taken to avoid the harm; their basicness – the degree to which the needs are grounded in unchangeable features of the person's condition; and finally their substitutability (Wiggins 1998: 14–16). I will deal with questions of substitutability in detail later in the chapter.

It is important that the concept of an absolute need is not confused with that of a biological need. Some biological needs are not absolute, for example those of the fashion model. More importantly some absolute needs are not biological. If a child is deprived of education or an adult is deprived of the chance to make choices about her own life, then they are harmed even if all their biological needs are met. Moreover, some absolute needs in the sense defined by Wiggins are relative to specific social arrangements. Consider the often quoted passage from Smith:

> By *necessaries* I *understand*, not only the commodities which are indispensably necessary for the support of life, but whatever the custom of the country renders it indecent for creditable people, even of the lowest order, to be without.

(Smith 1981 [1776]: 869)

The necessaries specified by Smith would count as absolute or categorical needs in the sense outlined. The worker would be harmed if he lacks those goods required for a decent life within a particular society. Not all absolute needs are biological needs. However, one important subset of absolute needs is that of basic needs grounded in 'laws of nature, unalterable and invariable environmental facts, of facts about human constitution' (Wiggins 1998: 15).

A second distinction that needs to be drawn is between dispositional and occurrent needs.[2] Dispositional needs are those needs which we ascribe to a class of beings by virtue of there being conditions of their living a minimally flourishing or decent life. All humans share certain needs, for example for food and water, in this sense. The claim that all human beings share the same needs is not true however if we use the term in the occurrent sense. An occurrent need refers to a particular lack of what is needed in the dispositional sense. Thus, while it is true that all humans need food and water in the dispositional sense, only the starving and thirsty have needs for food and water in the occurrent sense.

A third important feature of sentences describing needs is that they can take both noun-phrases and verb phrases as their object. One can specify a needs-claim by a noun phrase, for example 'Joe needs food' or by a verb phrase, for example 'Joe needs to be able to eat adequately'. The verb form is the more basic and as Wiggins has recently conceded, it should be wider than the particular verb-phrase 'to have x' which he employs in his characterisation of absolute needs (Wiggins 2005: 31–32). The point is important in closing the gap between needs-based and capabilities-based approaches to conceptualising human welfare. Two standard complaints against needs-based theories from the capabilities approach are (1) that needs are defined in terms of some bundle of goods and (2) need-based approaches are paternalistic. The argument runs that in contrast to the goods-focus of needs, the capabilities approach focuses on the functionings, with what people value doing and being. In contrast to the paternalism of the needs approach, the capabilities approach focuses on capabilities, that is with people's freedoms to achieve valuable functionings. It is not clear, however, that the gap between the approaches need be so wide. If one takes the use of the verb-phrase to be prior to the noun-phrase in characterisation of needs, then the first contrast between needs and capabilities become much more a matter of preferred modes of speech. With respect to the second, when it is granted that the capacity to make judgements and choices about one's own life is a condition of what it is to flourish as a human being, then many capabilities can be reformulated within a needs vocabulary. One can claim, for example, that individuals need to be free to pursue their own projects, to choose their own partner, to work for their own well-being and so on. What a needs approach will still emphasise in this context is the importance of the functionings themselves, not just the freedoms to achieve those functionings.[3]

With these distinctions in place, we can turn to the contrast between the logical properties of the concepts of 'need' and 'preference'. The concept of 'need' and the concept of 'preference' have different logical properties. First, sentences of the form 'a needs x' are extensional, whereas sentences of the form 'a prefers x to y' are in ordinary language intensional. The verb 'need' is extensional; if a needs x, and x is identical to y, then it follows that a needs y. For example, from 'Peter needs water', and 'water is H_2O' we can infer 'Peter needs H_2O'. The verb 'prefer' is an intensional transitive verb:[4] it is not the case that if a prefers x to z and x is identical to y then it follows that a prefers y to z. For example, from 'Oedipus prefers to marry Jocasta to any other woman in Thebes' and 'Jocasta is Oedipus's mother', one cannot infer 'Oedipus prefers to marry his mother to any other woman in Thebes'. The logical difference captures one way in which needs claims are objective whereas claims about preferences are subjective. The truth of the claim that a person needs something depends on the objective condition of the person and the nature of the object, its capacities to contribute to the flourishing or ends of a person. In contrast the truth of the claim that a person prefers one object to another depends rather upon the nature of the person's beliefs about and attitudes towards the object.

Second, the concept of an absolute or categorical need is a threshold concept; the concept of preference is not. The concept of need is a threshold concept in two distinct ways. First, to use the language of capabilities, there are lower levels to the functionings that characterise a minimally decent life for a particular human being. For example, an old person in a care home, drugged so that she is unable to think for herself or lacking the capabilities required for basic independent mobility falls below the minimal threshold for human functioning. Second, there are lower and often upper levels to the goods that are required to achieve those functionings. If a doctor says a patient needs 20mg of a drug per day, she is specifying roughly the right dose that the patient of that age, weight, etc. requires for her health. There is a level below this which will be ineffective – drugs in homeopathic quantities are useless. There is an upper level beyond which the drug may be dangerous. The patient will be harmed. Correspondingly needs are satiable. Preferences and desires are unlike this. It may be contingently the case that there are limits to the bundles of goods that are required to meet a particular agent's preferences. However, there are no necessary limits. There is nothing in the world or in the nature of a human agent that rules out an agent's never being satisfied and always preferring more if it is available. Indeed, this peculiarly avaricious agent is built into the assumptions of the nature of the consumer in modern neoclassical economics. Economic textbooks typically assume non-satiation: given a choice between a smaller and larger bundle of commodities, the agent always chooses the larger (Arrow and Hahn 1971: 78; Haussman 1992).

Third, there is a necessary link between the concept of categorical need and harm that is absent in the case of preference. One does not necessarily harm someone by failing to give them what they prefer. Harm is conceptually related to need rather than to preferences or wants. Some preferences tied to essential needs are such that if they are not satisfied a person is harmed. However, others are not.

Fourth, there is an epistemic difference between needs and preferences. Our needs can be opaque to us in ways that our desires and preferences are not. Consider the claims made in the following passage:

> The meeting of a need, unlike the satisfaction of a desire, always involves a confirmatory *recognition* of the nature of the need met, a recognition that retroactively determines the nature of the need that prompted the activity culminating in its fulfilling. The meeting of a need first makes the need recognizable for what it is; whereas that satisfying of a desire merely assuages the desire, without aiding us in its recognition. It was a desire only because there was no problem of recognition; we recognized what we wanted by it even before its satisfaction. We can thus be disappointed by getting what we desire
>
> (Todes 2001: 177, emphasis in the original)

The claims made here are not entirely right. It is not always the case that the meeting of needs involves 'confirmatory recognition of the nature of the need met'. We can and constantly do have biological needs met without recognising they are met or even that they exist at all. It is often when needs go unmet that there is a recognition of their nature. Dispositional needs are recognised when they become occurrent needs. Furthermore in this respect at least needs and desires are similar – both needs and desires are often recognised retrospectively when they are not met. However, the passage from Todes does point to import-ant contrasts. It is the case that while we sometimes retrospectively discover what a need is through its being met, we do not discover what we desire through its being satisfied. We can be disappointed in the satisfaction of a desire but not in the meeting of a need.

These are then the features of the logic of need concepts that distinguish it from that of preferences. Do the differences matter? In the following sections I will explore some of the ways in which they do. In Section 3 I consider the ques-tion of what is to be sustained for future generations. I suggest that a needs-based approach allows for much less substitutability between different kinds of goods that we need to pass on to future generations than a preference-based approach. In Section 4 I will suggest that conceiving of welfare in terms of preferences cannot capture the nature and seriousness of the ethical obligations we owe both to the poor in current generations and to future generations. In Section 5 I will argue that the needs-based approach better captures the limits to the goods required for human flourishing.

3 Needs, thresholds and substitutability[5]

I noted in the first section that in recent economic literature sustainable develop-ment is characterised in terms of economic and social development that at least maintains and if possible improves human welfare. The conditions for mainte-nance of human welfare over generations are typically characterised in the lan-guage of capital.[6] Each generation is to leave its successor a stock of capital assets no less than it receives. Given this account of the conditions for sustaina-bility, debates have subsequently often turned on the nature of the capital stock bequeathed to later generations. A distinction is drawn between human-made capital and natural capital. Human-made capital includes not just the physical items in the built and technological environment such as machines, roads and buildings, but also 'human capital' such as knowledge, skills and capabilities and forms of 'social capital'. Natural capital on the other hand includes organic and inorganic resources understood in a very broad sense to cover not just phys-ical resources but also for example genetic information, biodiversity, ecosys-temic functions and waste assimilation capacity. Given this distinction the literature normally focuses on two possible versions of the nature of the mix of capital goods that must be left to future generations. Proponents of 'weak sus-tainability' require only that 'overall capital – the total comprising both natural and human-made capital – should not decline', while proponents of 'strong sus-tainability' require that 'natural capital in particular should not decline' (Pearce *et al.* 1989: 34). The difference between the two positions is often taken to turn on the substitutability of human-made capital and natural capital. Daly for example offers the following characterisation of the differences: '[W]eak sustainability assumes that manmade and natural capital are basically substitutes. Strong sustainability assumes that manmade and natural capital are basically complements' (Daly 1995: 570).

The debate thus set up tends to degenerate into a battle of straw men. Proponents of strong sustainability are accused of holding an 'absurd' position of not allowing the use of any non-renewable resources or permitting any species to go extinct whatever the cost to human welfare (Beckerman 1994). Proponents of weak sustainability are accused of treating natural and human capital as infinitely substitutable. Both sides typically resist these characterisations. Defenders of strong sustainability reject the claim that their position denies the possibility of any loss of existing natural capital (Daly 1995). Neoclassical economists typically claim that it is substitution between natural and human capital at the margins that is at issue, not total substitutability of one for the other (Beckerman 2000; Arrow 1997: 579). What then is at stake in this debate? It would be easy to see it as turning into a series of local disputes about the substitutability of local marginal shifts in the total make up of natural and human-made capital.

There is however a prior issue at stake in the debate about the criteria that are employed for one good to be substitutable for another. Statements of the form 'A is substitutable for B' are elliptical. One good is substitutable for another with respect to something. The concept of a substitute in economic theory relevant in this context is that of substitutability with respect to welfare. For any particular agent a good, A, is a substitute for another good, B, if replacing B by A does not change the overall level of welfare of that agent. A loss in one good, B, can be compensated by a gain in another good, A, in the sense that the person's level of welfare remains unchanged. Two goods are substitutes for another not in the sense that they do the same job, but rather in the sense that, as Hillel Steiner puts it, 'although they each do a different job, those two jobs are *just as good* as one another' (Steiner 1994: 171). On this account the question of substitutability turns on what it is for one alternative to be as good for an agent as another in the sense of leaving their welfare level unchanged. One major reason for the assumption of ubiquitous substitutability of different kinds of 'capital' has its origin in the particular preference satisfaction account to welfare that it assumes.

If one assumes a preference satisfaction theory of welfare, the question of substitutability turns on the agent's overall level of preference satisfaction. A good A is a substitute for B if replacing B by A leaves the agent's overall preference satisfaction the same. The agent is indifferent between the two bundles of goods in the sense that they are equally preferred. Given additional assumptions about the structure of the agent's preferences, that they are transitive, complete, reflexive and continuous, one can draw the smooth continuous indifference curves of economic textbooks, which joins all the points of combination of goods which are equally preferred. The marginal rate of substitution between the goods, of how much of one good a person is willing to give up in order to gain an improvement in the other, is indicated by the slope of the curve. Central to the construction of these curves is an implication of the assumption of continuity, that 'given any two goods in a bundle, it is always possible – by reducing the amount of one fractionally and increasing the amount of the other fractionally – to define another bundle which is indifferent to the first' (Hargreaves-Heap *et al.* 1992: 6). This assumption can be questioned from within a preference satisfaction account of welfare. It might be that rational agents can have lexicographic preferences that are not consistent with this assumption (Spash 1998). However, one central reason for this is that preferences follow needs, and as far as the structure of needs is concerned there are strong reasons to doubt that an equivalent assumption about continuity holds.

I noticed in Section 2 that the concept of categorical need is a threshold concept in the way that the concept of preference is not. It is a threshold concept in two ways – there are lower levels to the functionings that characterise a minimally decent life; there are lower and often upper levels to the goods that are required to achieve those functionings. The existence of lower and upper levels creates problems for an assumption of continuity. Consider the following counter-example to the assumption of continuity offered by Vivian Walsh:

> [T]here are some important choice situations in which the object of choice must be available in exactly one form to be *any* good at all – where the idea of slightly more or less just does not apply. This can be so even when the thing chosen happens to be a physical thing which is highly divisible, like a chemical. Most of the drugs prescribed by physicians are highly divisible. Yet it is a matter of common practice that what he prescribes is some exact dose; quantities less than the right one may be useless and greater ones may be fatal.
>
> (Walsh 1970: 27, cf. 142)

The power of the example depends on an underlying appeal to a needs-based account of welfare. In offering the patient an exact dose, no more, no less, the doctor is concerned with what bundle of goods best meets the patient's health needs. The patient's own preference structure might be different. She might for example prefer to sell the drug to buy other goods, say a holiday, that satisfy other preferences she has. From the perspective of her preferences, the drug may have substitutes. However, from the point of view of the doctor concerned with her health-needs it does not. And if the patient's own preferences are about her health then the failure of substitutability will be reflected in her own preferences which may have a lexicographic structure.

What happens if we stay at the level of needs? The patient will have other needs, for example for education, social relations, leisure and so on. Is it possible that different goods can be substitutes so long as total needs-satisfaction stays the same? The fact that the concept of needs is a threshold concept blocks substitutability here as well. Where an agent suffers a loss in one dimension of need that takes her below a certain minimal threshold, there will not be a gain in some other dimension of need that will compensate for that loss. If a person is suffering from severe malnutrition then that immediate need must be satisfied. Goods that meet some other need, say for education or leisure, will not be substitutes. Where a person falls below some threshold of need, there is no reason to assume that anything like an assumption of continuity will hold.

The point can be stated more generally. Individuals have a variety of different categorical needs that are related to the distinct functionings that are constitutive of human welfare. Consider Nussbaum's list of the central human capabilities for functionings: bodily health; bodily integrity; senses, imagination and thought; emotions; practical reason; affiliation; other species; play; control over one's political and material environment (Nussbaum 2000: 78–80).[7] Each heading defines a space of functionings which will itself be internally plural. There are distinct dimensions of bodily health for example. Given this irreducible plurality of spaces of functionings there is no reason to assume that different goods are substitutable with respect to welfare understood in terms of the satisfaction of needs. For a marginal loss of a good in one space, such as bodily health, there may exist no compensating gain in another dimension, say practical reason or political freedom, that leaves the person's well-being unchanged. A loss in that dimension may only be addressed by a gain in the same dimension. The person who suffers from malnutrition requires immediate objects of nutrition – not better housing or a more satisfying leisure. There are, as people often say, no substitutes for good health, for good friends, for particular places and environments. A serious loss in one dimension of functionings must be made good by the provision of goods in that dimension.

Given the limits of substitutability across different dimensions of human functionings, the limits to the marginal substitutability of natural and human capital turns out to be a special case of a more general limit to substitutability of goods. If sustainability is about maintaining or improving human welfare over generations, and welfare is understood in terms of needs or capabilities to achieve functionings, then sustainability requires each generation to pass on a bundle of goods that is disaggregated across the different dimensions of human functioning. Each generation needs to pass down the conditions for livelihood and good health, for social affiliation, for the development of capacities for practical reason, for engaging with the wider natural world and so on. Different dimensions of human flourishing require different goods for their realisation. The development of capacities of theoretical and practical reason requires formal and informal institutions for education. There are specific cultural and physical conditions, including particular environments that are constitutive of communities that are necessary for sustaining human affiliation. In both cases an increase in the number and quality of leisure goods will be no substitute for those specific goods. The capacity to appreciate the natural world and to care for other species requires each generation to sustain particular natural environments. The existence of cultural goods requires a particular set of institutions and environments such as libraries and artworks. There is no rate of marginal substitution that will allow the growth of entertainment to compensate for their loss. In this respect there is more in common between passing on cultural goods and environmental goods than is often thought. Different human needs and functions require specific and non-substitutable goods for their realisation. The case of non-substitutability of 'natural' and 'human' 'capital' are a particular case of this more general limit on substitutability. Environmental goods are not substitutable by goods that satisfy distinct needs and preferences because they answer to quite distinct dimensions of human well-being.

Two clarificatory points need to be added here. First, none of this is to deny that there are important causal relations between different dimensions of human functionings. The existence of such causal relations is a source of compounded inequalities. Deficiencies in different dimensions of well-being will often reinforce each other. Ill health may be closely related to limits in an agent's capacity to control her life in the workplace (Marmot 2004). However, any remedies to those compounded deficiencies must ultimately address deficiencies in each dimension. The existence of causal relations is consistent with the claim about the limits of substitutability of goods across different dimensions of well-being. Second, the claims about the limits of substitutability across different dimensions of human functionings are quite consistent with there being considerable substitutability within any dimension. There are a variety of different ways in which the needs for nutrition, for affiliation and so on can be met. As other chapters in this volume make clear, this point matters for sustainability.[8] The possibility of such substitutability is a condition for the possibility of shifting to strategies of satisfying needs which have lower material and energy impacts and hence for sustainability.

4 Needs, harms and duties of justice

One problem with the specification of welfare entirely in terms of preferences is that it flattens moral distinction between the seriousness that different welfare demands make on both individual and social choices. The point is put well by Henry Shue:

> For standard economic analysis everything is a preference: the epicure's wish for a little more seasoning, the starving child's wish for a little water, the collector's wish for one more painting, and the homeless person's wish for privacy and warmth, all are preferences. Quantitatively, they are different because some are backed up by greater 'willingness to pay' than others, but qualitatively a preference is a preference. To choose, however, to discard all the qualitative distinctions built up during the evolution of human history is to deprive ourselves of a rich treasure of sophistication and subtlety. Some so-called preferences are vital, some are trivial. Some are needs, and some are mere wants (not needs). The satisfaction of some 'preferences' is essential for survival or human decency, and the satisfaction of some others is inessential for either survival or decency.
>
> (Shue 1993: 55)

As we noted in Section 2, while the concept of need is conceptually tied to that of harm, the concept of preference is not. If an individual or public body deprives an agent of objects that meet absolute needs, then the agent will be harmed. If an individual or public body deprives an agent of objects that would satisfy his preferences, then the agent is not necessarily harmed. It depends upon the nature of the preference. If a preference it tied to a vital need, then the agent will be harmed, but not necessarily otherwise. This feature of needs has important implications for the kinds of moral demands that needs make on agents. Claims of needs make moral demands on agents that preferences do not.

The point is important in understanding the demands of justice that sustainability calls upon. It is worth here returning to the Brundtland formulation of sustainable development. There are two components to the Brundtland formulation: the ability of future generations to meet their needs must not be compromised by the ways in which current generations meet their needs and within current generations the essential needs of the world's poor should be given 'overriding priority'. One way of interpreting the demands of justice that the Brundtland formulation invokes is in terms of negative duties of justice. We have duties of justice not to harm those who follow us. There is something prima facie unjust about our engaging in projects in which the benefits fall on ourselves while the harms fall on those who follow us. In this respect at least there is an asymmetry between the obligations not to harm future generations and duties to improve their welfare, which are also captured by the concept of sustainability. The negative duties not to harm are required by justice. In contrast, there are no requirements of justice to improve their lives, although it would be good of us to do so (Barry 1996: 244; Spash 1993, 1994, 2002). Similarly we have negative duties of justice not to harm the worst off within current generations in the pursuit of just policies with respect to future generations. Those who already fall below the threshold of a decent life are owed obligations in justice to have those vital needs met.

Consider for example the case of climate change. We have duties of justice towards future generations not to significantly risk damaging their fundamental interests by introducing dangerous levels of climate change. Our current patterns of production and consumption, which threaten an increase of four to six degrees Celsius, do not meet those standards of justice. At the same time, in the pursuit of policies that do meet these claims of justice, we have obligations of justice to the current poor to ensure that their interests are not adversely affected, but rather that their condition is improved so that it comes above minimal levels of human decency. Any policy on emissions should permit them to meet fundamental absolute needs for survival, self-respect and standing. The just policy will cut luxury emissions to allow both current and future generations to meet absolute needs (Shue 1993: 55).

There is a standard argument for there being an asymmetry between the cases of harming the future and harming current generations – the non-identity problem. The choice between different policies, for example between a high and low CO_2 emissions path of production affects not just the welfare states of future generations, but also their identity. Since the population that is consequent on the pursuit of the environmental non-benign policy would not have existed were it not for that policy, then, providing that their life is not so bad that they would have rationally preferred not to exist, they cannot be said to have been harmed, since they are not worse off than they would have been had they not existed. Our policies cannot be said to have harmed future generations. The conceptual relations between harms, needs and thresholds suggest a way in which this argument might be resisted. The argument relies upon a counterfactual account of the concept of harm: a person is harmed by an act if the act renders her worse-off than she would have been. On that account, if future generations are not so badly-off that it would have been better if they had not existed, then policies of current generations cannot be said to harm them. However, an alternative account of the concept of harm is to take it to be, at least in some uses, a threshold concept: a person is harmed by an act if it takes her below a certain threshold of human well-being. If we assume a threshold account of harm then the identity problem loses its sting. If our acts adversely affect the vital categorical needs of future generations then we harm them, even if causing that harm was a condition of their existence. The counterfactual situation in which they did not exist is not relevant.

5 Needs, dependence and agency[9]

One reason for the unpopularity of needs-claims in political theory and public policy is that neediness is associated with human dependence and seeing a person as a patient, rather than with human agency and seeing a person as an actor. Sen offers one version of the complaint in contrasting needs with capabilities:

> 'Needs' is a more passive concept than 'capability' and it is arguable that the perspective of positive freedom links naturally with capabilities (what can the person *do*?) rather than with the fulfilment of their needs (what can be *done for* the person?). The perspective of fulfilling needs has some obvious advantages in dealing with dependents (e.g. children), but for responsible adults the format of capabilities may be much more suitable.
>
> (Sen 1984: 514)

While Sen goes on to claim that the distinction is one of 'outlook and emphasis' rather than one of fundamentals, it does capture an important worry about needs. Coupled with the objectivity of needs, the worry goes that it can lead to various forms of paternalism, where some expert is able to judge and act on behalf of the actor. The doctor or social worker determines her patient's or client's needs without reference to the patient's and client's own conception of their good. In public policy it can lead at worst to 'a dictatorship over needs' where the state imposes its conception of needs upon citizens without reference to their own account of the good life (Fehér *et al.* 1983). This feature of the language of needs underpins one of the attractions of the appeal to preferences in welfare economics, that it avoids paternalism. Sen's own shift to capabilities to achieve valuable functionings is in part aimed at similarly avoiding paternalism. It is the agent's freedoms to realise those functionings that matters for public policy. Hence, in part, the distance he places between needs and capabilities, despite their commonalities.

There is much that can be said in defence of the needs perspective, some of which I have already rehearsed above. First, not all needs should be understood in a passive form. The verb phrase that a need statement introduces can be active. Individuals have needs to be able to feed and nourish themselves, to form bonds of affiliation and so on. Thus stated, as Wiggins notes, the gap between needs and capabilities is narrowed (Wiggins 2005: 32). Second, autonomy itself is a vital interest, and correspondingly individuals have needs to be able to shape their own lives, not merely to be served by others. Nothing in the language of needs rules out the fact that human beings are active agents and not just passive recipients of goods. However, not all needs are like this – and here the language of needs may have virtues. It is possible to reverse some of the charges made against the needs theorist. There is also a danger of forgetting the other side of human life that is lost if focus is put purely on the facts of agency – the existence of dependence and vulnerability.[10] The wider fact of human dependence and vulnerability is liable to be forgotten. The very achievement of independence, the creation of conditions in which people can significantly shape their own lives, takes place only against a background in which the needs that are a precondition of agency are met.

Part of the difficulty here lies in the way that the virtues of autonomy or independence have been characterised. The virtue of autonomy for example is usually characterised in opposition to the vice of heteronomy. The heteronomous agent is one whose will is determined by another, who is excessively dependent on the authority of others, who does not exercise her own judgement, whose whole life and identity is shaped by a pre-given role or a role that is determined by another: her choices are not her own. In contrast the choices and judgements of the autonomous agent are her own; she is able and willing to depend upon her own capacities of thought and decision, to shape to a significant extent her own life and character. The contrast is often coupled with an account of the achievements of modern commercial societies as creating the conditions for the development of independence and autonomy, the freeing of individuals from the pre-determined roles and personal dependence of pre-commercial society. The account is shared by theorists as different as Smith, Marx and Sen (Marx 1973: 163ff.; Sen 1995: Chapter 5; Smith 1982 [1762–1764], 1981[1776]). There is a great deal that is right about this account. The vices of heteronomy are vices. An achievement of modern commercial society has been the degree to which, as Marx puts it 'ties of personal dependence ... are in fact exploded' (Marx 1973: 163). However, there are good reasons for thinking that the account of autonomy needs to be more Aristotelian than this characterisation suggests.

The virtues of autonomy need to be contrasted not just with the vices of deficiency, those of the heteronomous character, but also with vices of excess, with the vices of unacknowledged dependence (MacIntyre 1999). Hubris and arrogance are typical instances of these vices. The point is developed as follows by John Benson:

> The virtue of autonomy is a mean state of character with regard to reliance on one's own powers in acting, choosing and forming opinions. The deficiency is termed heteronomy, and there are many terms which may be used to describe the heteronomous person, some of which suggest specific forms of the vice: credulous, gullible, compliant, passive, submissive, overdependent, servile. For the vice of excess there is no name in common use, but solipsism might do, or arrogant self-sufficiency.
>
> (Benson 1983: 5)

These vices of excess are not only often unrecognised, they are sometimes confused with the virtues of autonomy. Consider for example Harsanyi's principle of Preference Autonomy: 'The principle that, in deciding what is good and what is bad for a given individual, the ultimate criteria can only be his own wants and his own preferences' (Harsanyi 1982: 55). Something like this principle underpins the anti-paternalism to which preference theories of welfare in economics appeal. However, the claim that the ultimate criteria for determining what is good and what is bad for an individual are his wants and preferences expresses a conception of autonomy according to which the autonomous person is not only the author of his own projects but also of the standards by which they should be judged. This looks implausible. Authoritative standards that are independent of the preferences of individuals are a condition of education within a variety of practices that are necessary for a condition of autonomy. The acceptance of such standards is a condition of the very capacity to rationally reflect upon one's own projects that is required for autonomy. (O'Neill 1998, 2005; Keat 2000).

The vices of unacknowledged dependence are of particular significance in consideration of the relations of humans with the background natural conditions of human life that are at the centre of recent debates on sustainability. The vice of excess in this context does have a name, that of hubris, which is often invoked in this context. Another phrase that is used in popular culture to capture at least some of worries about unacknowledged dependence is that of 'playing God'. The phrase tends to be dismissed by philosophers and in public policy debate. However, there is one way of understanding the metaphor that goes back to Aristotle that is rationally defensible. We are human beings with an animal nature with all the forms of neediness and limits in capacities that this involves. We are not gods who transcend the natural world and can control it. There is hubris in the failure to acknowledge our dependence on natural processes and the limits of our knowledge of these processes and our capacities to control them.[11] In this context, to the extent that Sen is right that the concept of 'needs' is 'a more passive concept', it may have its own virtues in drawing attention to the vulnerabilities and dependence that are constitutive of human life.

6 The overshadowing of needs

My central aim in this chapter has been to suggest that the original Brundtland formulation of the concept of sustainability in terms of needs has both theoretical and practical virtues which disappear in the shift to the language of preferences. A needs-based approach is more alive to the plurality of different constituents of well-being, and the limits to the substitutability between different kinds of goods that current generation must pass on to future generations if human welfare is to be maintained. It better captures the nature and seriousness of the ethical obligations that are owed both to the poor in current generations and to future generations. It provides a more adequate starting point for the acknowledgement of forms of human dependence and vulnerability that informs basic concerns with sustainability. Something important is lost from the conceptual, political and moral landscape in the replacement of 'need' by 'preference' in the characterisation of sustainability.

Notes

* There is also the distinct approach offered by recently revived hedonic theories of welfare. There has been an influential argument that recent hedonic research promises the possibility of a decoupling of consumption and happiness, and hence offers the promise of a sustainable economy. See, for example, Porritt, 2003. I criticise this approach and defend an Aristotelian alternative closer to needs-based and capabilities-based approaches in O'Neill, 2006 and 2008. For other discussions of the differences between hedonic and capabilities approaches see Robeyns and van der Veen, 2007, Jackson, 2009 and Chapter 4 of this book.

1 My discussion draws heavily on the work of David Wiggins 1998, 2005.
2 On the distinction between dispositional and occurrent needs see Reader 2007a: 71–72 and Thompson 1987: 13.
3 For a fuller discussion of these issues see Wiggins 2005; Alkire 2005 and Reader 2005.
4 For discussion of intensional transitive verbs see Forbes 2002 and Saul 2002.
5 The arguments in this section draw on O'Neill 2007: Chapter 6 and O'Neill *et al.* 2008: Chapter 11.
6 I criticize the use of this metaphor in O'Neill 2007: Chapter 6.
7 Nussbaum's list is of course one of many similar lists. The authors of Chapter 1 appeal to the list offered by Max-Neef. John Finnis offers another influential list of 'basic aspects of ... well-being' (Finnis 1980: 85ff). For a useful discussion see Alkire 2002. Crucial to the argument here is the fact that the different dimensions of well-being are irreducible to each other and unforsakeable.
8 See in particular the arguments in Chapters 1 and 3.
9 For a more detailed discussion of some of the main claims here see, O'Neill 2005 and 2009.
10 Compare Reader 2007b.
11 These failures to acknowledge our dependence are not simply cognitive errors. Their origins are in part social. The networks of care and support that are a condition of meeting our dispositional needs are often rendered socially invisible in modern society. Needs are often met in ways that often go unobserved and unnoticed. The fact of human dependency is apparent only among those with pressing occurrent needs, paradoxically often the very people whose labour is required to meet basic dispositional needs of those who appear above common human dependencies. In contrast the occurrent needy are often humiliated in their neediness, their need for social independence not acknowledged in social policy. The meeting of occurrent needs of the

dependent and vulnerable in turn often fails to recognise their own needs for social independence (O'Neill 2005). Hence the resistance to means testing that involves humiliation of neediness.

> Let me advise you. I was wounded in both arms and the shrapnel is still there. I have thirty-three and a third per cent disability. But I was like thousands ... I was so glad to get out of the army. I didn't claim. I was an independent man. I am an independent man I didn't want anything from anybody; and I don't want charity now. I didn't clam income support, or whatever they called it then, until I was forced to ... I've been opposed to means testing all my life. It is no less degrading today than it was in the time of the Poor Laws. I *paid* for my pension in contributions all my working life; no one has a right to question that now and to interrogate me, no matter how poor I am.
>
> (Interview with a pensioner in Pilger 1998)

The social invisibility of particular networks of support that meet needs has been a theme of recent work on environmental justice. Environmental justice concerns not just the ill-distribution of environmental benefits and harms, but also failure of recognition, in particular the lack of social recognition of forms of labour such as domestic labour and subsistence agriculture that fall outside the market realm. Within a market system, those forms of labour which have been central to sustaining human life and agricultural biodiversity tend to go unrecognised and unvalued (Martinez-Alier 1997, 2002; Shiva 1992).

References

Alkire, S. (2002), Dimensions of human development, *World Development*, 30(2): 181–205.

—— (2005), Needs and capabilities, in Reader (2005) pp. 229–251.

Arrow, K. (1997), Invaluable goods, *Journal of Economic Literature*, 35(2): 757–765.

Arrow, K. and Hahn, F. (1971), *General Competitive Analysis*, Holden-Day: San Francisco, CA.

Barry, B. (1996), Circumstance of justice and future generations, in R. Sikora and B. Barry (eds), *Obligations to Future Generations*, White Horse Press: Cambridge.

Beckerman, W. (1994), Sustainable development: is it a useful concept? *Environmental Values*, 3(3): 191–209.

—— (2000), Review of Foster J. (ed.). Valuing Nature? Ethics, Economics and the Environment *Environmental Values*, 9(1): 122–124.

Benson J. (1983), Who is the autonomous man? *Philosophy*, 58(223): 5–17.

Daly, H.E. (1995), On Wilfred Beckerman's critique of sustainable development. *Environmental Values*, 4(1): 49–55.

Fehér, F., Heller, A. and Márkus, G. (1983), *Dictatorship over Needs: An Analysis of Soviet Societies*, Blackwell: Oxford.

Finnis, J. (1980), *Natural Law and Natural Rights*, Clarendon Press: Oxford.

Forbes, G. (2002), Intensionality, *Proceedings of the Aristotelian Society*, Supplementary 76: 75–99.

Hargreaves-Heap, S., Hollis, M., Lyons, B., Sugden, R. and Weale, A. (1992), *The Theory of Choice: A Critical Guide*, Blackwell: Oxford.

Harsanyi, J. (1982), Morality and the theory of rational behaviour, in A. Sen and B. Williams (eds), *Utilitarianism and Beyond*, Cambridge University Press: Cambridge.

Haussman, D. (1992), *What Are General Equilibrium Theories? Essays on Philosophy and Economic Methodology*, Cambridge University Press: Cambridge.

Jackson, T. (2009) *Prosperity without Growth*? Sustainable Development Commission: London, online, abailable at www.sd-commission.org.uk/publications/downloads/prosperity_without_growth_report.pdf.

Keat, R. (2000), *Cultural Goods and the Limits of the Market*, Macmillan: Basingstoke.

MacIntyre, A. (1999), *Dependent Rational Animals*, Duckworth: London.

Marmot, M. (2004), *The Status Syndrome*, Bloomsbury: London.

Marx, K. (1973), *Grundrisse*, Penguin: Harmonsdworth.

Martinez-Alier, J. (1997), The merchandising of biodiversity, in T. Hayward and J. O'Neill (eds), *Justice, Property and the Environment: Social and Legal Perspectives*: Avebury: Aldershot.

—— (2002), *The Environmentalism of the Poor*, Edward Elgar: Cheltenham.

Nussbaum, M. (2000), *Women and Human Development: The Capabilities Approach*, Cambridge University Press: Cambridge.

O'Neill, J. (1998), *The Market: Ethics, Knowledge and Politics*, Routledge: London.

—— (2005), Need, humiliation and independence, in S. Reader, 73–98.

—— (2006), Citizenship, Well-Being and Sustainability: Epicurus or Aristotle? *Analyse & Kritik* 28: 158–172.

—— (2007), *Markets, Deliberation and Environment*, Routledge: London.

—— (2008), Happiness and the good life, *Environmental Values*, 17(2): 125–144.

—— (2009), Labour, nature and dependence, in S. Moog and R. Stone (eds), *Nature, Social Relations and Human Needs: Essays in Honour of Ted Benton*, Palgrave: London.

O'Neill, J., Holland, A. and Light, A. (2008), *Environmental Values*, Routledge: London.

Pearce, D. (1993), *Economic Values and the Natural World*, Earthscan: London.

Pearce, D., Groom, B., Hepburn, C. and Condor, P. (2003), Valuing the future: recent advances in social discounting, *World Economics* 4(2): 121–141.

Pearce, D., Markandya, A. and Barbier, E. (1989), *Blueprint for a Green Economy*, Earthscan: London.

Pilger, J. (1998), *Hidden Agendas*, Vintage: London.

Porritt, J. (2003), *Redefining Sustainability*, Sustainable Development Commission: London.

Reader, S. (ed.) (2005), *The Philosophy of Need: Royal Institute of Philosophy Supplement 57*, Cambridge University Press: Cambridge.

—— (2006), Does a basic needs approach need capabilities? *The Journal of Political Philosophy*, 14(3): 337–350.

—— (2007a), *Needs and Moral Necessity*, Routledge: London.

—— (2007b), The other side of agency, *Philosophy* 82(4): 579–604.

Robeyns, I. and Van der Veen, R.J. (2007), Sustainable quality of life: Conceptual analysis for a policy-relevant empirical specification, Netherlands Environmental Assessment Agency (MNP): Bilthoven.

Saul, J.(2002), Intensionality, *Proceedings of the Aristotelian Society*, Supplementary 76: 101–119.

Sen, A. (1984), *Resources, Values and Development*, Blackwell: Oxford.

—— (1995), *Development as Freedom*, Oxford University Press: Oxford.

Shiva, V. (1992), Recovering the real meaning of sustainability, in D. Cooper and J. Palmer (eds), *The Environment in Question*, Routledge: London.

Shue, H. (1993), Subsistence emissions and luxury emissions, *Law and Policy*, 15(1): 39–59.

Smith, A. (1982 [1762–1764]) *Lectures on Jurisprudence*, Liberty Press: Indianapolis, IN.

—— (1981 [1776]), *An Inquiry into the Nature and Causes of the Wealth of Nations*, Liberty Press: Indianapolis, IN.

Spash, C.L. (1993), Economics, ethics, and long-term environmental damages, *Environmental Ethics*, 15(2): 117–132.

—— (1994), Double CO_2 and beyond: benefits, costs and compensation, *Ecological Economics*, 10(1): 27–36.

—— (1998), Investigating individual motives for environmental action: lexicographic preferences, beliefs and attitudes, in J. Lemons, L. Westra and R. Goodland (eds), *Ecological Sustainability and Integrity: Concepts and Approaches*, Kluwer Academic Publishers: Dordrecht, pp. 46–62.

—— 2002. Greenhouse Economics: Value and Ethics. Routledge: London.

Steiner, H. (1994), *An Essay on Rights*, Blackwell: Oxford.

Thompson, G. (1987), *Needs*, Routledge and Kegan Paul: London.

Todes, S. (2001), *Body and World*, MIT Press: Cambridge, MA.

Walsh, V. (1970), *Introduction to Contemporary Microeconomics*, McGraw-Hill: New York.

Wiggins, D. (1998), The claims of need, in D. Wiggins (ed.), *Needs, Values, Truth*, Clarendon Press: Oxford.

—— (2005), An idea we cannot do without, in Reader (2005): 25–50.

WCED (United Nations World Commission on Environment and Development) (1987), *Our Common Future*, online, available at: www.un-documents.net/wced-ocf.htm [accessed 3 April 2010].

3 Sustainability as a challenge to the capability approach

Ortrud Leßmann*

The basic concepts

The Capability Approach (CA), developed by Amartya Sen and Martha Nussbaum, defines a person's well-being in terms of the beings and doings (the *functionings*) a person achieves and her *capability* to choose among different combinations of such functionings. The 'doings and beings' a person achieves are constitutive of her well-being and can be used to describe her life situation.[1] Examples of functionings range from elementary ones like being adequately nourished to rather complex ones like being able to take part in the life of the community and having self-respect (Sen 1999a: 75). The achievement of a functioning typically presupposes on the one hand the availability of certain commodities and on the other hand the ability of the individual to use these commodities accordingly. Take as an illustration the functioning to move about (Figure 3.1). It presupposes the availability of a bike (or a car) or of the money for public transport on the one hand and on the other hand the ability to ride a bike (or drive a car) or to go by bus, i.e. the ability to convert a resource into a functioning. The individual budget set comprises all commodity bundles feasible for a person and the set of conversion functions is composed of all modes of utilization a person is able to exercise. Hence, the feasibility of functionings for a person depends on (a) the budget set and on (b) the set of (individual) conversion functions (Sen 1985a: 11; Robeyns 2005: 98–99).

Those ways of life (bundles of functionings) that are feasible for the person, in terms of both material conditions and her personal features, constitute the elements of her *capability set* (see Box 3.1 for the difference between capability and functionings). The capability set thus reflects a person's *freedom* to lead one way of life or another. Each way of leading a life is one element or option of a person's capability set. One option may consist of riding a bike and another option going by bus (Figure 3.1). The person is thought to be free to choose among these options. The functionings the person actually chooses from this set are her *achievements*. In Figure 3.1 the option that encompasses 'riding a bike' is chosen.

The person's well-being is now taken to be a function of both – the functionings achieved as well as the capability set, i.e. the options open to her. Put differently, the freedom to choose affects well-being positively in the sense that it is

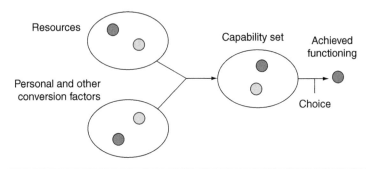

Symbol	●	○
Mode of moving about	Riding a bike	Going by bus
Resources	A bike	Money for the bus
Personal conversion factor	Ability of riding a bike	Ability of going by bus
Other conversion factors	Streets suitable for bikes	Availability of public transport

Figure 3.1 An illustration of capability and functionings: two modes of moving about.

an end in its own right (Sen 1988: 270) and thus the well-being of a person depends on the life she leads and the freedom of choice she enjoys. Sen (e.g. 1999a: 148) speaks of the intrinsic value of the opportunity to choose in contrast to its instrumental value.

Box 3.1 Functionings and capability in Sen's CA

Functionings are doings and beings, they are constitutive of well-being, examples range from eating, working, being healthy, to taking part in the life of a community, to appearing in public without shame. These are the dimensions of well-being.

Bundles or combinations of functionings describe a way of life. The interdependency of functionings is reflected by considering combinations and not single functionings or dimensions.

The capability set consists of all combinations of functionings feasible for a person. Formally, it is a subset of the multidimensional functioning space. Each element of the capability set thus describes multidimensionally a way of life open to the individual. The person can choose among these options.

Though well-being is an important variable for moral analysis – perhaps the most important one – it is not the only one as Sen argues (1985b: 186). People pursue goals other than well-being and sometimes their activities do not contribute to their well-being. In order to take a broader perspective than e.g. utilitarianism that focuses on self-interest, Sen introduces the distinction between *well-being* and *agency* in addition to the distinction of freedoms and achieve ments (see Box 3.2). Thus he arrives at four categories: (1) well-being achieve-ments, (2) well-being freedom, (3) agency achievements and (4) agency freedom. In drawing these distinctions Sen (1985b: 203) explains that 'agency freedom refers to what a person is free to do and achieve in pursuit of whatever goals or values he or she regards as important' and concludes that 'agency freedom is more general' than well-being freedom, 'since it is not tied to any one type of aim' whereas the latter is confined to a particular aim, namely that of well-being. While he points out that '[t]he importance of the agency aspect, in general, relates to the view of persons as responsible agents' (Sen 1985b: 204), his use of the term agency is more specifically confined to following motives 'closely connected with one's morals' (Sen 1977: 93).

Box 3.2 Well-being and agency in Sen's CA

The distinction between well-being and agency does not confine the former to per-sonal well-being. If we act for reasons of sympathy, e.g. because we care for others, we aim at well-being whereas acting for reasons of commitment is a case of agency (Sen 1987: 28). 'It can be argued that behaviour based on sympathy is in an important sense egoistic' (Sen 1977: 92) and can be analysed along the lines of self-interest as Sen (1987: 28) notes:

> In helping another person, the reduction of the other's misery may have the net effect of making one feel and indeed be – better off. This is a case of action that can be promoted on grounds of 'sympathy' ..., and this falls within the general area of promotion of one's own well-being.

The case of sympathy can be included in a traditional utility function by allowing the well-being of those we care for to be an argument of our personal utility func-tion. Sympathy might be subsumed under a broader conception of personal welfare. Commitment, however, involves ideas that conflict with personal welfare. It 'drives a wedge between personal choice and personal welfare' (Sen 1977: 94). In contrast to standard economic theory Sen identifies motives other than personal welfare as reasons for personal choice. Sen (1985b: 206) gives the example of a person who sits on a bench next to a river eating a sandwich when she observes someone falling into the river. Rescuing this other person will not serve her per-sonal well-being since she has to spring into the water, become wet and cold and leave the sandwich behind. Hence, the difference between commitment and sym-pathy can best be seen by asking whether the motivation is ultimately self-interested or not: 'Sympathy is combinable with self-interested behaviour.... But if one is committed ... then that *is* a clear departure from self-interested behaviour' (Sen 2009: 189).

In contrast to Sen, Nussbaum (2000: 14) does not distinguish well-being from agency or freedoms from achievements. She believes 'that all the important dis-tinctions can be captured as aspects of the capability/function distinction'. Aiming at capabilities means according to Nussbaum (1988: 153) aiming at making people 'able to live and act in certain concrete ways'. Because of the value of choice 'we will define our goal in terms of capabilities, not actual functioning'. Thus she reserves the term 'functioning' to indicate actual achievements and emphasises the freedom aspect by referring to capabilities. She does not consider it necessary to speak of agency since the term functioning already implies actively pursuing something rather than passively receive it (Nussbaum 2000: 14). Hence, there are major differences in the understanding of the terms between Sen and Nussbaum (see Box 3.3). The chapter follows Sen's use of the terms.

Specific to Nussbaum's approach is the distinction between basic, internal and combined capabilities that hints at how capabilities develop in the course of time. Basic capabilities refer to the innate potential – for example to speak. Internal capabilities indicate the achieved level of talents and skills and combined capabilities denote the combination of what a person is able internally with the external conditions which may enhance or hinder the exercise of her internal capabilities. Further Nussbaum concludes that 'of course we need to specify the list of things that we want people to be capable of doing' (Nussbaum 1988: 153–154). Hence, she developed a list of ten 'central functional capabilities' in order to give 'a partial, not a comprehensive, conception of the good life, a moral conception selected for political purposes only' (Nussbaum 2000: 77).

Sen has resisted the idea of specifying a similar list mainly for two reasons: the context-dependency of functionings and the need for continued public reasoning (Sen 2005: 157). Nussbaum (2000: 77) responds to these arguments by pointing out that her list is open-ended and highlighting that the capabilities might be realized in various ways according to the specific context and in line with public debate in the particular society (see Leßmann 2007).

Box 3.3 Sen versus Nussbaum

Dimensions are called 'functionings' by Sen and 'central functional capabilities' by Nussbaum. The evaluative space, the space for evaluating the wellbeing of people is the functioning space in Sen and the space of capabilities in Nussbaum.

Multidimensionality of the approach: Sen considers combinations of functionings and defines capability as a subset in the multidimensional space of functionings. Nussbaum considers a multitude of capabilities. For normative reasons she demands to treat the capabilities separately, but acknowledges some interdependency by using the concept of combined capability.

A list of relevant dimensions is not provided by Sen because the relevance of dimensions depends on the context and has to be determined in a public discussion. Nussbaum provides a list of ten central functional capabilities. She allows for changes of the list and points at multi-realizability of the elements depending on the specific context.

Problems for conceptualizing sustainability within the CA

The CA lends itself to conceptualizing sustainable development insofar as both aim at achieving and sustaining well-being. Yet the conception of sustainability so far has been developed on a different footing. In the following, three differences are discussed with respect to the question whether and how the CA may encompass these issues. The first concerns the understanding of well-being. In the context of sustainability well-being is related to needs and therefore one can ask whether the understanding of well-being in terms of functionings and capability can be reconciled with well-being in terms of needs. Second, intertemporal or intergenerational issues are at the core of sustainability. The CA so far does not provide a dynamic model of how capability comes about and has no definite answer to the general question known as the 'non-identity problem' of future generations (Parfit 1984). Third, though the CA criticizes standard economic theory it does so from a different point of view from the discussion on sustainability which particularly points at the peculiarities of the ecosystem services that are not accounted for in standard economic theory.

Needs or capability?

The Brundtland definition of sustainability is still frequently quoted and considered as a cornerstone of the sustainability discussion. The definition reads: 'Humanity has the ability to make development sustainable – to make sure that it meets the needs of the present without compromising the ability of future generations to meet their own needs' (WCED 1987: 8).

Thus, needs are referred to as the central measure for evaluation. The Brundtland report does not elaborate in much detail on what is meant by 'needs'. As examples for 'essential needs' it lists food, clothing, shelter and jobs. The report also mentions 'aspirations beyond basic needs' and the 'opportunity to satisfy aspirations for a better life' (WCED 1987: 43–44). Thus, the focus is on 'essential' or 'basic needs' and these are linked to commodities or resources. This is a general pitfall of the needs-concept: needs are usually linked to the commodities or resources needed for their fulfilment (as Rauschmayer *et al.*, Chapter 1, and O'Neill, Chapter 2, both in this book, state as well[2]). It should be noted, however, that by referring to needs the Brundtland commission has also raised the question of quality of life. Since the report does not conceptualize either needs or quality of life in great detail there is room for filling the gap in different ways.

The understanding of needs displayed by the Brundtland report is close to that of the Basic Needs Approach (BNA in the following, Streeten 1981) which was a leading new approach to human well-being in that decade. '[T]he basic needs concept is a reminder that the objective of the development effort is to provide all human beings with the *opportunity* for a full life' (Streeten 1981: 21). Though the BNA tried hard to avoid a concentration on commodities (the pitfall of needs theories mentioned above (Streeten 1984: 973–974)) it was driven in that direction fairly soon.[3] In some important ways the CA has been inspired by the BNA. Sen (1987: 24) approves of the direction BNA takes insofar as it tried to refocus the debate on the 'basis of good living conditions'. But he also takes the 'unsettled questions' Streeten (1984) himself raises further by asking for the foundation of the concern for basic needs: 'Are basic needs important *because and only because* their fulfilment contributes to utility? If not, *why* are they important?' (Sen 1987: 25). Thus, Sen's (1983: 515) main criticism is that the BNA needs to be embedded in a more general approach and he claims that the CA is suitable for that task.[4] This implicitly means that the conception of capability is not opposed to a focus on needs but goes beyond it in important ways.

First of all, the distinction between means and ends is important. Needs are often defined as 'the necessary conditions for the pursuit of the good' (Qizilbash 1997: 261). As such they are seen as the means for achieving the end of a good life (without necessarily distinguishing needs from strategies as Rauschmayer *et al.*, Chapter 1, do). One justification for invoking the concept of needs is that they are universally accepted and that otherwise there cannot be a consensus among persons with conflicting conceptions of the good (Qizilbash 1997). There are two problems with this argument: on the one hand even if we shared a conception of the good life there could be interpersonal variation in the conditions necessary for the pursuit of the good – our needs – to achieve such a good life. People are heterogeneous, they live in different environments, they face different social conditions and sometimes the achievements have to be seen in relation to the society they live in rather than in absolute terms. These are the factors Sen (2009: 255) considers to have an influence on the conversion of resources into functionings (well-being). On the other hand if we do not even share a conception of the good life it seems all the more implausible that we can rely on the same means in order to achieve well-being. However, this is exactly what Rawls (1971) claims to hold for his primary goods. In analysing this argument, Qizilbash (1997: 274) comes to the conclusion that in the end the 'excessive informational demands' is what keeps Rawls from judging well-being directly in terms of opportunities.

Thus, second, we have to investigate whether needs can be understood as ends themselves (see also O'Neill, Chapter 2 above). David Wiggins (1987, 2005) has advocated needs as a core category of ethics. Though he acknowledges that needs are often understood in a 'purely instrumental sense' (Wiggins 2005: 29) he claims that needs can go beyond that and assume an absolute sense by relating the notion to 'unforesakeable' ends. He then, however, goes on to inquire 'how to understand the unforesakeable' and considers two proposals. His own proposal is that things are unforesakeable if the subject who is in need of them 'will be seriously harmed or else … will live a life that is vitally impaired' (Wiggins 2005: 31). This seems like a negative version of the other proposal, namely that things are unforesakeable if the subject who is in need of them 'won't flourish unless it has [them]'.[5] Hence, even when Wiggins defines needs in an absolute sense he invokes some other 'unforesakeable' ends. The concept is derivative of these other ends. Reader (2006: 342) sees this as an advantage of needs theories since they do not prescribe anything beyond meeting needs and, thus, leave room for people's deliberation about their ultimate ends. Hence, most needs theories agree[6] that needs are at best a subset of the ends of human beings and do not deliver a comprehensive list of these ends.

Finally, we have to analyse how the idea of opportunity relates to the end of well-being. The term opportunity turns up in two contexts: (1) the context of deliberation about one's ends e.g. about which ends are 'unforesakeable' or about the conception of 'a good life' including ends beyond meeting one's needs; (2) the context of how to meet one's ends e.g. when the Brundtland report refers to the 'opportunity to satisfy aspirations of a better life' or as BNA puts it the 'opportunity for a full life'. The CA takes opportunity in both contexts into account. Sen (1993: 50) states: '[T]he capability approach is concerned with showing the cogency of a particular *space* for the evaluation of individual opportunities and successes.' The CA does not prescribe a certain way of life as 'the good life' but always emphasizes that everyone should have the opportunity 'to choose a life one has reason to value' (Sen 1999a: 74) – thus leaving the deliberation about what life to value deliberately to people themselves.[7] Sen (2009) points, in fact, out that the CA is not a full theory of justice exactly because it lacks a 'transcendental ideal' of good living or a just world. He even insists on a plurality of spaces in which equality matters apart from capabilities (Sen 2009: 297). By strictly defending the space of functionings as the right space for assessing human advantage and disadvantage – human well-being for short – the CA nevertheless gives some guidance of how the end of a flourishing life is to be described: in terms of functionings and the capability to do and be certain things.

Wiggins (2005: 32) alludes to this phrasing by saying:

> If the ... form of needs claims [as the need to do or to be something] had been consistently and carefully emphasized, moreover, there would have been far less cause for the 'Capability Theory', advocated by Amartya Sen and his allies and associates, to be seen as a rival to 'Needs Theory'. The concerns of these theories are entirely consonant – though I do myself think that the needs framework is better sustained by ordinary significations of the words of natural language.

Opportunity matters also in the context of different strategies to achieve given ends. When needs are considered, there are often different means for satisfying one and the same need. Therefore the notion of different strategies for satisfying needs came about in needs theories (Rauschmayer *et al.* Chapter 1; Cruz Chapter 5 both in this volume; Reader 2006: 341). The CA uses a slightly different perspective by looking at bundles or combinations of functionings. For example, various ways of life may coincide with respect to the achievement of 'being well nourished' but differ profoundly with respect to other functionings such as being educated' and 'having self respect'. Hence, the interdependence of the various functionings – the interdependence of being nourished, being educated and having self-respect – is captured by focusing on combinations of them. Since the capability set by definition comprises all feasible functioning bundles it is up to the individual to choose among these different options (Box 3.1). This is similar to the choice between different satisfiers or different strategies in some ways, but we have to keep in mind the procedural aspect of the notion of 'strategies'. Reader (2006: 341) distinguishes between satisfiers and 'the process by which the need is to be met'. A strategy might refer to both (Rauschmayer *et al.* Chapter 1, above, use the term strategies in both meanings though they define it as an instrumental means which is closer to a satisfier). The CA, however, is especially suitable for assessing the opportunity aspect, but Sen (2009: 296) points out that 'it cannot possibly deal adequately with the process aspect of freedom' which refers mainly to rights and liberties that enable people to get certain things. This seems a very harsh and absolute way to put it, but processes definitely are not modelled but only described within CA. In particular, capability sets are not modelled as an outcome of some process, but as the result of interaction between resources and conversion factors at one moment in time.

In summary, the CA and needs theories both evaluate the well-being of people by looking at their lives. They are not opposed to each other, but the CA goes beyond needs theories by (1) defining and justifying an evaluative space for well-being, namely the space of functionings, and (2) taking freedom of choice explicitly into account and modelling it.

Intergenerational concerns

The process of enhancing the capability of people – their opportunity to live a full life – is at the very heart of the idea of sustainability. Sustainable development, however it is defined, is focused on the process of sustaining something – be it 'nature', the ability of meeting the needs of people or the capability of people to lead a life they value. Hence, if we understand sustainable development in terms of the CA it is important to know how the capability of people develops and in particular what impact the lives of the current generation has on the capability of future generations.

Thus far we can only say that whatever has an impact on the resources (the budget set) or on the conversion factors (the set of individual conversion functions) of future generations will influence their capability to live a life they value. But the definition of sustainability asks more concisely about balancing the capability of the current and that of future generations. Hence, it asks how the current generation has to behave in order to preserve certain conditions for later generations. It is important to note that two assumptions are implicit in the definition of sustainable development – and not given by the CA: (1) the assumption that mankind has an impact on the development of life on earth and (2) the idea that the current generation might have to restrict itself in some ways (e.g. restrict its consumption) in order to ensure the preservation of the opportunity for a full life for future generations.

The CA shares the belief in the power of mankind to change life on earth, but its stance on the issue of the necessity to limit oneself today in order to preserve capabilities for the future is more differentiated. The CA reminds us that there may be several routes to take and that it is not always possible to say which one is the best. The reasons for this indeterminacy are manifold: the CA refrains from defining a 'good life' in concrete terms since each person should have the opportunity to deliberate on the kind of life she values and wants to lead. Further, the CA opts for sustaining the capability of people, i.e. the set of options feasible for them, not one specific option. Even if one specific option could be defined as the goal there might be several routes to achieving this option given the multiple interdependencies between functionings. In consequence, it is not at all clear whether today's generation would consider sustainable development measures as limiting or as empowering. The thought of limiting oneself is misleading in that it views the status quo as an ideal that has to be cut down while sustaining the opportunity of future generations, which might require the active removal of the current ideal. Given the indeterminacy in the 'production' of capabilities (see below) and keeping in mind that it is not necessary (and may be impossible!) to preserve life as it is today it is not clear as well in what way the current generation would have to limit itself in order to sustain the capability of future generations.[8]

Sen (in Sen *et al.* 2003: 330) hints at these important distinctions in saying that 'the Brundtland-Solow approach may be too aggregative'. He goes on to explain that a high overall standard of living can be sustained even though particular freedoms like the freedom from secondary smoking or the freedom to breathe fresh air are impaired. He further points out that the process of achieving certain goals is important in itself. He gives the example of China's one child policy for achieving the goal of lowering fertility rates as an illustration. Though the goal of lowering fertility rates can be justified by the needs of future generations, the coercive one child policy of China's government impairs the freedom of the current generation.

This illustration may also serve as an example for a rather general problem concerning intergenerational justice which has first been described under the name of 'non identity problem' by Derek Parfit (1984). Not only the circumstances of the lives of future generations depend on the activities of the current generation, but in the first place they owe their very existence to their ancestors – the current generation. For that reason we do not know their identity yet – neither their number nor who will come into being and much less what kind of life they will value. Parfit draws the conclusion that the meaning of harming future generations is unclear since they come into being through our very activities. Thus, we do not have a clear moral obligation towards them.

If this argument was accepted the whole question of sustainable development would become pointless: whichever opportunities of life we sustain for future generations, these generations should not complain since they owe their life to us. Hence, Parfit's 'non identity problem' urges us to justify our concern for future generations and for sustainable development.

Sen (2009: 145–149) uses Parfit's argument against contractarian approaches to justice which rely on justifying moral principles in a hypothetical agreement (the 'contract'). In Rawls' theory of justice (1971), for example, the members of society arrive at a hypothetical agreement on principles of justice in an imaginary 'original position' behind a 'veil of ignorance'. This procedure is used to ensure impartiality, but – as Sen (2009: 148) points out – it restricts the agreement to the represented society which may well change depending on the decisions taken. Thus, the question of future generations is difficult to tackle in contractarian approaches, Sen concludes.[9] He favours the 'impartial spectator' of Adam Smith (1976 [1790]); Sen 2009: 44–46) for ensuring impartiality and claims that it has no 'immediate analogue' to the difficulty of dealing with future generations that contractarian approaches have. However, he does not tell how an impartial spectator may help to show that we have a moral obligation towards future generations.

The CA offers two perspectives that matter in this context: (1) an universalist approach towards intragenerational justice and (2) the inclusion of altruism in the idea of well-being. The former matters insofar as intergenerational and intragenerational justice share the problem of taking the well-being of people outside one's own society into account. If the reason for caring about people who live far away is that we are all human beings and share some universal characteristics like being needy this argument readily applies also for future generations. The difference between intra- and intergenerational justice lies exactly in the 'non identity problem': one society does not cause another contemporary society in the way it causes its own future. Nevertheless, intra- and intergenerational justice both concern justice towards people far away either in terms of space or time.

The inclusion of altruistic concerns in the definition of personal well-being matters because the current generation might care about their offspring. Hence, we do not have to know the identity of a future generation and their values in order to care for them and aim at sustaining certain opportunities (Pasek 1993: 19–20).

Sustainability poses the question of intergenerational justice. Development over time plays a crucial role for answering this question. The CA does not model the dynamics of capability so far (cf. Boulanger, Chapter 5, below). Further, time involves path-dependency and this leads to the 'non identity problem'. This problem challenges the idea of intergenerational justice in a fundamental way and urges us to justify our concern for future generations. There is no simple answer to this problem and it has yet to be seen how the CA can meet this challenge.

The role of the ecosystem in the production of capability

The CA does not explicitly mention ecosystem services and their role in the 'production' of capability, but implicitly the intention to model interaction between resources, goods and human well-being in a more complex and comprehensive way is present. The term 'ecosystem services' hints at the interaction between 'nature' and human life. Daily (1997: 3) gives the following definition:

Ecosystem services are the conditions and processes through which natural ecosystems, and the species that make them up, sustain and fulfill human life. They maintain biodiversity and the production of *ecosystem goods* such as seafood ... and many pharmaceuticals.... In addition to the production of goods, ecosystem services are the actual life support functions, such as cleansing, recycling, and renewal, and they confer many intangible aesthetic and cultural benefits as well.

Thus, they can be classified to fulfil three functions: (1) provisioning, (2) regulating and (3) enriching or cultural (see UNEP/iisd 2004: 13–14).

The CA, in contrast, focuses on the characteristics of goods and on the diversities of human beings in explaining how human well-being comes about. As outlined above the CA takes resources and conversion factors into account. Ecosystem services can be both: natural resources seem to be a typical example of resources while climate is one of the examples Sen (1999a: 70) gives for conversion factors since someone living in a hot climate needs different food, clothes and shelter from someone living in a cold climate. Robeyns (2005) summarizes the CA in Figure 3.2.

This representation of the CA alludes to ecosystem services under the headings 'non-market production' and 'environmental factors'. It further hints at the complexity of effects by drawing a two-way arrow from the social context to preference formation. However, there is no straightforward way in which 'non-market production' and 'environmental factors' relate to the three functions of ecosystem services as provisioning, regulating and enriching. Ecosystem goods can be regarded as non-market products, but the role of biodiversity in enhancing capability has yet to be investigated. (However, the CA holds that other species should be preserved, see below.) The regulating services of the ecosystem may be

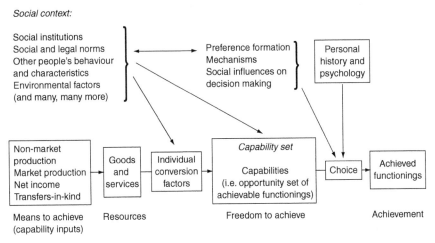

Figure 3.2 A stylized non-dynamic representation of a person's capability set and her social and personal context (adapted from Robeyns 2005: 98).

regarded as environmental factors or environmental conditions that influence the conversion of goods and services into capability since they convert used or polluted air into fresh and breathable air. But they could as well be viewed as 'non-market services', thus entering as resources for the production of capability as well. In this case they are what standard economic theory calls public goods: there is neither rivalry in consumption nor excludability from consumption. Mostly, these services have not been mentioned explicitly – and though the CA gives a more complex explanation of the role of goods and services in achieving well-being, it has yet failed to notice the special characteristics of the regulating services of the ecosystem as much as the more traditional economic approaches.

Further, the regulating function of ecosystem services is realized in the course of time. The ecosystem needs time to deliver these services and the time it needs might elongate the more damaged the ecosystem is. As Robeyns rightly emphasizes, her figure is a 'non-dynamic representation' and, thus, cannot display these processes correctly. However, there is no dynamic model of the ramifications of realizing one combination of functionings today on the future or more specifically on one's future capability (Leßmann 2009) at all.

Although the cultural and enriching function of ecosystem services is missing in the figure the CA is aware of this function. Both, Nussbaum (2000, 2006) and Sen (2004) refer to other species and their value for the human species. Sen points to the imbalance of power and refers to Buddha's view that the powerful should act for those who have less power thereby taking the cultural value of other species as given. Nussbaum (2000: 80) includes other species in her list of central functional capabilities because some people convinced her of their importance. Further, she reflects on just relations between human beings and other species (Nussbaum 2006). Anand (2007: 117–126) infers the cultural and enriching role of nature more directly, when he points to the role of rivers in shaping the identity of those living at riversides. Thus, the CA alludes to the cultural function of the ecosystem but not in a uniform or systematic way.

All in all the 'production' of capability and the role of ecosystem services therein has yet to be explored.

The demands of sustainability challenge the CA

Though the ideals of sustainable development and the CA seem close, they differ profoundly with respect to the unit of evaluation: sustainable development is about ensuring well-being for generations, for a nation, the world or whatever agglomeration of people you may think of. In contrast, the CA focuses on individual well-being[10] and provides a definition thereof. Thus the CA first and foremost provides a measure for evaluating well-being (on the individual level). Opposed to that, the issue of sustainability urges us to go beyond mere evaluation and ask for a (political) remedy. To take up the question of sustainability means to introduce a particular criterion into the evaluation: the criterion of sustainability.

Since this criterion points to problems well beyond the scope of the life of one individual the usual reflex is to relegate the responsibility for sustainable development to the society as a whole. Even Anand and Sen (2000: 2034) write that 'the state should serve as a trustee for the interests of future generations'. This solution is unsatisfying since (a) it relies on the existence of social interests independent from individual ones, (b) builds a contrast between the interests of today's and those of future generations and (c) suggests that some social body (like 'the state') has to enforce the interests of future generations against the current generation. This last idea is at odds with the political ideal of democratic decision making.

The CA offers one way to reconcile the individual and the social perspective on sustaining life on earth by pointing to the social nature of human beings. Sen's conception of individuals as social individuals is sketched below.[11]

The CA strives for the ideal of well-being of all people and defines well-being as follows: well-being is a plural concept and cannot be reduced to achievements in one dimension such as utility or wealth in terms of money. Further, the CA emphasises the role of freedom for the well-being of a person. Without the opportunity to choose from a set of options, options which the person values, the person cannot be regarded as being well. Has the concern for sustainability an influence on individual well-being?

The individual in Sen's CA is a social individual (Davis 2004) in the sense that its aims are not restricted to 'self-interest' or 'self-welfare goals' or 'self-goal choice' (Sen 1985c: 213–214). Sen allows for sympathy to others as a motive and for commitment to goals other than well-being (see Box 3.2). Sympathy, however, does not do the trick we are after. Sympathy may be a motive for sustaining one's home for one's children, but it cannot motivate acts of benevolence towards people one does not know. At least the motivation for this behaviour is not the concern for their well-being but the concern for one's own well-being:

> If the knowledge of torture of others makes you sick, it is a case of sympathy; if it does not make you feel personally worse off, but you think it is wrong and you are ready to do something to stop it, it is a case of commitment
>
> (Sen 1977: 91–92)

As outlined above commitment may conflict with personal well-being. In the example of a person who sits on a bench next to a river when she observes someone falling into the river her rescuing the drowning person does not serve her personal well-being. Yet, she decides to do just that out of a sense of duty. Doing one's duty and having a clear conscience may be said to contribute to one's well-being. In contrast to consuming a good (which is the economist's standard idea of improving one's well-being) doing one's duty cannot be sought and much less be bought. Either a situation imposes a duty on us and provides the opportunity to attend to the duty or it does not.

Sen calls acts of commitment agency. As outlined above he distinguishes in both cases – that of well-being and that of agency – achievements and the freedom to achieve the goals (Figure 3.3). He states: '[A]gency freedom includes inter alia the freedom to pursue your own well-being', but 'even though agency freedom is "broader" than well-being freedom the former cannot subsume the latter' (Sen 1985b: 207). There are goals which are sought out of both commitment and sympathy. For instance, I might feel committed to the idea of stopping torture *and* feel sick if others are tortured. Thus my agency against torture is motivated by both commitment and sympathy. As mentioned above there are, as well, cases where agency goals are in conflict with well-being goals. The goals are overlapping but cannot be subsumed to either one motive (see Figure 3.3). In consequence agency freedom and well-being freedom are overlapping, too, but neither can subsume the other.

This is especially true since agency goals will differ from individual to individual. Though Sen assumes agency to be a characteristic of all human beings in general the goals are not specified and may vary a good deal. In contrast to that the goal of well-being is more specific. Sen tacitly assumes more agreement concerning this goal. This is one reason for distinguishing well-being and agency goals since the distinction allows a more complex concept of human beings and their preferences (Sen 1977: 99–104) while ensuring the comparability of well-being at the same time. Agency and the freedom to achieve either well-being or agency goals is assumed by Sen to be a precondition of achieving both. Further, he ascribes a positive impact on well-being to agency (Figure 3.3). Thus, it does not matter what goals we are striving at: if we are able to strive at these goals this has a positive effect on our well-being.

As stated above sustainable development is a goal that cannot entirely be based on sympathy since it is not restricted to sustaining the world for those we know and care about. There is an element of commitment involved. Anand and Sen (2000: 2034) speak of 'the obligation of sustainability' and hence also think of sustainability as a commitment since obligations are one type of commitment: 'In fact, some types of agency roles, e.g. those related to fulfilling obligations, can quite possibly have a negative impact on the person's well-being.' (Sen 1985b: 187). The negative impact of acting in accordance with sustainable development on our own well-being is well reflected in the discussions about abandoning consumption and adopting a new life style in order to contribute to sustainability. '[A] case of 'commitment' is observed when a person decides to do a thing ... despite it not being, in the net, beneficial to the agent himself'

Figure 3.3 Interdependence of well-being and agency.

(Sen 1987: 28). This is exactly the case when we do without certain comforts here and today for sustaining the life of others living elsewhere or in the future.

But let us not forget about the positive impact of being able to act in accordance with agency goals. Our agency freedom contributes to our well-being. Human beings are social beings. The conflicting claims of sustainability and well-being are not in such a sharp contrast as it seems on the first glance because humans have interests other than 'self-welfare goals' and even than 'self goal choice' (Sen 1985c). Our interest in choosing goals other than that of ourselves arises in the pursuit of our loyalties and affiliations: 'between the claims of oneself and the claims of all lie the claims of a variety of groups – for example, families, friends, local communities, peer groups, and economic and social classes' (Sen 1977: 85; see also Sen 1985c: 344).

The pursuit of our loyalties and affiliations shapes our identity (see Sen 1999b; 2006) and often we do not actually reflect carefully before we act but rely on some rules of behaviour that has evolved in our peer-group. As Sen (1977: 104) points out '[s]ometimes the lack of personal gain in particular *acts* is accepted by considering the value of *rules* of behavior.' Our moral behaviour is mediated by the social context (cf. Boulanger, Chapter 5 below). Hence, even though sympathy is seen in traditional welfare economics as the only rational motive for behaviour, commitment is not irrational but sometimes drives us to act in opposition to our immediate self-interest in the pursuit of some group interest. The social rules of behaviour take a universalist form and do not specify exactly whose interest is supported. The specification will take place in the specific context and the rule may also apply one day to each of us (see Sen's 1991 exchange with Frank Hahn on benevolence on that). This characteristic of universal rules is especially relevant in the context of sustainability: 'For example, we may not know exactly *who* will live in the future, but long-run actions to protect the environment may still do a lot more good than disregarding the interests of *unknown* people in the future' (Sen 1991: 16).

For two reasons the conception of sustainable development presents a special challenge to the CA: first, sustainable development takes the well-being of people all over the world, now and in the future, into focus whereas the CA is allegedly individualistic. Second, the concern for sustainability requests political strategies whereas the CA provides mainly a measure for evaluating well-being. However, agency takes a prominent position in Sen's framework. If agency provides a path for reconciling the individualistic character of the CA with the global demands of sustainability and for underpinning political strategies towards sustainable development has yet to be explored in more depth.

Conclusion

The chapter identifies and addresses some of the difficulties that arise when sustainable development is conceptualized from a capability perspective. Since well-being is understood in the context of sustainability in terms of needs the chapter first asks whether this understanding contradicts the idea of well-being in terms of capability. This issue has already been discussed in some length by needs theorists such as Streeten (1994) as well as capability theorists like for example Alkire (2005a). The capability perspective goes beyond needs in some ways, but there is a lot of common ground.

The peculiarities of the way nature influences the production process of (marketable) goods and services have been brought to the fore under the name of 'ecosystem services' in the context of sustainability. Though the CA does not follow traditional economic thought in evaluating well-being in terms of the utility brought about by goods and services it has not taken up this issue properly so far. In general, the 'production process' of doings and beings cannot be determined as concise as that of goods, but this should not stop capability theorists from exploring this process in more detail and analysing the contribution of the ecosystem to human well-being in particular.

The most difficult issue when conceptualizing sustainability arises, however, from the explicit concern with future generations. Considering future generations constitutes a challenge both from a theoretical point of view as well as from a political point of view. The CA offers a theory that respects the freedom of choice of people whether they live today or in the future. Thus, the CA does not prescribe a certain type of life for either the current or future generations and in consequence does not schedule sustaining a certain state of the world. However, the CA does not provide an intertemporal model of functionings and capability. The problem of 'non identity' related to future generations presents a general challenge to sustainability theorists since it urges us to justify the concern for future generations. Thereby it also prompts us to ask why anyone should care about future generations and in what sense this care can be said to be rational. It is possible to describe this problem as a conflict between individual and collective interests. The chapter suggests that viewing the individual as a social being may prove to be the key for meeting this challenge. It should be noted that by emphasizing the social character of individuals Sen leaves the understanding of rationality embraced by traditional economics behind. In his latest book he calls this socially sensitive sort of rationality reasonableness (Sen 2009: 196). The idea of reasonableness as well as its potential to resolve the 'non-identity' problem has to be scrutinized carefully.

Notes

* I would like to thank Andrew Crabtree, Martin Rechenauer, Tobias Lorenz, Sophie Spillemaeckers and the editors for their helpful comments. The usual disclaimer applies.

1 Well-being in the CA is, thus, a concept that may include subjective views. For example 'being happy' can be regarded as one functioning among others (Sen 1987:14). The CA aims, however, at basing the evaluation of well-being on more objectivist grounds (Sen 1987: 14–16). Thus, my use of the term 'well-being' is never restricted to subjective elements in contrast to Rauschmayer et al. Chapter 1 and Spillemaeckers et al. Chapter 4 in this volume.

2 Note that John Rawls thought of his theory of primary goods as a generalization of the notion of needs (Rawls 1975 in 1999: 284).

3 Sabina Alkire (2005b: 116) describes this process as a result of the desire for operationalizing the concept.

4 Streeten (1994: 234) confirms that the general idea of BNA is close to Sen's capability concept.
5 Wiggins (2005: 29, 31) quotes from Anscombe and mentions that a friend of his, Sira Dermen embraces this meaning. Reader (2006) refers to Anscombe's notion of flourishing as well. See also Rauschmayer *et al.* Chapter 1 above.
6 In contrast to Rauschmayer *et al.* and Spillemaeckers *et al.* (Chapters 1 and 4 in this book) I do not consider psychological needs theories, but only economic and philosophical ones.
7 Nussbaum is more determinate than Sen on that matter, because she gives a list of 'central functional capabilities'. She insists, however, that her list is open-ended.
8 Nevertheless, Breena Holland (2008) suggests 'capability ceilings'.
9 See as well Nussbaum's (2006) discussion of contractarian solutions to the problem of representing dependent members of society.
10 There is an ongoing debate within the CA community about this issue. Robeyns (2005: 107–110) and Alkire (2008: 34–41) summarize the dispute and the proposed solutions of collective or group capabilities (e.g. Deneulin and Stewart 2001; Ibrahim 2006; Ballet *et al.* 2007). Sen has discussed the issue in his latest book (2009: 244–246). See as well Boulanger, Chapter 5, below.
11 Martha Nussbaum (2000: 82) speaks of social affiliation an 'architectonic capability' in the sense that all other capabilities are suffused by this one. She does not, however, share Sen's view that we should differentiate between agency and well-being.

References

Alkire, S. (2005a), Needs and capabilities, in S. Reader (ed.), *The Philosophy of Need*, Cambridge University Press: Cambridge, pp. 229–251.
—— (2005b), Why the Capability Approach? *Journal of Human Development*, 6(1): 115–134.
—— (2008), Using the Capability Approach: prospective and evaluative analyses, in F. Comim, M. Qizilbash and S. Alkire (eds), *The Capability Approach: Concepts, Measures and Applications*, Cambridge University Press: Cambridge, pp. 26–50.
Anand, P.B. (2007), Capability, sustainability, and public action: an examination of a river water dispute, *Journal of Human Development*, 8(1): 109–132.
Anand, S. and Sen, A.K. (2000), Human development and economic sustainability, *World Development*, 28(12): 2029–2049.
Ballet, J., Dubois, J.-L. and Mahieu, F.-R. (2007), Responsibility for each other's freedom: agency as the source of collective capability, *Journal of Human Development*, 8(2): 185–202.
Boulanger, P.-M. (2011), The life-chances concept: a sociological perspective in equity and sustainable development, Chapter 5, this volume.
Cruz, I. (2011), Human needs frameworks and their contribution as analytical instruments in sustainable development policymaking, Chapter 6, this volume.
Daily, G.C. (1997), *Nature's Services: Societal Dependence on Natural Ecosystems*, Island Press: Washington, DC.
Davis, J.B. (2004), *Identity and Commitment: Sen's Conception of the Individual*, Tinbergen Institute Discussion Paper TI 2004–055/2: Amsterdam.
Deneulin, S. and Stewart, F. (2001), *A Capability Approach for Individuals Living Together*, online, available at: www.st-edmunds.cam.ac.uk/vhi/sen/papers/ deneulin.pdf [accessed 3 March 2010].
Hahn, F. (1991), Benevolence, in J. Meeks and T. Gay (eds), *Thoughtful Economic Man:*

Essays on Rationality, Moral Rules and Benevolence, Cambridge University Press: Cambridge, pp. 7–11.

Holland, B. (2008), Ecology and the limits of justice: establishing capability ceilings in Nussbaum's Capability Approach, *Journal of Human Development*, 9(3): 401–426.

Ibrahim, S. (2006), From individual to collective capabilities: the Capability Approach as a conceptual framework for self-help, *Journal of Human Development*, 7(3): 397–416.

Leßmann, O. (2007), *Effective Freedom and External Capabilities: Two Different Conceptions of Capability*, Beiträge zur Wirtschaftsforschung Nr. 152 des Sozialoekonomischen Seminars (Institute of SocioEconomics), Universität Hamburg: Hamburg.

——— (2009), Capability and learning to choose, *Studies in Philosophy and Education*, 28: 449–460.

Nussbaum, M.C. (1988), Nature, function, and capability: Aristotle on political distribution, *Oxford Studies in Ancient Philosophy*, (supplementary volume): 145–184.

——— (2000), *Woman and Human Development: The Capabilities Approach*, Cambridge University Press: Cambridge.

——— (2006), Education and democratic citizenship: capability and quality education, *Journal of Human Development*, 7(3): 385–396.

O'Neill, J. (2011), The overshadowing of needs, Chapter 2, this volume.

Parfit, D. (1984), *Reasons and Persons*, Oxford University Press: Oxford.

Pasek, J. (1993), *Environmental Policy and 'the Identity Problem'*, CSERGE working paper GEC 93–13, University of East Anglia: Norwich.

Qizilbash, M. (1997), Needs, incommensurability and well-being, *Review of Political Economy*, 9(3): 261–276.

Rauschmayer, F., Omann, I. and Frühmann, J. (2011), Needs, capabilities and quality of life: refocusing sustainable development, Chapter 1, this volume.

Rawls, J. (1971), *A Theory of Justice*, Harvard University Press: Cambridge, MA.

——— (1975), Fairness to goodness, *Philosophical Review* 84(4): 536–554, reprinted in J. Rawls (1999), *Collected Papers*. Harvard University Press: Cambridge, MA.

Reader, S. (2006), Does a basic needs approach need capabilities? *Journal of Political Philosophy*, 14(3): 337–350.

Robeyns, I.(2005), The Capability Approach: a theoretical survey, *Journal of Human Development*, 6(1): 93–114.

Sen, A.K. (1977), Rational fools: a critique of the behavioural foundations of economic theory, reprinted in: A.K. Sen (ed.) (1982), *Choice, Welfare, and Measurement*, Blackwell: Oxford, pp. 84–106.

——— (1983), Goods and people, in A.K. Sen (ed.), *Resources, Values and Development*, Blackwell: Oxford, pp. 509–532.

——— (1985a), *Commodities and Capabilities*, Elsevier: Amsterdam.

——— (1985b), Well-being, agency and freedom: The Dewey Lectures, 1984, *Journal of Philosophy*, 82(4): 169–221.

——— (1985c), Goals, commitment and identity, *Journal of Law, Economics and Organizations*, 1(2): 341–355, reprinted in A.K. Sen (2002), *Rationality and Freedom*, Oxford University Press: Oxford, pp. 206–224.

——— (1987), *The Standard of Living: The Tanner Lectures 1985*, Cambridge University Press: Cambridge.

——— (1988), Freedom of choice: concept and content, *European Economic Review*, 32(2–3): 269–294.

——— (1991), Beneconfusion, in J. Meeks and T. Gay (eds.), *Thoughtful Economic Man:*

Essays on Rationality, Moral Rules and Benevolence, Cambridge University Press: Cambridge, pp. 12–16.

—— (1993), Capability and well-being, in A.K. Sen and M.C. Nussbaum (eds), *The Quality of Life*, Clarendon Press: Oxford, pp. 30–53.

—— (1999a), *Development as Freedom*, Alfred A. Knopf Inc.: New York.

—— (1999b), *Reason Before Identity*, Oxford University Press: Oxford.

—— (2004), Why we should preserve the spotted owl? *London Review of Books*, 26(3): 10–11), online, available at: www.lrb.co.uk/v26/n03/sen_01_.html [accessed 7 April 2010].

—— (2005), Human rights and capabilities, *Journal of Human Development*, 6(2): 151–166.

—— (2006), *Identity and Violence: The Illusion of Destiny*, Penguin Books: London.

—— (2009), *The Idea of Justice*, Belknap Press: Cambridge, MA.

Sen, A.K. and Agarwal, B. (2003), Continuing the conversation, *Feminist Economics*, 9(2–3): 319–332.

Smith, A. (1976 [1790]), *A Theory of Moral Sentiments*, Oxford University Press: Oxford.

Spillemaeckers, S., Van Ootegem, L. and Westerhof, G. (2011), From individual well-being to sustainable development: a path where psychologists and economists meet, Chapter 4, this volume.

Streeten, P. (1981), *First Things First: Meeting Basic Human Needs in Developing Countries*, Oxford University Press: New York.

—— (1984), Basic needs: some unsettled questions, *World Development*, 12(9): 973–978

—— (1994), Human development: means and ends, *American Economic Review*, 84(2): 232–237.

UNEP/iisd (2004), *Exploring the Links: Human Well-Being, Poverty and Ecosystem Services*, The United Nations Environment Programme/International Institute for Sustainable Development: Nairobi.

WCED (United Nations World Commission on Environment and Development) (1987), *Our Common Future* [Brundtland Report], Oxford University Press: Oxford.

Wiggins, D. (1987), *Needs, Values, Truth: Essays in the Philosophy of Value*, Blackwell: Oxford.

—— (2005), An idea we cannot do without, in S. Reader (ed.), *The Philosophy of Need*, Cambridge University Press: Cambridge, pp. 25–50.

4 From individual well-being to sustainable development

A path where psychologists and economists meet

Sophie Spillemaeckers, Luc Van Ootegem and Gerben J. Westerhof*

Introduction

There is growing (scientific and political) support for the position that the measurement of well-being requires indicators going beyond income- or resource-based indicators. Discussions about these criteria are being held in economic sciences as well as in psychology. For some time, happiness had been promoted in both disciplines as a utilitarian-based criterion to monitor the quality of life from the perspective of citizens themselves. However, serious doubts about the use of happiness as a measure arose and alternatives to this utilitarian approach are being sought in both disciplines. In this chapter, we will address the short-comings of the happiness approach, describe alternatives proposed in both disciplines and discuss where these converge.

1   From an economic perspective, the chapter elaborates on a conceptual framework of well-being based on the capabilities approach and current research on basic needs. In order to integrate sustainable development into the capabilities approach, this framework was broadened. One of the challenges is how to use and adapt the capabilities model such that it can be used for those aspects of sustainable development that go beyond individual well-being. Both a capabilities model for well-being and for sustainable development are proposed. These can be used to analyse the strategies chosen on different levels to satisfy human needs, and to study the capabilities needed to enable human flourishing and social equity.
2   From a psychologist's perspective, we introduce a second framework that has been developed in research on human flourishing and mental health. This approach also goes beyond happiness and takes into account the individual's self-realization as well as social integration and contribution in defining a good life. The challenge here will be to integrate this psychological perspective with the capabilities and sustainable development approaches.

It must be noted that the concepts of happiness, quality of life and well-being used in this chapter are somewhat different from those proposed in the first chapter of this book (Rauschmayer *et al.*). *Happiness* is considered a more or less temporary and subjective sensation of feeling well. In the psychological literature, happiness has also been described as subjective, emotional or hedonic well-being. In economic terms, *quality of life* indicates the extent to which needs are met enabling human flourishing in its fullest sense. From a psychological point of view human flourishing consists of the fulfilment of individual strivings towards self-realization and social integration. The subjective evaluation of the fulfilment of these two needs is designated as psychological well-being and social well-being respectively. Together, these two forms of well-being constitute what has been called *eudaimonic well-being*. Hence, well-being consists of happiness and quality of life from an economic perspective, whereas it is made up of happiness, psychological, and social well-being from a psychological perspective.[1]

In the second section of this chapter the classical economic and psychological theories based on consumption and/or individual preferences are criticized. In both scientific branches new tendencies claim that other indicators must be added or found. The third section presents the example of the capability approach of Sen, some theories on needs and the eudaimonic approach in psychology that were also developed in the first chapter of this book (Rauschmayer *et al.*).The last part of this section expands on the similarities of the capabilities approach and the eudaimonic view when considering human flourishing. A capabilities model for well-being is proposed, enabling the understanding of the way individual strategies are conceived to reach a good life. Up to this section, the capabilities and self-realization approach were applied to the conceptualization and the measurement of individual well-being in a specific society. The fourth section focuses on sustainable development by broadening the capabilities point of view on individual well-being to well-being worldwide and in the future. Again a capabilities model is proposed, this time adapted to sustainable development. The aim of these models is to enable a structural analysis of how well-being or sustainable development is achieved, and which strategies should be chosen. The difficulty of the transition to sustainable development is discussed in the light of the needs theory and the concept of 'agency'. Furthermore the importance of adding social well-being in order to transcend the individualistic approaches to hedonic and eudaimonic well-being in psychology will be elaborated. The section ends with a discussion of what the disciplines can learn from each other. In the final section a conclusion is drawn.

Welfarism and happiness

Traditional quality of life

Many of the traditional (economic) indicators look exclusively at what a person has in terms of material commodities or consumption goods or what a person could have, when looking at disposable income. Macroeconomic policy is traditionally mainly concerned with real GDP or real income growth. The problems surrounding this approach have been discussed on several occasions (e.g. Stiglitz *et al.* 2009; Cassiers and Delain 2006; Van den Bergh 2007). One problem is that the approach does not worry too much about what income or income growth does to 'the way of life' people are living. A further problem is that an 'aggregate' approach is not a good assessment of individual lives. To give a good picture of 'the kind of life people are living', qualitative and quantitative data at the household or at the individual level are needed.

The use of income or consumption expenditure to evaluate quality of life is sometimes justified using a behaviourist, or revealed preference, interpretation of choice. This view rests on an ordinal preference ordering done by individuals. This ordering is represented in a utility function that depends on commodity bundles or services. Revealed preference theory holds that preferences are revealed by the choices individuals make. Utility maximization is not the only guide for individual choice making, however, as individual choices are biased by other factors such as adaptation and comparison to others (Schwartz 2005; Diener and Biswas-Diener 2008). Therefore observed choices cannot be the only basis to assess quality of life.

Next to income/GDP and the behaviourist theory, there is the utilitarian approach to quality of life. This view assumes that utility has a real descriptive content, based on the mental reaction of an individual to the kind of life he or she is living. At the beginning of this new century there seems to be a 'real return' of the belief in the possibilities of the measurement and use of utility (or happiness) in a cardinal way. Subjective individual or utilitarian indicators are used to look at what a person is 'feeling' in terms of utility, pleasure, desire- or needs-fulfilment and happiness. Research on happiness especially has known an exponential growth (see, among many others, Frey and Stutzer 2002; Layard 2005; Van Praag 2007).

The traditional economic approaches to quality of life are summarized in Figure 4.1, which shows the three levels of interest. First there is income, GDP or wealth that offers the opportunity for consumption. Endorsing the behaviourist assumption, preferred consumption is as such an expression of well-being. Utilitarianism considers happiness to be a relevant measuring rod for well-being.

At this point, there is an interesting convergence with psychological scientific theories on happiness. During the past decades, there has been in psychology an increasing interest in measuring the quality of life from an individual's point of view. In the 1960s and 1970s, large-scale surveys started to document the well-being of individuals (Andrews and Withey 1976; Bradburn 1969; Campbell *et al.* 1976; Cantril 1965; Gurin *et al.* 1960). The goal of these studies was to monitor the well-being of the population and to improve social policies. Well-being was measured in these kinds of studies as the satisfaction with life in general as well as with specific domains of life such as income, health or social relations. Furthermore, the emotional state of an individual in terms of happiness or the balance between positive and negative affects is being used as a measure of well-being. Diener (1984), Diener *et al.* (1999) and Veenhoven (2000) provide overviews of studies in this field.

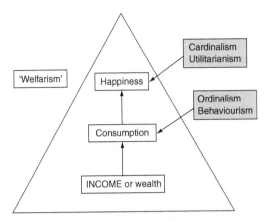

Figure 4.1 Welfarism and the traditional approaches to well-being.

Recently, this tradition of well-being research has been described as *hedonistic* because it concerns the maximization of pleasure and the minimization of pain – much like hedonistic Greek philosophers such as Aristippus described the good life (Waterman 1993). This term can also be applied to the traditional economic approach as it is focused on the positive utility for the individual.

Critique of the traditional approach

Evaluating an individual's quality of life cannot be limited just to looking at the happiness or hedonic well-being of that person, however. Nobel Prize winner Amartya Sen (1985) is one of the most prominent academics insisting on the fact that valuing a life is more than just looking at the amount of happiness in this life. Sen mentions two main problems with this approach. First, there is the problem of 'adapted preferences'. A poor woman in a developing country can be happy, because she lowered her expectations in such a way she has the impression to have enough capabilities to enable her to satisfy her needs, even if she lives in the slums of India. The second problem is the problem of 'valuation neglect': the valuation of a life must have something to do with a judgement about the real content of that life, not with temporary feelings of 'pleasure or pain'.

Psychological scientific studies on hedonic well-being provide further support for Sen's critical evaluation of the use of happiness as a measure for the quality of life. Several studies indicate that there are only low to moderate correlations of more objective standards of quality of life, such as income, education and health with the subjective evaluation of life satisfaction and happiness (Diener *et al.* 1999; Veenhoven 2000; Westerhof 2001). Together, such objective indicators account for only about 10 per cent of the variance in life satisfaction and happiness. These findings are also interpreted in terms of adaptive preferences and valuation neglect. Probably because psychologists are traditionally interested in the biases and illusions of people's cognitive systems that are supportive to their mental health, these scholars evaluate adaptation in a positive way. The personal interpretation of standards and their adaptation in order to enhance subjective feelings of well-being is generally seen as a sign of human resilience, and of human strength.

Nevertheless, there is also some discontent in psychology with the hedonistic approach. Some researchers argue that hedonic well-being is only a minimal empirical measure. It is not well-grounded in psychological and social theories when it comes to defining the 'good life' (Ryff and Essex 1991; Waterman 1993). In a similar way as Sen criticized utilitarianism or welfarism, these scholars argue that other criteria are to be used to define and assess human flourishing. They started to reflect on the notion of well-being in terms of individual strivings and optimal psychological functioning, giving rise to a new strand of research, focusing on eudaimonic well-being. The concept of eudaimonia dates back to Aristotle, for whom not happiness, but the realization of one's own potentials within the values of society was the essential element of a good life (Waterman 1993). Positive affects and life satisfaction are important dimensions of mental health, but they are not the only ones. In the following we will describe Sen's capabilities approach and the psychological approach of self-realization and discuss how they can inform each other.

Capabilities and self-realization

Capability approach

The growing body of evidence and agreement that the measurement of well-being or quality of life requires additional indicators leads us to the capabilities approach, as pioneered by Amartya Sen and Martha Nussbaum.

As far as happiness cannot be bought in a supermarket nor given to the population as a product, it basically remains a personal responsibility. Still, some features increase the likelihood of feeling good. The relevance of these features depends upon their potential to increase people's quality of life by offering them more capabilities to realize themselves. Sen defines these capabilities as all possible combinations of functionings an individual can achieve, representing the positive real freedom of an individual. Capabilities are opportunities or 'potential functionings'. What an individual is really doing or being is called his or her achieved functionings. Capabilities are necessary for the realization of the aspired functionings of each individual. These aspired functionings are what is called the 'good life'. The more opportunities one has, the greater the chance for a good quality of life.

Capabilities can also be described as the real possibilities for persons to satisfy their needs, to have a good standard of living and to have the choices that are open for this. A distinction has to be made between individual or personal resources (personal responsibility) and social resources (opportunities, diversity of supplies, adequate provision of public goods and services). 'The idea of "capability" is ... the opportunity to achieve valuable combinations of human functionings – what a person is able to do or to be' (Sen 2005: 153). These achieved functionings can be seen as how people used their capabilities to achieve a good life. The way people valuate their lives will be based on the difference between their aspirations in life, the way they actually live and the way they perceive this. Nussbaum states that

> we can only have an adequate theory of gender justice, and of social justice more generally, if we are willing to make claims about fundamental entitlements that are to some extent independent of the preferences that people happen to have, preferences shaped, often, by unjust background conditions.
> (Nussbaum 2003: 34)

Furthermore she writes that 'Sen argues that the space of capabilities provides the most fruitful and ethically satisfactory way of looking at equality as a political goal.' (Nussbaum 2003: 35).

Within the capabilities approach, following Anand it is 'the opportunity to live a good life, rather than the accumulation of resources, that matters most for well-being, and that opportunities result from the capabilities that people have' (Anand *et al.* 2005: 10). Alkire refers to human development when talking about well-being in the capabilities context. She describes well-being as 'human flourishing in its fullest sense – in matters public and private, economic and social and political and spiritual' (Alkire 2002).

To understand how well-being can be achieved in the context of the capability approach, a capabilities model for well-being was developed (see Van Ootegem and Spillemaeckers 2010). This model can be summarized as in Figure 4.2. The perception people have about (a good) quality of life is culturally defined and dependent on the resources available. It is also related to comparisons people make, their adaptation to the circumstances and their personality, so the concept of well-being reflects the (moral) values of individuals and society. As most people aim to achieve well-being in their lives, the way they consider a good life determines their aspirations.

Based on these aspirations a list of relevant capabilities can be elaborated, reflecting what people need to be able to do and to be in order to realize well-being. Within the capability approach, what people realize in life is called the achieved functionings. These are related to the choices people make in life in function of their capabilities. So capabilities, personality and values will define the strategies chosen to fulfil aspirations in life. These choices reflect which dimensions and categories are considered important, and why people live the (way of) life they are living. Based on the achieved functionings, the life one is living will be valuated by the individual. It is not uncommon for people to take a step aside and to compare what they have achieved in life with their original aspirations and to adapt goals in life.

The basic idea is that capabilities lead to achieved functionings, which are valuated in judging the quality of one's life. As in Figure 1.1 (Rauschmayer *et al.*

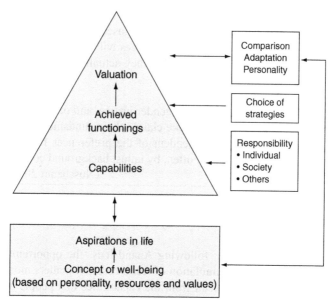

Figure 4.2 Capabilities model for well-being.

Chapter 1, above), that proposes a process-based understanding of quality of life: quality of life and well-being are seen as a dynamic process. In our model the concept of well-being and the aspirations in life, and thus the capabilities needed and the strategies used, are continuously adapted in function of the way individuals evaluate their own life. Both figures show the interaction between capabilities, well-being, strategies and need. In the following, we will further develop this capabilities model using the theories of Amartya Sen and Manfred Max-Neef.

Capabilities and the satisfaction of needs

Values and valuation are an important part of capability approach. For Sen the selection of capabilities is a value judgement that should be 'subject to the test of public reasoning' (Sen 2005: 160). By contrast, Alkire writes that a set of universal values would help to identify which capabilities are more valuable than others in a given context. She hereby refers to a list by Finnis, which she describes as a 'discrete heterogeneous set of most basic and simple reasons for acting which reflect the complete range of human functionings' (Alkire 2002: 185). It consists of the reasons why people act in seeking wholeness or well-being in pursuing human development, such as health, knowledge and friendship. Equity and social justice lie in the fact that all individuals should be able to integrate these values in their lives.

Alkire links this conception of basic human values to the conception of basic human needs as developed in the works of Manfred Max-Neef as described in Chapter 1 (cf. also to Alkire 2002: 187). His list of basic human needs consists of subsistence, protection, affection, understanding, participation, idleness, creation, identity and freedom. These needs are considered as the fundamental answers to the question 'Why are you acting this way?' All are seen as equally important with the sole exception of the most basic need, 'the need of subsistence, that is, to remain alive' (Max-Neef *et al.* 1991: 17). However, not all needs have to be equally satisfied. Trade-offs will be made in the satisfaction of needs, and individuals will choose depending on their values and the presence of capabilities.

Individuals use different strategies to fulfil their needs and to achieve human flourishing (see Leßmann, Chapter 3 in this volume). Max-Neef explains that

> food and shelter, for example, must not be seen as needs but as satisfiers of the fundamental need for Subsistence. In much the same way, education (either formal or informal), study, investigation, early stimuli and meditation are satisfiers of the need for Understanding.
>
> (Max-Neef *et al.* 1991: 17)

The choice of those satisfiers or strategies will in the first place depend on what people consider as a good life, as well-being and on their aspirations to obtain it.

While needs as described by Max-Neef can be considered as universal human values, the concept of well-being, of the 'good life', on the contrary is individually and culturally defined. Robeyns confirms that what is meant by quality of life is 'highly sensitive to the specific context and the areas of social life within which that question is asked' (Robeyns and Van der Veen 2007: 11). So the goal settings of each individual and the choice of strategies to achieve this goal are influenced by cultural values and personality.

Strategies will of course also be related to one's capabilities. To be able to develop strategies for achieving the 'good life', people need to be able to make choices in life. Having the freedom to choose depends on the possibilities one has, thus on the capabilities one has allowing to satisfy needs and aspirations.

Sen also never sought to make a definitive enumeration of capabilities. He considers that 'a "fixed forever" list of capabilities would deny the possibility of progress in social understanding, and also go against the productive role of public discussion, social agitation, and open debates' (Sen 2005: 160). For Alkire 'lists are useful not if they are universally acclaimed but if they are effectively used to confront the many challenges of this generation' (Alkire 2002: 194). Rather, they are tools used in specific circumstances, for specific goals and will give better results if adapted to the context, preferably through participatory processes.

The responsibility of the institutions in deciding in a democratic way about capabilities is important because of the 'valuation neglect' and the 'adaptive preferences' (see above), which were some of Sen's main reasons for developing the capability approach. As people adapt to their situation and do not always valuate acquired rights, individual standards for judging well-being cannot be used to define a list of necessary capabilities. A central focus on well-being will make policies 'less sensitive to signalling and combating social injustices' (Robeyns and Van der Veen 2007: 40). As poor people have lower expectations in life, taking only into account individual preferences or hedonic well-being, they will seem to need less to live a good life, and consequently will be provided with less. So taking into account 'valuation neglect' and 'adaptive preferences' allows one to avoid possible injustices induced by a utilitarian approach.

From a capabilities point of view, society is also 'tasked to make available the resources which are necessary for the capabilities of individuals' (Robeyns and Van der Veen 2007: 9). Governments alone are not responsible for the creation of the capabilities. Individuals, families, corporate companies, non-governmental organizations (NGOs) and multinationals are also involved. Each has a role to play, but eventually people are at least responsible for making use of the existing capabilities for their own well-being, of making choices according to what kind of life they want to live. More capabilities imply more freedom, which increases the importance and the responsibility of the individual choice.

Eudaimonic well-being in terms of self-realization

As said before, psychologists also have tried to tackle the problem of human needs, but they have taken a different route. The traditional hedonic approach only uses criteria of subjective individual well-being. Some researchers argue that this approach of well-being is inadequate, because it does not take into account some of the basic criteria of human flourishing (Ryff and Essex 1991; Waterman 1993). According to them, human flourishing has to be defined in terms of the potential of individuals to realize their own capacities – in other words in terms of eudaimonia. We can distinguish between two somewhat different approaches here.

The first approach stems from self-determination theory (Ryan and Deci 2001, 2002). The basic tenet of this theory is that human beings are active, growth-oriented organisms. Three basic psychological needs are distinguished which are to be satisfied in order to grow and realize oneself: autonomy, competence and relatedness. *Autonomy* refers to the possibility to choose activities, make decisions and regulate behaviour in accordance with one's own goals. *Competence* is the fact that one's behaviours result in the intended outcomes and effects. *Relatedness* refers to the fulfilment of the basic need to belong and be close to others. All three are connected to the needs as defined by Max-Neef. Autonomy is linked to freedom and identity; competence is close to creation and understanding and relatedness implies affection and participation. Self-determination theory sees these three needs as the psychological equivalent of physical needs such as hunger, thirst or sexuality. When the fulfilment of these needs is compromised, this will result in a decrease in the quality of life. Interestingly, there is some research indicating that these intrinsic psychological needs are related to hedonic well-being whereas more extrinsic needs, such as financial success, material possessions or popularity are related to less satisfaction with life and less vitality as well as more anxiety, depression and addiction problems (Kasser and Ryan 1993, 1996).

The second approach studies psychological well-being (Ryff 1989; Ryff and Essex 1991; Ryff and Keyes 1995). Ryff reviewed earlier psychological theories on optimal lifespan development (Erikson, Jung, Neugarten), on optimal functioning and self-actualization (Allport, Maslow, Rogers), and on positive mental health (Jahoda). She found six elements of psychological flourishing in this literature which together make up her definition of *psychological well-being*: autonomy, environmental mastery, positive social relations, self-acceptance, personal growth and purpose in life. Each of these six dimensions is important in the striving to become a better person and to realize one's potential.

Positive relations   Has warm, satisfying, trusting personal relationships and is capable of empathy and intimacy.
Purpose in life   Holds goals and beliefs that confirm a sense of direction in life and feels that life has a purpose and meaning.
Autonomy   Exhibits self-direction that is often guided by socially accepted and conventional internal standards resisting unsavoury social pressures.
Environmental mastery   Exhibits the capacity to manage a complex environment, and to choose or manage and mould environments to suit needs.
Personal growth   Shows insight into own potential, sense of development, and is open to new and challenging experiences.
Self-acceptance   Holds positive attitudes toward oneself and one's past life; concedes and accepts varied aspects of self.

It can be seen from these definitions that the approach to psychological well-being is concerned with the process of agency in self-realization. In a context of positive relations people can autonomously choose their own purpose in life which can be realized when individuals have mastery over their environment, resulting in a process of personal growth and self-acceptance. This theory thus focuses on what is necessary for self-fulfilment, drawing attention to the motivational process that results in eudaimonic well-being rather than to hedonic feelings of happiness and satisfaction.

Researchers in the hedonic tradition have focused only on emotional well-being and they have thereby implicitly assumed that satisfaction and happiness are the most important psychological states that individuals strive for in realizing a good life. The eudaimonic approach takes a different normative view on happiness. In general, the fulfilment of basic psychological needs and the presence of psychological well-being will be accompanied by positive feelings of satisfaction and happiness. However, it is possible that leading a life towards fulfilment does not always bring positive affects as it might call for personal sacrifices in terms of hedonic feelings. On the other hand, being happy and satisfied with one's present life might even result in inertia and a lack of striving towards individual fulfilment. In studying optimal experience, Fave and Bassi (2009) found that productive activities, like working and studying, are characterized by lower levels of happiness and short-term desirability, but also by a higher perceived relevance to future goals. On the other hand, passive entertainments, such as watching TV, are perceived as highly enjoyable and desirable, but scarcely relevant to future goals. It should therefore be concluded that individual fulfilment and happiness are related but distinct phenomena. Several empirical studies have indeed shown that hedonic well-being and eudaimonic, psychological well-being can be distinguished from each other, even though they are moderately related (Keyes *et al.* 2002; Waterman *et al.* 2008; Westerhof and Keyes 2008).

Capabilities and self-realization

The capability and self-realization approaches share a mutual interest in defining the good life as more than the presence of hedonic well-being and happiness. They both search for answers with regard to the conditions that encourage human flourishing while being aware of the valuation problem. Furthermore, they both see human flourishing in terms of realizing latent possibilities.

Having pointed out this common source of inspiration, the two approaches have taken rather different routes in the way they elaborated on this. Therefore they might mutually inform and strengthen each other. The capabilities approach can learn from the description of basic psychological values and the criteria for defining human flourishing. We argue here that self-realization as defined in psychological studies plays an important role in the achievement of functionings on the basis of existing capabilities. The focus of self-determination theory makes clear that the achievement of functionings should be based on the basic psychological needs. Aspiring for functionings that are not grounded in these basic needs would be considered an idle endeavour, which in the end might hinder the strivings for personal growth. Whereas self-determination theory thus provides a normative perspective on aspirations, the theory of psychological well-being provides a formulation of the psychological make-up which is necessary for a successful achievement of aspired functionings: personal growth will only follow when individuals feel autonomous enough to choose a purpose in life which is commensurate with one's own competencies, when they have the sense of mastery to realize that purpose, and when they are functioning in a positive context of social relations and self-acceptancy. In other words, psychological well-being is the subjective evaluation of the individual agency, which is necessary to achieve functions by choosing strategies and realizing one's individual responsibility.

On the other hand, the psychological approach to self-realization might learn from the broader context in which the capabilities approach is defined. In this sense, the capabilities approach provides a better description of the societal arrangements necessary for self-realization. Furthermore, although the self-realization approach defines psychological criteria for the good life, it does not in itself provide a valuation of the functionings that are achieved in the process of self-realization. Again, the capabilities approach draws more attention to the societal processes needed for such a valuation.

Sustainable development and social functioning

A capabilities approach to sustainable development

The concept of needs is essential for sustainable development, as the aim is to enable current and future generations to meet their needs in an equitable way across the planet (see Rauschmayer *et al.*, Chapter 1 in this book). The sustainable development perspective is challenging in its spatial and temporal dimensions: it aims at spreading well-being worldwide, now and in the future.

Satisfying the needs of a generation means that all people have sufficient capabilities allowing them to ensure their well-being. Achieving sufficient capabilities for the entire present generation is not possible without intra-generational solidarity. This issue was taken up in the recent documentary film 'The End of Poverty?' featuring contributions by Nobel Prize winners Amartya Sen and Joseph Stiglitz, and other distinguished academics and politicians (Diaz 2008). It shows that the well-being of a society can influence the well-being of others in both positive and negative ways. One of the examples is the strong interconnection between the wealth of some countries and the poverty in others, that have continued to exist ever since colonization.

As we do not know what the needs of the future generations will be, we must leave them as many 'capabilities' as possible. To prevent harm being done to future generations the precautionary principle must be applied. This principle was taken up by the Rio Declaration of the Earth Summit of 1992 (principle 15). It states that 'where there are threats of serious or irreversible damage, lack of full scientific certainty shall not be used as a reason for postponing cost-effective measures to prevent environmental degradation'. This principle can be enlarged by considering possible threads for the well-being of future generations, other than environmental damage. Furthermore the development of knowledge and new technologies are precious legacies to enhance the capabilities for well-being of future generations.

It is possible to translate the capabilities model for well-being into a model for sustainable development (see Figure 4.3). This implies a shift from an individual approach to a more societal viewpoint, where nevertheless the needs of individuals stay central (see Table 4.1). Here the model differs more from Figure 1.1 (Rauschmayer *et al.* Chapter 1 in this volume), where sustainable development is considered as one of the influences of the quality of life process. We put sustainable development as a central goal, subsuming the dynamic process of individual well-being. We have described the concept of well-being as being based on the satisfaction of individual needs in the functioning of the personality of the individual, the existing resources and the cultural values. The concept of sustainable development is equally based on the satisfaction of needs, but considers those

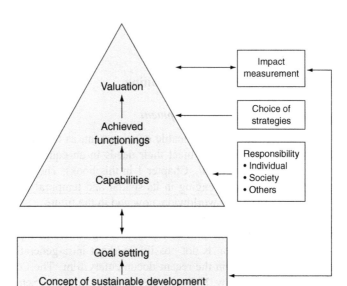

Figure 4.3 Capabilities model for sustainable development.

Table 4.1 Differences between a capabilities approach of well-being and of sustainable development

	Well-being	*Sustainable development*
Concept	Individual	Society
Goal setting	Individual	Society
Capabilities	Individual/Society	Society
Strategies	Individual	Individual/Society
Achieved functionings	Individual	Individual/Society
Valuation	Individual	Society

needs in a broader interpretation. Not only the needs of a specific individual count, but also those of current and future generations. Resources and values stay crucial but personality will have less influence. Goal setting for sustainable development is more a matter of society and highly determined by existing resources, as the precautionary principle has to be applied. We do not know how future generations will perceive well-being: therefore resources must be protected and/or created to enable a wide range of opportunities. Individual preferences are less relevant, considering the multitude of cultures involved. Goal setting will be based on international values. International agreements such as the Universal Declaration of Human Rights, Agenda 21 and the fundamental International Labour Organization conventions can be used to define these values.

Goals cannot be realized without the necessary capabilities. Capabilities for achieving sustainable development will reflect the goal setting for well-being in a worldwide intertemporal context. As said before, Sen argues that these capabilities must be determined in a process of public reasoning. Not only individuals, but certainly also governments, international organizations, NGOs and companies are responsible for the presence of capabilities. These capabilities can be called 'collective capabilities'. Ballet *et al.* say a collective capability 'can be represented by a structure' and

> is composed of the various personal capability structures. Collective capability may then raise the issue of collective agency where, by joining or participating in a group with similar goals, the person acts in concert with the others to achieve these goals.
>
> (Ballet *et al.* 2007: 13)

The decisions on the strategies will be taken by institutions, but also individuals play an important role, as their way of life has an important influence. Sustainable consumption for example is a powerful lever for sustainable development. As individuals often have the impression their actions are just a drop in the ocean and are meaningless, it is more interesting that their actions are situated in a larger framework, provided by societal actors, as governments, institutions, the business world or NGOs. The valuation of what is achieved is of the utmost importance as the world is changing rapidly. We do not know how the environment will react to certain actions or how future generations will conceive well-being. We do not even know how the aspirations of our own generation will change in the next ten years. Sustainable development requires a close monitoring of these changes and a continuous adaptation of sustainable strategies. The valuation will not only be based on the achieved well-being but also on scientific impact measurements such as environmental impact studies. These allow researchers to try to estimate the influence of the achieved functionings on the well-being of current generations worldwide. Simulations can be established, too, of the possible effects on the well-being of future generations.

The difficulty of transition towards sustainable development

In the previous section, we argued that meeting the needs of the current generation can be interpreted as providing people with the opportunity to achieve well-being. If applied to a specific society or country, the issues are already complex. Providing well-being worldwide is an even more difficult objective. Not all people achieve an adequate standard of living although as humans they have the right (United Nations 1948: Article 25).

Some authors claim that both well-being and sustainable development are constitutively independent, because if one aims for a viable and fair distribution of well-being for individuals across time and space, this will diminish the opportunities of quality of life for the current generation (Robeyns and Van der Veen

2007: 23). The objective to attain an acceptable quality of life at home while respecting the rights of people elsewhere and future generations is often regarded as a constraint as, consequently, material wealth at home will diminish.

If one interprets needs in the terms of Max-Neef by referring to the ultimate drive behind the actions, this feeling of constraint can be put into perspective. If other cultures and future generations are taken into account, the strategies to achieve individual well-being will have to change. This means that the concept of well-being most cultures have must be adapted. Most probably there will be a loss of material wealth in well-off countries, but in Chapter 1 (Rauschmayer *et al.*) it was explained that this does not mean a loss of well-being in the long run. In principle all needs, with the exception of subsistence, can be fulfilled through mostly non-material strategies. If the fight for subsistence is not taking all our time and if one has good social relationships, then protection, affection, understanding, participation, idleness, creation, identity and freedom can be achieved without input of money or material objects. Therefore an equal satisfaction of needs can be maintained through the introduction of less material strategies.

Research done by the New Economics Foundation confirms that constraints on the material level should not have an influence on well-being. They refer to the Easterlin paradox, observing that once a certain income level is reached, a higher income will not increase well-being. The consultation of several scientific studies led them to the conclusion that:

> There is considerable evidence from psychology that well-being is much less strongly influenced by income than by other key aspects of people's lives. A review of the extensive research in this area suggests that only a small proportion of the variation in subjective well-being is attributable to material and environmental circumstances – perhaps as little as 10 per cent. Around 50 per cent is due to relatively stable factors such as personality, genes, and environment during the early years. The remaining 40 per cent is linked to the 'intentional activities' in which people choose to engage: what they do and how they behave (both on their own and with others), their attitudes to the events in their lives, and the sorts of goals they are motivated to pursue.
>
> (New Economics Foundation 2008: 13)

This implies that it is possible to take into account future generations and to satisfy at least the need of subsistence worldwide without diminishing the well-being of affluent countries.

Furthermore the well-being of individuals is not only dependent on the satisfaction of individualistic needs. Sen states that people do not always act out of self-interest, but that they also gain well-being from altruistic feelings or actions. Therefore he introduced the concept of *agency*, which is the individual's freedom to act in pursuit of goals other than self-interest (Sen 1985). Introducing sustainable development responds to the will of taking others into account.

Also, in psychology, individual pleasure is not considered as the only objective of the majority of citizens, nor is it the sole component of human well-being. Here as well it is recognized that individuals can act for social reasons.

The importance of social well-being in psychology

We have seen that the tradition of hedonic well-being has been criticized and complemented by studies on eudaimonic well-being. Hedonic and eudaimonic well-being share a focus on individual functioning and in general both neglect the societal embeddedness of a person (Keyes 1998). Recent studies however try to include social well-being into the eudaimonic approach. Social well-being is seen as an essential component of mental health, just like happiness and psychological well-being. Together, they build the three core elements in the definition of mental health of the World Health Organization (1) well-being, (2) effective functioning for an individual and (3) effective functioning for a community (WHO 2004).

Just as Ryff studied the classical psychologists, Keyes (1998) studied the work of major sociologists and social psychologists, like Marx, Durkheim, Seeman and Merton, to find indicators of what it means to prosper socially. His conceptual analysis indicates that *social well-being* consists of at least five dimensions: social acceptance, social actualization, social contribution, social coherence and social integration.

> *Social contribution* Feels that one's life is useful to society and the output of his or her activities are valued by or valuable to others.
> *Social integration* Has a sense of belonging to a community and derives comfort and support from community.
> *Social actualization* Believes that people, social groups, and society have potential and can evolve or grow positively.
> *Social acceptance* Has a positive attitude toward others while acknowledging and accepting people's differences and complexity.
> *Social coherence* Is interested in society or social life; feels society and culture are intelligible, somewhat logical, predictable and meaningful.

At the individual level, Keyes' work shows what it means to flourish in terms of living a life of social value. The work of Keyes thus adds a distinct dimension to the studies on hedonic and psychological well-being. Existing studies show indeed that social well-being is related to, but different from both hedonic and psychological well-being (Keyes *et al.* 2008; Westerhof and Keyes 2008). Whereas hedonic and psychological well-being focus on the emotions and psychological functioning of the individual, social well-being adds a societal component by studying evaluations of how well an individual is functioning in society. Social well-being is indeed related to an individuals' civic engagement, the transmission of personal experiences and values to other generations, and pro-social behaviours (Keyes 1998; Keyes and Shapiro 2004). Social well-being might therefore be related to the spatial and temporal dimensions that are added in sustainable development. In the next paragraph, we will therefore address how social well-being and sustainable development are related.

Sustainable development, capabilities, and social well-being

The main concept of sustainable development broadens the perspective of the quality of life in time and space to global and intergenerational equity. We have seen that this perspective broadens the capabilities approach and makes an impact measurement beyond the here and now necessary. Interestingly, the psychological approach has broadened its perspective from individual flourishing in terms of happiness and self-realization to social flourishing in terms of being integrated and contributing to society at large.

We have argued before that self-realization provides a formulation of what is psychologically necessary for the achievement of functionings. In a similar vein, it can be argued that social well-being is a necessary individual corollary in promoting sustainable development. A higher social well-being implies that individuals evaluate their societal functioning in a more positive way, i.e. they have a better understanding and acceptance of how society is functioning and developing, and they feel part of society. This mindset will then function as a motivation to contribute to society in general rather than staying focused on their own happiness and self-realization. Individuals with a stronger sense of social well-being will subsequently be more motivated to take the needs of other people of their own and of coming generations into account.

Although the size of society implicit in this approach might not be the globalized society intended by sustainable development, nor the time perspective in terms of the generations to follow, the approach thus clarifies what is necessary on the part of the individual to broaden the scope to the flourishing of society in general and to sustainable development. This understanding is especially important because some of the main barriers to sustainable development seem to be psychological.

In the first chapter of this book (Rauschmayer *et al.*), it was said that, currently, sustainable development is associated with more technocratic restrictions on freedom, which makes it hard to motivate people to change their lifestyle. We agree that if lifestyles have to change drastically, people need to be involved socially and transcend their individual happiness and fulfilment for which high levels of social well-being provide the necessary psychological insight.

Conclusion

This chapter aimed to understand individual well-being and how it can be achieved. Traditional economic welfarist approaches such as looking at GDP, behaviourism and utilitarianism do not provide sufficient answers to this question, as they assess an individual's well-being only by looking at a person's mental state (utility or happiness) or consumption level. This was equally the case in psychology, where quality of life was mostly measured from a hedonistic viewpoint. But valuing a life is more than looking at the amount of happiness in this life, however. Recent tendencies in economics and in psychology tend to consider happiness or hedonic well-being as only one dimension of an individual's being or well-being. The importance of happiness remains to be weighed against other dimensions, such as sufficient health care or education.

Sen's capability approach states that only assessing the individual's valuation does not lead to well-being, because of 'adaptive preferences', and 'valuation neglect'. This means that individuals are inclined to adapt themselves to their situation and to neglect some important causes for their well-being because they take them for granted. The 'adaptive preferences' explain why poor people will claim less for their well-being than the more well-off population, and the 'valuation neglect' makes clear why citizens often disregard the importance of objectively important issues as democracy and freedom of speech. The capability approach allows us to overcome those biases and to gain a broader view on human well-being. In recent psychological theories, the hedonic viewpoint is replaced by an eudaimonic approach of well-being by the self-realization theories. They define the good life as the realization of one's own potentials within the values of society.

The human needs theory developed by the economist Max-Neef and the psychological self-realization theories give a number of basic conditions for human flourishing. How human flourishing can be achieved was summarized in the capabilities model for well-being (see Figure 4.2). It describes the correlation between an individual's concept of well-being and his aspirations in life. Furthermore it shows that the freedom to choose strategies to realize these aspirations is dependent on the available capabilities. Sustainable development aims at the well-being of current generations here and elsewhere, and is directed at worldwide intergenerational equity. Accordingly it is possible to translate the capabilities model for well-being to sustainable development (see Figure 4.3). As individual preferences are less relevant, considering the different cultures involved, goal setting for sustainable development will be based on available resources and international values. It is up to societal actors to provide capabilities. The responsibility for the choice of the strategies aiming at a sustainable world lies more in the hands of societal actors and less in those of individuals, even if ultimately it is the lifestyle of individuals that decides upon the realization of such a sustainable world.

The realization of sustainable development should be possible: equal opportunities for all human beings will mean less material consumption in affluent countries, but this does not mean less satisfaction of their needs. Most needs do not require material strategies to be fulfilled and humans derive satisfaction from securing the needs of others. Furthermore the concept of 'agency', the individual's freedom to act in pursuit of goals other than self-interest, developed by Sen, and the studies on social well-being show that human flourishing is related to individuals' civic engagement, solidarity with other generations, and pro-social behaviours. It transcends individual happiness and self-realization to forms of societal realization.

Using less material strategies for the satisfaction of needs requires rethinking some of our society's values and strategies. Such changes are hard to introduce, however. Some of the main barriers to change seem to be psychological. As, in principle, a sustainable world is capable of providing even more well-being than current societies, the reasons behind the current reluctance to adopt transition processes are crucial for further research. The proposed economic and psychological models provide theoretical concepts and empirical measures that can drive this research and thereby contribute to a sustainable choice of strategies to satisfy our present and future needs.

Note

* Part of this research benefits from the project WELLBEBE (SD/TA/09A) of the Belgian Science Policy. With special thanks to Anne Laurence Lefin, Nicolas Prignot, Paul Marie Bonlanger and Tom Bauler.
1 In Chapter 1 (Rauschmayer *et al.*) well-being is divided in hedonic and eudaimonic well-being, however quality of life comprises capabilities and well-being.

References

Alkire, S. (2002), Dimensions of human development, *World Development*, 30(2): 181–205.
Anand, P., Hunter, G. and Smith, R. (2005), Capabilities and well-being: evidence based on the Sen-Nussbaum approach to welfare *Social Indicators Research*, 74(1): 9–55.
Andrews, F.M. and Withey, S.B. (1976), *Social Indicators of Well-Being: Americans' Perceptions of Life Quality*, Plenum: New York.
Ballet, J., Dubois, J. and Mahieu, F. (2007), Responsibility for each other's freedom: agency as the source of collective capability *Journal of Human Development*, 8(2): 185–202.
Bradburn, N.M. (1969), *The Structure of Psychological Well-Being*, Aldine: Chicago.
Campbell, A., Converse, P.E. and Rodgers, W.L. (1976), *The Quality of American Life: Perceptions, Evaluations and Satisfactions*, Russell Sage: New York.
Cantril, H. (1965), *The Pattern of Human Concerns*, Rutgers University Press: New Brunswick, NJ.
Cassiers, I. and Delain, C. (2006), La croissance ne fait pas le bonheur: les économistes le savent-ils? *Regards Economiques* 38: 1–14.
Diaz, P. (2008), The End of Poverty? (documentary) Cinema Libre Studio, related website available at: www.theendofpoverty.com [accessed 7 August 2009].
Diener, E. (1984), Subjective well-being, *Psychological Bulletin*, 95(3): 542–575.
Diener, E and Biswas-Diener, R. (2008), Happiness: *Unlocking the Mysteries of Psychological Wealth*, Blackwell Publishing: Malden, MA.
Diener, E., Suh, E.M., Lucas, R. and Smith, H.L. (1999), Subjective well-being: three decades of progress, *Psychological Bulletin*, 125(2): 276–302.
Fave, A. and Bassi, M. (2009), The contribution of diversity to happiness research, *Journal of Positive Psychology*, 4(3): 205–207.
Frey, B.S. and Stutzer, A. (2002), What can economists learn from happiness research? *Journal of Economic Literature*, 40(2): 402–435.
Gurin, G., Veroff, J. and Field, S. (1960), *Americans View Their Mental Health*, Basic Books: New York.

Kasser, T. and Ryan R.M. (1993), A dark side of the American dream: correlates of financial success as a central life aspiration, *Journal of Personality and Social Psychology*, 65(2): 410–422.

—— and —— (1996), Further examining the American dream: differential correlates of intrinsic and extrinsic goals, *Personality and Social Psychology Bulletin*, 22(3): 280–287.

Keyes, C.L.M. (1998), Social well–being, *Social Psychology Quarterly*, 61(2): 121–140.

Keyes, C.L.M. and Shapiro, A.D. (2004), Social well-being in the United States: a descriptive epidemiology, in O.G. Brim, C.D. Ryff and R.C. Kessler (eds), *How Healthy Are We: A National Study of Well-Being at Midlife*, University of Chicago Press: Chicago, pp. 350–373.

Keyes, C.L.M., Shmotkin, D. and Ryff, C.D. (2002), Optimizing well-being: the empirical encounter of two traditions, *Journal of Personality and Social Psychology*, 82(6): 1007–1022.

Keyes, C.L.M., Wissing, M., Potgieter, J., Temane, M., Kruger, A. and Rooy, S. (2008), Evaluation of the mental health continuum – short form (MHC-SF): Swetsana-speaking South Africans, *Clinical Psychology and Psychotherapy*, 15(3): 181–192.

Layard, R. (2005), *Happiness: Lessons From a New Science*, Allen Lane: London.

Leßmann, O. (2011), Sustainability as a challenge to the capability approach, Chapter 3, this volume.

Max-Neef, M.A., Elizalde, A. and Hopenhayn, M. (1991), Development and Human Needs, in *Human scale development: conception, application and further reflections*, Apex: New York.

New Economics Foundation (2008), *National Accounts for Well-being*, online, available at: http://cdn.media/0.com/national-accounts-of-well-being-report.pdf [accessed 28 August 2009].

Nussbaum, M.C. (2003), Capabilities as fundamental entitlements: Sen and social justice, *Feminist Economics* 9(2–3): 33–59.

Rauschmayer, F., Omann, I. and Frühmann, J. (2011), Needs, capabilities and quality of life: refocusing sustainable development, Chapter 1, this volume.

Robeyns, I. and Van der Veen, R.J. (2007), *Sustainable Quality of Life: Conceptual Analysis for a Policy-Relevant Empirical Specification*, Netherlands Environmental Assessment Agency and University of Amsterdam: Bilthoven and Amsterdam.

Ryan, R.M. and Deci, E.L. (2001), On happiness and human potentials: a review of research on hedonic and eudaimonic well-being, *Annual Review of Psychology*, 52: 141–166.

—— and —— (2002), Overview of self-determination theory: an organismic dialectical perspective, in E.L. Deci and R.M. Ryan (eds), *Handbook of Self-Determination Research*, University of Rochester Press: Rochester.

Ryff, C.D. (1989), Happiness is everything, or is it? Explorations on the meaning of psychological well-being, *Journal of Personality and Social Psychology*, 57(6): 1069–1081.

Ryff, C.D. and Essex, M.J. (1991), Psychological well-being in adulthood and old age: Descriptive markers and explanatory processes, *Annual Review of Gerontology and Geriatrics*, 10: 144–171.

Ryff, C.D. and Keyes, C.L.M. (1995), The structure of psychological well-being revisited, *Journal of Personality and Social Psychology*, 69(4): 719–727.

Schwartz, B. (2005), *The Paradox of Choice: Why More is Less*, Harper and Collins: New York.

Sen, A. (1985), *Commodities and Capabilities*, Oxford University Press: New Delhi.
—— (2005), Human rights and capabilities, *Journal of Human Development*, 6(2): 151–166.
Stiglitz, E., Sen, A. and Fitoussi, J.P. (2009), *Report by the Commission on the Measurement of Economic Performance and Social Progress*, online, available at: www.stiglitz-sen-fitoussi.fr/en/index.htm [accessed 2 March 2010].
United Nations (1948) *Universal Declaration of Human Rights*, online, available at: www.un.org/en/documents/udhr.
—— (1992), *Rio Declaration on Environment and Development*, A/CONF.151/26 (Vol. I), UN.
Van den Bergh, J. (2007), *Abolishing GDP*, Tinbergen Institute Discussion Paper TI 2007-019/3, online, available at: www.tinbergen.nl/discussionpapers/07019.pdf.
Van Ootegem, L. and Spillemaeckers, S. (2010), With a focus on well-being and capabilities, *Journal of Socio-Economics*, 39(3): 384–390.
Van Praag, B. (2007), Perspectives from the happiness literature and the role of new instruments for policy analysis, *CESifo Economic Studies*, 53(1): 42–68.
Veenhoven, R. (2000), The four qualities of life: ordering concepts and measures of the good life, *Journal of Happiness Studies*, 1(1): 1–39.
Waterman, A.S. (1993), Two conceptions of happiness: contrasts of personal expressiveness (eudaimonia) and hedonic enjoyment, *Journal of Personality and Social Psychology*, 64(4): 678–691.
Waterman, A.S., Schwartz, S.J. and Conti, R. (2008), The implications of two conceptions of happiness (hedonic enjoyment and eudaimonia) for the understanding of intrinsic motivation, *Journal of Happiness Studies*, 9(1): 41–79.
Westerhof, G.J. (2001), Wohlbefinden in der zweiten Lebenshälfte [Well-being in the second half of life], in F. Dittmann-Kohli, C. Bode and G.J. Westerhof (eds.), *Die zweite Lebenshälfte – Psychologische Perspektiven. Ergebnisse des Alters-Survey*, Kohlhammer: Stuttgart, pp. 79–128.
Westerhof, G.J. and Keyes, C.L.M. (2008), Geestelijke gezondheid is meer dan de afwezigheid van geestelijke ziekte [Mental health is more than the absence of mental illness], *Maandblad Geestelijke Volksgezondheid*, 63(10): 808–820.
World Health Organization (2004), *Promoting Mental Health: Concepts, Emerging Evidence, Practice*, Summary Report, WHO: Geneva.

5 The life-chances concept

A sociological perspective in equity and sustainable development

Paul-Marie Boulanger[1]

Introduction

Beyond the vague affirmation that ultimately it is the well-being and quality of life of current and future generations that constitute the subject matter of sustainable development (SD), it remains to decipher what are the precise requirements of SD as both an intragenerational and intergenerational concern. What are the rights and duties of current generations, what use can they make of the scarce and non-substitutable resources of the environment, what can they consume for their own well-being and what should they save for the well-being of the future generations? Answering all these questions supposes that a more fundamental one has been addressed first: what exactly does human well-being mean? On what does it depend? How can it be improved and what hampers it? These questions are addressed by all the chapters in this book, in one way or another, directly or indirectly. For instance, in the opening chapter, Rauschmayer, Omann, and Frühmann define quality of life as composed of well-being and capabilities. The former is seen by them as a mix of subjective perceptions (with emotional, cognitive and evaluative components) and objective conditions (capabilities) linked to the satisfaction of Max-Neef's (1991) nine fundamental human needs, considered as the most fundamental dimensions of human flourishing. For their part, Spillemaeckers, Van Ootegem, and Westerhof propose in Chapter 4 an enlarged conception of the capability approach integrating some elements of the basic needs discourse. Despite their differences, the different chapters in this book share a common starting point: the rebuttal of the welfarist, utilitarian and subjectivist conception of well-being and of justice that prevailed until very recently in economics, political philosophy and ethics and whose most renowned adversaries today are, each in his own way, John Rawls and Amartya Sen. In this chapter, we will mobilize an older intellectual tradition which has also struggled from the outset against strictly economical as well as purely psychological conceptions of well-being and to which it opposed a category:

> somewhere between the philosophy of money and the philosophy of happiness, that is the assumption that everything can be measured in dollar terms, and the other assumption that the individual alone knows what has got value

– in short, a category which expresses human wants and needs, interests and hopes in a way that does not suppress the subjective element but makes it clear that one is seeking more than the personal sensation of happiness, namely socially structured ways of individual life. The category which serves these multiple purposes is that of life chances.

(Dahrendorf 1979: 52)

Life-chances and the life course

We maintain that the 'life chances' concept, together with other descendants of the same mother ('life') such as life course, lifestyle or livelihood, provides a plausible alternative (or complementary?) discourse on well-being, justice and sustainability. Our aim, in this chapter, is to explore the possibilities opened by these categories and, in so doing, to connect the discussion on capabilities, needs and sustainable development to the sociological tradition of analysis of social inequalities.

The chapter is structured in two sections. The first is devoted to the definition and discussion of the life-chance concept and the related notion of life course. After some semantic considerations, we turn to what constitutes and what determines life chances according to the sociological tradition. Then, we analyse the similarities and the differences between the life chances discourse and the capability approach. The second section is devoted to the implications of the life-chances perspective for sustainable development and SD policies. Drawing on the similarity between Rawls' notion of life prospects[2] or expectations (of the representative individuals in the various social positions) and the life chances concept, it is argued that adoption of a life chances perspective leads naturally to adopt a Rawlsian conception of justice. We then discuss the plausibility of 'sufficient life chances' as the subject matter of the inter- and intragenerational requirements of sustainable development. The notion of sufficient life chances is interpreted in a twofold way: as a minimum set of options and opportunities in terms of livelihoods, and as options and opportunities guaranteeing the satisfaction of an extended Rawlsian set of basic needs.

Life chances made their apparition in sociology with Max Weber's *Economy and Society*, published in 1921. Contrary to Marx, who defined social class by the relation to the means of production and, more precisely, the property thereof, Max Weber defined social class as a group of people with similar life chances, that is, similar biographies in term of what they will actually achieve in a given society because of a communality of access to scarce economic and social resources:

'Class position' shall mean the typical chance: 1. Of supply of goods, 2. Of external position in life, 3. Of internal destiny in life, which arises from extent and kind of command power (or its absence) over goods or achieved qualifications and from the given manner of its utility for attaining a wage or an income within a given economic order.

(Weber 1921: translation Dahrendorf 1979: 70)

Also, he distinguished life chances linked to the position a person holds in the process of production and distribution of scarce goods (class position), from life chances as dependent on a person's position in networks of social relations. In more modern terms, we would say he distinguished three different sources of life chances: economic capital (a 'kind of command power over goods'), human capital ('achieved qualifications') and social capital (networks of social relations).

In fact, as Abel and Cockerham (1993) showed, Weber discussed together three intimately related concepts: *Lebensstil* (or *Stilisierung des Lebens*) which means 'lifestyle, *Lebensführun*' which translates in 'life conduct' and *Lebenschancen* which correspond to 'life chances'. *Lebensführung* refers to the choices people have in their selection of lifestyles and *Lebenschancen* is the probability of realizing these choices. With the upsurge of modernity and the rise of a consumption society, the concept of lifestyle has acquired a more cultural meaning associated almost exclusively to consumption behaviour (Slater 1997). Therefore it seems preferable, in a sustainable development context, concerned also – actually in priority – with all those who do not participate in the consumption society to use, instead of lifestyle, the more comprehensive notion of 'livelihood' or the still more general 'way of life'. Unlike lifestyle, they refer to production as well as consumption, to material as well as to cultural phenomena.

Chance, as Weber understood it, means probability on the ground of causal relations, structurally anchored probabilities of the occurrence of certain circumstances or events such as reaching a desired educational level, joining a given organization or corporation, obtaining a job or a given social position, etc. The relevant circumstances and events are chronologically ordered, hence the idea of 'life course'. The 'life course' is the sequence of states (statuses) and activities (roles) through which individuals pass from birth to death, the sequence of socially defined events and roles that the individual enacts over time (Elder 1985).

The easiest way to grasp what 'life chances' means is to resort to some extensional definition by giving actual examples of differences in life chances within and across societies. For instance, perhaps the most important characteristic of the life course, its length, as measured by life expectancy, varies dramatically across countries: there is no less a gap than 30 years between the life expectancy of Japanese women and Russian men. There are also important differences in life expectancy within countries, including Western developed states. For example, Americans in the top 5 per cent of the income distribution can expect to live nine years longer than those in the bottom 10 per cent and in Britain, professional men live 9.5 years longer than unskilled manual workers (Barry 2005: 72). Differences in life chances in the UK have been the concern of a report, titled *Life chances and social mobility: an overview of the evidence* presented by UK's Prime Minister Strategy Unit in March 2004.[3] The report begins by stating that life chances refer to the opportunities open to individuals to better the quality of life of themselves and their family. It insists on the fact that a life-chances approach focuses attention on the life cycle (or life course) and that life chances (as well as social mobility) can be considered both intra- and intergenerationally (a feature particularly resonant in a sustainable development context). Next, the report exposes some salient facts about life chances in UK, amongst which:

- People in unskilled or semi-skilled occupations are at much higher risk of unemployment than those in managerial and professional occupations;
- Persistence of high rates of gender inequality;
- Ethnic minority groups are more likely to have lower incomes;
- Deprivation tends to be concentrated in certain geographical areas;
- The infant mortality rate and the incidence of mental illness are higher in unskilled and lower income households;
- There has been no narrowing of differences in life expectancy by social class over the past 30 years;
- Households on lower incomes are more likely to be victims of crime and less able to protect their property from theft;
- There is a significant correlation between parents' position in earnings distribution and the position of their children, etc.

All these facts highlight the existence of correlations between positions in the social 'pecking order' and objective conditions for well-being (health, longevity, security, income, unemployment) or the correlations between successive positions within the life course or across generations.

Sociology and the more recent discipline called 'social epidemiology' have shed light on the process through which first the circumstances of birth and, afterwards, the various social experiences that follow, accumulate in life course and constrain life chances in health and longevity. Sociological and social epidemiological surveys and studies (Wilkinson 2006; Marmot 2005; Marmot and Wilkinson 2006) show very clearly that even in our so-called 'meritocratic' societies, life chances, including probably the most crucial and valuable property of existence, life expectancy in good health, depends dramatically on the social and family background of individuals, or, in other words, the human, economical and social capital inherited from one's parents. Of course, social institutions such as schooling and health care systems play a crucial role in limiting the influence of these background factors but they seldom eliminate it totally. Likewise, individuals, by their own efforts and actions can and sometimes do, overcome their initial disadvantage but most often it is at the expense of sacrifices and trade-offs more advantaged persons never have to concede, as we will illustrate below. However, the two Whitehall studies, the longitudinal epidemiological surveys led by Marmot (Marmot et al. 1997; Marmot 2005) on British civil servants demonstrated that even amongst that relatively privileged social category, both mortality and morbidity vary according to the rank in the organizational hierarchy. In other words, each grade has higher levels of morbidity and mortality than the one above it and this remains true for a wide range of causes of death, both those that might be influenced by medical care and those that may not.

To sum up:

Life chances, life course and the social state space

> The life course may be regarded as combining biological and social elements which interact with each other. Individual biological development takes place within a social context which structures life chances so that advantages and disadvantages tend to cluster cross-sectionally and accumulate longitudinally ... Cross-sectionally, advantage or disadvantage in one sphere of life is likely to be accompanied by similar advantage or disadvantage in other spheres.... Social organization also structures advantages and disadvantages longitudinally. Advantage or disadvantage in one phase of the life course is likely to have been preceded by, and to be succeeded by, similar advantage or disadvantage in the other phases of life.
>
> (Blane 2006: 55)

Figure 5.1 pictures this synchronic and diachronic relation between social positions, living conditions and well-being.

It shows that well-being depends simultaneously on the occupied positions and the conditions attached to them. The sociological tradition highlights two different but related inequalities in almost every known society: inequalities of conditions attached to the different positions (correlations between positions at t_n and conditions at t_n) and inequalities of access to these positions (correlations between position at t_n and position at t_{n+1}) so that life chances designate both the probabilities of occupying a given position knowing preceding ones, and the correlative probabilities of experiencing more or less favourable conditions given the occupied positions. Occupancy of various positions during the life course is a dynamical process characterized by path dependency and sensitivity to initial

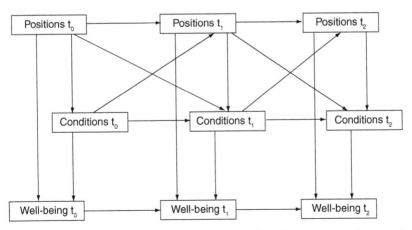

Figure 5.1 Life course and life chances as a succession of interacting positions and conditions (adapted from Gershuny 2001: 14).

conditions. In other words, individuals' life course is determined from the outset by the circumstances surrounding birth:[4] the country and the generation to which one belongs, gender, race, ethnicity, parents' wealth, status and educational level etc. All these circumstances, which are obviously independent of individuals' will and efforts are called in sociological jargon 'ascribed' characteristics. They contrast with 'achieved' characteristics, the ones individuals acquire through their actions, efforts and endeavours. It is one of the less contentious results of sociology that ascribed characteristics limit and orient the kind and level of characteristics people will be able to achieve through their life course, or, in other words, their life chances. Furthermore, people occupying similar positions in the stratification system form social groups whose living conditions, way of life and life chances are also more or less similar.

Figure 5.2 illustrates the main ideas behind the life-chances approach. It pictures the life courses of three typical or representative individuals (A, B, and C) as trajectories in the state space (the enclosing white rectangle) delimited by the possible values of two relevant social-personal characteristics, be they functionings (beings and doings) or needs satisfaction levels or even, in a welfarist perspective, arguments of a utility function. Of course, real, relevant social state spaces are actually n-dimensional, not just 2-dimensional. The trajectories are (in a highly stylized way) represented by arrows between original positions O and destination positions D. They are enclosed in circles that figure the life chances attached to the different original positions. In the capability-functioning language, the O-D line would correspond to the history of achieved functionings but the life-chances set is larger than the capability set which includes only the valued and aspired-to functionings. We will return to this later when comparing

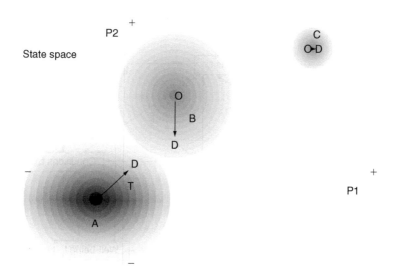

Figure 5.2 Three examples of life chances.

capability with life chances. If the state space contains the different combinations of P1 and P2 existing in a given social and historical context, only those contained in the circle are the most likely for the individuals whose life trajectory is pictured by the lines O-D. Of course, it is not impossible, at least in most contemporary societies, to reach any point of the social state space from whatever initial position but in general, as was stated above, depending on their starting position (for instance, the parents' one), people are most likely to occupy only a limited subspace of the existing social positions. This means that knowing the initial position of any individual in the social state space, one can predict, not with absolute certainty but with reasonable confidence, in which region of the social space their life trajectory will take place. Or, otherwise stated, of all the people starting in a similar position, the majority will end up in positions close to one another.

Thus life chances have two fundamental properties: their size (as proportion of total state space) and their situation with respect to reference point T. Individual C, for instance, is characterized by a relatively limited set of life chances located in the upper-right quadrant of the state space. On the contrary, individual A has larger life chances mainly located in the lower-left quadrant. Individual B is somewhere between A and C with average life chances located near the reference point T but in the positive portion of the state space. The reference point T can mean different things: the modal position with respect to P1 and P2 (the one where the majority of the population is located) or a given deprivation threshold such as a (multi-dimensional) poverty level. Abstracting from their trajectories, B's life chances would certainly be evaluated by an external observer as better than A's ones because, even if the latter is facing a larger set of possibilities, a major part of them corresponds to inferior functionings or needs satisfaction. On the contrary, B's chances are more limited but they are generally of better quality and, at least, above the 'good enough' threshold. However, and this is very important, it does not mean that B will be happier or more satisfied than A. On the contrary, if one takes into consideration their life courses, it is very likely that at any point between origin and destination A could be happier or more satisfied than B, even if most of his/her living conditions are below the reference threshold. This is likely, because A is improving his/her situation while B is experiencing a decline in his/her living conditions. The example illustrates the framing problem which, together with the adaptive preferences problem, plagues subjective well-being assessment and helps understanding why it is not a reliable guide in ethics and social policy, including sustainable development matters. Not only do people adapt to their current situation, their level of satisfaction depends also on their relative situation compared either to preceding ones or to one's reference group well-being. The problem it poses is the following: supposing individual A to be rather satisfied, does it mean that there is no moral and social duty to help him reaching a higher level of needs satisfaction or of achieved functionings? For instance, from the fact that people in Columbia report the highest level of subjective well-being and happiness in the world, can it be concluded that nothing needs to be done to improve their living standard and security levels?

And, symmetrically, supposing individual B to be unhappy, is there a moral social duty to do something for him/her notwithstanding his/her objectively satisfying living conditions?

Life chances and trade-offs

Figure 5.3 illustrates another aspect of life chances.[5] The example shows that the wealthier you are, the less you need to trade free time (which means leisure, family life and other opportunities) against consumption. Being very wealthy gives the real freedom to combine a high standard of living with plenty of free time. Of course, the rich and wealthy are also free to overwork if they want to, but they are not forced to in order to satisfy their subsistence needs. On the contrary, the very poor must sacrifice much leisure time just to reach a moderate standard of living.

In general, unfavourable life chances manifest themselves in the difficulty if not the impossibility of achieving high functionings or high levels of needs satisfaction in a given domain of life without sacrificing satisfying functionings or basic achievements in another domain. For instance, living under totalitarian regimes or dictatorships means trading safety against dignity and self-esteem because voicing opinions exposes individuals to severe repression; people forced to migrate to make a living trade family life and affiliation against subsistence; miners in Russian or Chinese mines trade health and life expectancy against minimum income, and so on. All these are forced trade-offs because those people have no real alternatives. On the contrary, in the rich Western industrial and liberal-democratic countries, trade-offs correspond generally to deliberate

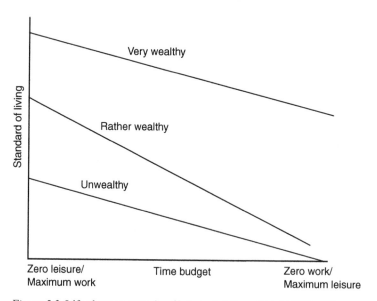

Figure 5.3 Life chances as trade-offs (adapted from Wright 1997: 32).

choices (which correspond to the 'choice of strategies' in Rauschmayer, Omann and Frühmann's Figure 1.1) because accessible alternatives always exist and, at any rate, they do not, as a matter of fact, entail people falling under what is considered the decent threshold of human needs satisfaction, thanks to the safety nets provided by the social security and the securing of human rights.[6]

Life chances and capabilities[7]

At this point in the discussion, the reader might ask: what is the difference, if any, between life chances and capabilities? Unfortunately, to distinguish what the two perspectives have in common and where they depart from one another is a challenging task for several reasons. The first is that both are fundamentally abstract notions whose precise meaning is difficult to express in ordinary language.[8] Second, the two perspectives stem from the same dissatisfaction with 'both of subjective states and command over resources as concepts or measures of well-being or advantage...' (Gasper 2007: 356), so it should not come as a surprise that they look so similar. Returning to Weber's original categories, one could understand capability as something between *Lebensführung* and *Lebenschancen*, between open options for individuals in terms of livelihoods and lifestyles and the probability to succeed (achieve well-being) in them. This would make life chances equivalent to what Gasper (2002) calls O-Capability (opportunity-capability) as distinguished from S-Capability (skill-capability). Likewise, Roche (2006) suggests understanding life chances in terms of capabilities but, unless one considers the two concepts as pure synonyms, the most plausible way to follow Roche's suggestion is to interpret life chances as kinds of metacapabilities, i.e. as distributions of probabilities over the set of capabilities. Indeed, as Gasper (2007: 351) argues: 'What matters for the measurement of capabilities is not only the possibility, but also the *probability* to achieve an n-tuple of functionings'. This raises several methodological difficulties justifying using 'simplifying and standardizing assumptions. In particular, one might have to look at representative standard individuals, not idiosyncratic real individuals, and use standard human values, not idiosyncratic individual preferences' (Gasper 2007: 351). In this perspective, life chances would correspond to the operationalization of O-capability in terms of probabilities referring to standard representative individuals and standard human values. Despite its seductive character, this option will not be explored further here. Instead we will just pinpoint some salient differences between the capabilities and life-chances traditions.

- The life-chances tradition carries a more comparative, differential approach than the capability one. What matters in a life-chances perspective is the differences between people, according to their positions in social and cultural hierarchies, and depending on the circumstances of their birth. It is not to deny that the capability approach is also concerned with inequalities – Sen's as well as Nussbaum's concern with equity and justice is paramount – but the social and cultural underpinnings of inequalities are more present in the life-chances approach than in the capability one. The sociological tradition is less sensitive to individual differences not caused by social stratifications and relations, and the capability approach is much more concerned with persons as reasoners as well as with individual diversity in 'conversion factors'. One could say that if the capability approach seems sometimes to endorse an 'undersocialized' conception of man, the life-chances' one can be said to have the opposite drawback: endorsing an oversocialized conception of man.

- Though it does not make much sense to speak of the capabilities of a child, let alone a toddler, because the idea of freedom to choose amongst alternative vectors of being and doings looks strange when applied to non-adults (Gasper 2002: 457),[9] it is perfectly sensible, on the contrary, to look at their life chances. This observation is resonant with the criticism sometimes addressed to Sen[10] about the somewhat 'athletic' character of his human agent. With its insistence on freedom, choice and reason, the capability approach concentrates more on the active, (young) adult portion of the life cycle than on the states of dependency, relative weakness, and passivity that characterizes those important and inescapable parts of a human life and fate that are infancy, childhood, old age, and episodes of mental and physical illness and disability. In particular, it emphasizes the crucial importance for life chances of the satisfaction of the infant and child's physical (nutrition) and psychological (affection) needs (Wadsworth and Butterworth 2006).
- Indeed, the full life-course (and intergenerational) perspective is probably what distinguishes most sharply the two frameworks. With the recent exception of Yaqub (2008) who advocates and initiates a life-course approach to capabilities and Comim (2003) who insists on the dynamical character of capabilities and on the importance of 'becoming' besides 'beings and doings', the capability approach (and the needs satisfaction as well) has been hitherto more static than dynamic.
- Whilst the operationalization of the capability framework is particularly difficult (Sugden 1993; Anand and van Hees 2006; Gasper 2007), life-chances let themselves rather naturally translate into conditional probabilities, facilitating the gathering of empirical material. Actually, even the United Nations Development Programme's 'Human Development Index' which is supposed to have been inspired by Sen's theories has a more natural interpretation in terms of differential life chances across countries than in terms of capabilities. In particular, life expectancy at birth, which counts for one third of the index, is closer to the idea of life chance than to the one of capability.

Conclusion on life chances

To sum up our discussion:

- Life chances account for both capabilities and well-being in a probabilistic, diachronic and structural perspective. They can be defined as the most likely trajectories (life courses) for individuals in a given society, or as the set of most likely vectors of functionings or of needs satisfaction level for a given individual in a given society, looked at in a diachronic perspective and knowing his/her birth's circumstances. As such, it is a fundamentally prospective notion.

- Life chances can be interpreted as 'rational expectations of well-being' over the whole life cycle taking first into account initial conditions of the life course and other ascribed characteristics linked to the circumstances of birth (country of origin, race, religion, sex, genetic endowment, parents' position ...) and the following succession of positions in social hierarchies. As such they are very close (but more comprehensive than) to what Rawls (1971: 64) calls the 'expectation of well-being' for representative individuals holding social positions or offices established by the basic structure.
- Life chances refer usually to objective conditions of well-being more than to happiness or subjective well-being in general. The life-chances perspective focuses on the socially instituted system of expected contributions, legitimate practices, rewards, gratifications and entitlements attached to characteristics such as gender, race, geographical origin, educational level, position in the social division of labour etc. Income and material conditions are only one part of the 'information set' of life chances assessment. Non-material benefits such as power, authority, influence, prestige, honour – all concepts that play a minor role, if any, in the capability and needs satisfaction approaches are also important elements of this information set. Therefore, the life-chances discourse addresses frontally the inequities in the distribution of those 'positional' goods (Hirsch 1977) whose scarcity is socially organized through the institutions that constitute societies' 'basic structure' (Rawls 1971).

Sustainable development as sufficient life chances

Two principles of morality underpin the idea of sustainable development: the principle of universalism which states that 'place and time do not provide a morally relevant basis on which to differentiate the weight to be given to the interests of people' (Barry 1999: 100), and the principle of responsibility which maintains that

> unless people in the future can be held responsible for the situation that they find themselves in, they should not be worse off than we are. And no generation can be held responsible for the state of the planet it inherits
>
> (Barry 1999: 106)

These two principles are mixed in SD in a manner that 'ingeniously rivets together the major concerns of inter- and intragenerational justice with the demand for environmental protection' (Benton 1997: 202). Therefore, as a global justice endeavour, sustainable development aims at minimizing the influence of two very general but nevertheless decisive circumstances of birth on life chances: the country where and the generation in which you are being born. Its translation on a national scale commits each country to ensure that life chances of their inhabitants will depend less and less on the contingency of regional, social and even biological circumstances of birth, now and tomorrow.

Letting the interests of people and the well-being of future generation be defined as life chances, these principles translate in two major objectives for SD:

- In the name of universalism, struggling against the current unequal (and unjust) distribution of life chances across countries. Indeed, the Human Development Index gives ample evidence that education, income and health (longevity) which are amongst the most important resources for (or indicators of) well-being are very unevenly distributed across countries.
- In the name of responsibility, whilst increasing life chances for the less advantaged today, caring not to jeopardize those of future generations.

Yet, these objectives are not precise enough to help designing actual policies. The formulation leaves unaddressed important issues, notably the following: what does 'increasing life chances' mean? How far should we go in increasing life chances, or when do we decide that life chances are 'sufficient'? Whose life chances have priority? Etc.

It is obviously impossible to give complete answers to all these questions here. All we can do is to open avenues in view of further and more systematic discussions of these difficult issues.

To recall, in Figure 5.2, two properties of life chances were symbolized: their size as portion of the social state space reasonably (or statistically) reachable from a given starting position and their location with respect to a reference point T whose interpretation was at that moment left open. Now, we suggest interpreting T as a threshold of basic needs satisfaction considered in a Rawlsian perspective, i.e. in terms of – augmented – Rawlsian primary goods.

Primary goods and basic needs

Rawls argues that in a well-ordered society there exists a public interpretation of the claims expressed by the citizens when issues of justice are raised and of the way they should be advocated. A political conception of justice provides the framework of such an interpretation enabling the citizens to reach an agreement on the way to assess their respective claims and evaluate their relative importance. This framework consists of a conception of the needs of the citizens, of the needs of persons qua citizens. Thus, a politically effective conception of justice involves a political interpretation of what must be publicly acknowledged as the citizens' needs and therefore as profitable for all. However, in a context of conflicting conceptions of the good, how can we reach a political (that is a public) interpretation of what can be considered as legitimate claims, assuming that the government cannot aim at maximising the satisfaction of the citizens' rational preferences or needs (as for utilitarianism) nor at fostering human flourishing or perfectionists values, nor at promoting a particular religion?

The idea of primary goods is, according to Rawls, a solution to this problem.[11] t is based on the discovery of a partial similarity in the structure of the different acceptable (i.e. those whose realization is compatible with the principles of political justice) conceptions of the good. The similarity in citizens' conception of the good lies in, first, an identical conception of themselves as free and equal persons; and second, the fact that these different conceptions of the good – whatever their differences – share similar needs in terms of freedoms, fundamental rights, opportunities, income and wealth and social basis of self-respect. Indeed, Rawls argues that these goods are what citizens need as free and equal persons and therefore that claims on them is fully justified.

More precisely, the primary goods identified (and ranked) by Rawls are:

a First, the basic liberties: freedom of thought and liberty of conscience, freedom of association; the freedom defined by liberty and integrity of the person, political liberties.
b Second, freedom of movement and choice of occupation against a background of diverse opportunities.
c Third, powers and prerogatives of offices and positions of responsibility, particularly those in the main political and economic institutions.
d Fourth, income and wealth.
e Finally, the social bases of self-respect.

In Rawls's conception of justice, the only permissible differences among citizens are in their share of goods of the (c), (d) and (e) categories. In a well-ordered society, goods of categories (a) and (b) are equally shared by all citizens. However, on several occasions, Rawls admits that the basket of equally shared goods could be enlarged (provided the necessary precautions are taken) to other goods such as, for instance, leisure and even some psychological states. Actually, in a footnote of Section 4 (Lecture V) of *Political Liberalism* (Rawls 1993), Rawls adds some important remarks which throw more light on his conception of citizens' needs. First, as the needs of free and equal persons, they differ from those of patients or students, i.e. of persons unable to cooperate fully and normally with society. Second, because of their objective nature they differ from wants, desires, wishes or preferences which are inherently subjective (cf. O'Neill, Chapter 2, above). Contrarily to desires or preferences, they express necessities for persons having higher order interests with a given status and role and such that 'if these necessities aren't met, they cannot keep their role and status nor achieve their essential aims.' (Rawls 1993: 189).

In sum, Rawls' theory of primary goods is a partial theory of basic needs restricted to needs of fully participating citizens. It should be complemented with a theory of the needs of those permanently or temporarily unable to play a role as full citizens. Rawls is of course totally aware of this and refers to Daniels' (1981, 1985) ethical theory of health care as a model of what is needed to complement it. In particular, he endorses Daniels' conception of 'just' health care as aiming at restoring the capacity of persons to fully cooperate anew to society.

Daniel's naturalistic theory of needs

Daniels extends Rawls' primary goods (the ones that have a moral importance) to 'those things we need in order to achieve or maintain *species-typical normal functioning*' (1981: 153). Such things are objectively ascribable assuming we can come up with the appropriate notion of species-typical functioning and they are objectively important because, whatever our specific chosen goals or tasks, our ability to achieve them (and consequently our happiness) will be diminished if we fall short of normal species-functioning. So, just like Rawls' primary goods, we need them whatever else we need but, furthermore, if we do not have enough of them, the range of opportunity within which to construct our life plans and conceptions of the good will be significantly reduced. The list of things Daniels is ready to add to Rawls' primary goods is quite large. It includes (Daniels 1990: 280):

- adequate nutrition and shelter;
- sanitary, safe unpolluted living and working conditions;
- exercise, rest, and some other features of life-style;
- preventive, curative, and rehabilitative personal medical services; and
- non-medical personal and social support services.

The problem now is to come up with an appropriate notion of 'species-typical normal functioning'. In some way, diseases and illness give us clues to this because they point to 'deviations from the natural functional organization of a typical member of a species.' (Daniels 1981: 155). It is therefore the task of bio-medical sciences to characterize the natural functional organization of man. However, Daniels argues, the biomedical sciences 'must include evolutionary theory since claims about the design of the species and its fitness to meeting bio-logical goals underlie at least some of the relevant functional ascription' (ibid.). Thus, basically, the task of characterizing species-typical normal functioning is the same for man and for other animals except that it is a bit more complicated for man because of (a) the complexity of human apparatus underlying cultural functions such as knowledge acquisition, linguistic communication and social cooperation; and (b) the problem of mental diseases and health, and the fact that we have a less well-developed theory and knowledge of species-typical mental functions and organization. On the other hand, the consequences of impairment in species-typical normal functioning for real life chances depend on the level of economic, social and political development of the society. We have given here above examples of the way social structures influence the chances of functioning at the 'species-typical normal' level, notably for persons ranking low in the social 'pecking order'.

It should be clear that Daniels conceives his theory of needs not as a critique of Rawls' conception of primary goods but as a complement to it, a 'fleshing out' of the Rawlsian primary goods. How can all those goods fit into Rawlsian theory of primary goods? By their relation with one of them: opportunity. 'Impairments of normal species functioning reduce the range of opportunity open to the individual in which he may construct his "plan of life", or conception of the good' (Daniels 1990: 280). Disease or handicaps make it impossible for individuals to develop plans of life that belong nevertheless to what a given society considers 'normal opportunity range', defined as the array of life plans reasonable persons are likely to construct. Such an array is highly dependent on the level of development, the culture and the wealth of the society and, as such, is socially relative. On the other hand, the share of that normal opportunity range each individual can aspire to depends heavily on his/her personal resources (talents and skills). Equality of opportunity does not require that opportunities should be made equal for all persons. They should only be equal for persons with similar talents and skills. Indeed, in 'justice as fairness' (Rawls 1971), there is nothing wrong with these inequalities as long as they benefit the least well-off in terms of talents and skills, which is provided by the difference principle. To come back to health care as primary goods, they can only make the case that individuals are made capable of reaching the share of the normal opportunity range[12] their talents and skills would have given them access to. The 'normal opportunity range' has both similarities and differences with Sen's capability set. Indeed, Daniels argues:

> What is of urgent moral concern to us is not assuring equality of capability in some global way, in all its dimensions, but the more modest goal of protecting individuals from certain impairments of their capabilities. The reference to a normal range of functioning is crucial and captures what I believe underlies our sense of the urgency of meeting health care needs for disease and disability. We are not, concerned with shortfalls from some notion of optimal or enhanced capabilities; if I cannot run a 3:50 mile, I do not view myself as handicapped in ways that give rise to claims on society for assistance or compensation for my lack of optimal capabilities.
>
> (Daniels 1990: 283)

Daniels' conception of needs is also compatible with a life-chances, life-course perspective where the individual is not considered only as a 'fully cooperating member of society' but as a future or past cooperator not yet or not anymore able to fully cooperate but nevertheless still fully member of society.

Sustainable development: generation neutral priority of needs

In a recent essay, Clark Wolf (2009) gives a similar interpretation of Rawls' later discussions of needs and primary goods than the one outlined here above. He argues that taking seriously the changes Rawls has brought to his theory would lead to giving the principle of basic-needs satisfaction a lexical priority over the two other principles of justice for several reasons, notably the fact that satisfaction of basic needs is a precondition for the significance of the equal liberty principle and the value of rights and liberties it guarantees. 'Without prior satisfaction of basic needs, rights and liberties would be valueless to those who possess them, but who would lack any ability to exercise or understand them' (Wolf 2009: 354). Wolf goes on to argue that a lexically prior needs principle should be generation neutral: it should give no special weight to the needs of the members of any particular generation, including the present one. He advocates a 'Min-Deprivation' (MD) formulation of the principle of basic needs satisfaction which stipulates that priority should be given to minimizing deprivation with respect to basic needs. This principle requires that, when deciding between alternative policies, we choose the one which minimizes the likely bad consequences. It also makes it impermissible to promote the less basic interests of some at the expense of the needs of others.

> A generation-neutral needs principle would prohibit such trade-offs between generations as well as among contemporaries. Thus it will be impermissible to promote the less basic interests of members of the present generation if this would compromise the needs of future generations
>
> (Wolf 2009: 367)[13]

What we understand by guaranteeing 'sufficient life chances' should be clearer now. The notion of 'sufficient life chances' carries two requirements: the possibility for individuals to develop life-course strategies for satisfying one's needs (the 'chances' element of life-chances) irrespective of the contingent circumstances of place and time of birth, and the assurance that, whatever these circumstances, individuals' life courses will enable basic needs satisfaction allowing 'full typical-species normal functioning' according to the then relevant social standards in terms of satisfiers. As for existing generations, we are able to assess if their life chances include or not likely states of basic needs thwarting and try to correct things accordingly. For future generations, we can only try to ensure that the circumstances (above all, environmental circumstances) they will face do not make it impossible to preserve both sufficient freedom for exercising one's right to choose one's lifestyle (in the respect of others' freedom to do likewise irrespective of their generation) and to make the case that this freedom is not traded against other fundamental needs satisfaction. It is clear that an impaired environment is only a *sine qua non*, a necessary but not sufficient condition for preserving future life chances. Just institutions, cultural traditions promoting decency and respect in human relations and an enhanced public morality are also parts of the public goods that must be cared for. However as the only resources that cannot be recreated by man, the natural environment must be given lexical priority over those that can be, even if painfully, reinvented by human ingenuity.

Conclusion

According to Dahrendorf:

> Human societies and their history are about life chances, not about the great-
> est happiness of the greatest number, but about the greatest life chances of
> the greatest number. Life chances are (in principle) measurable possibilities
> to realize needs, wants and interests in, or at time, against a given context.
>
> (Dahrendorf 1979: 52)

Sustainable development has already been defined and conceptualized, with
much plausibility, in terms of needs satisfaction (WCED 1987; Cruz, Chapter 6,
below) in terms of capabilities (Sen 2000; Leßmann, Chapter 3 in this volume)
and in terms of both capabilities and needs (Rauschmayer *et al.*, Chapter 1;
O'Neill, Chapter 2; and Spillemaeckers *et al.*, Chapter 4, all in this book). Here
we have explored another possibility, the one offered by the life-chances and
life-course tradition. Our aim was not to urge scholars and policymakers to
endorse a different conception of sustainable development but more modestly to
help strengthen and refine the existing conceptualizations based on needs and
capabilities through their confrontation with a close but slightly different perspective. Admittedly, the life-chance discourse is no less under-specified, ambig-
uous, and fuzzy than the capability-functionings or the needs-satisfaction ones.
It has its seduction and its weaknesses and would require much more elaboration
before being able to compete with the two other discourses. Unfortunately or
not, sociologists have been much more preoccupied with the accumulation of
empirical evidences on the reality of unequal life chances than with its theoretical and semantic clarification. Without doubt, should it have benefited from the
same infatuation as the capability approach, it would probably have more to
offer in terms of sophistication and depth. However, despite thousands of pages
of commentaries and elicitations, neither the capability nor the needs-satisfaction
approaches can be considered finished, uncontroversial pieces of knowledge.
Both have probably to gain in paying more attention to what the life-chances and
life-course approach has to offer: a more prospective accent, concern for human
life as an ongoing process unfolding itself in duration from conception to death;
attention to mankind not only as an agent but also as a patient but always a
'social animal', a tireless concern for unjust inequalities linked to contingent circumstances of birth and for all discriminations.

It appears that neither the capability discourse (as others chapters of this book
testify, notably Leßmann in Chapter 3) nor the life-chances can dispense with
the concept of needs, at any rate when applied to sustainable development and
global justice. This raises an upsetting question: does the need-satisfaction discourse, as Max-Neef conceived it (cf. Cruz, Chapter 6) and in the enriched
version proposed here by Rauschmayer *et al.* (Chapter 1) really need the complement of capabilities or life chances? Are not freedom, participation, understanding, creativity, identity, affection, protection and leisure capabilities also

needs? The capability theory maintains (rightly) that well-being depends as much on the real freedom to choose one's livelihood and lifestyle as on achieved functionings. Is it not the same to affirm that it does not suffice that a lifestyle or livelihood satisfies needs of subsistence, security, understanding and so on: it is also necessary that it satisfies the need for freedom, and first of all, the freedom to choose one's own way to satisfy the other needs (i.e. strategies, in the terminology of Chapter 1)? Could not the capability idea be subsumed under a kind of distinction between substantive needs and procedural needs, the latter referring to the processes through which the former are satisfied? Freedom, for instance, would be such a procedural need, as well as participation, understanding, creativity …. If the answer is yes, then the capability concept could be dispensed with but not necessarily the life chances one. We would still need a way to express the fact that expectations and possibilities of needs satisfaction (including procedural ones) may be unequally distributed and depend on external (environmental, social and political) conditions out of reach of individual control but resulting from collective and social passivity, irresponsibility or sheer immorality, today or in the past.

Notes

1 Institut pour un Développement Durable. E-mail: pm.boulanger@skynet.be. This chapter has been written as part of the WellBeBe (SD/TA/09A) project financed by Belgian Science Policy. It has benefited from discussions with my colleagues and partners in the project: Anne-Laurence Lefin, Tom Bauler, Sophie Spillemaeckers and Luc Van Ootegem. This is a widely revisited version of the first draft in response to remarks, criticisms and suggestions from Felix Rauschmayer, Johannes Frühmann and Ines Omann. If they can be held responsible for all the improvements, if any, between the two successive versions, they cannot be blamed for the possible remaining errors, ambiguities or inconsistencies. I want also to thank especially Ivonne Cruz for her friendly and forgiving appreciation of the first draft and for suggesting a better title.

2

> Another thing to bear in mind is that when principles mention persons, or require that everyone gain from inequality, the reference is to representative persons holding the various social positions, or offices, or whatever, established by the basic structure. Thus, in applying the second principle I assume that it is possible to assign an expectation of well-being to representative individuals holding these positions. This expectation indicates their life prospects as viewed from their social station
> (Rawls 1971: 64)

These expectations of well-being or life prospects are exactly what, following Max Weber, the sociological tradition calls life chances.

3 There is only a web reference for this document at the following address: www.cabinetoffice.gov.uk/media/cabinetoffice/strategy/assets/lifechances_socialmobility.pdf. Last consultation on 27 July 2010.

4 Inequalities in life chances begin even before conception as Barry (2005: 14–15) reports:

> morally arbitrary inequities begin before conception, since the health and nutritional status of the mother at the time of conception is critical. In the womb, the future child is vulnerable to lack of essential nutrients (…), exposure of the mother

to a toxic environment and her own use of tobacco, alcohol and drugs (...). The social structure is implicated in all of these events.

5 Figures 5.2 and 5.3 are not directly comparable. The former adopts a dynamical perspective, the latter a static comparative one.
6 However, I am fully aware that the safety nets can have many and large holes.
7 Cf. Leßmann, Chapter 3, for a discussion of capabilities and sustainable development.
8 Several authors have highlighted the fact the capability view has many versions and interpretations. See for instance Gasper (2007) and Vallentyne (2005).
9 Gasper, expressing his 'doubts and alternatives' concerning the capability approach remarks: 'Even as a prescriptive stance, a criterion of assessing only people's opportunities is not appropriate for children, especially younger children; and it is inappropriate for adults too in any situations where they lack the capacity to understand or cope' (Gasper 2004: 180). But see Yaqub (2008).
10 Nussbaum's version of capabilities is less vulnerable to this criticism than Sen's, at least in several of his writings.
11 Primary goods play an important role in Rawls's theory of justice as fairness, but their role or more exactly their conception has slightly evolved since its first formulation in *A Theory of Justice*. Actually, Rawls came back to primary goods at several occasions. First in 1982 with *Social Unity and Primary Goods*, then in 1987 with *The Priority of the Right and Ideas of the Good* and finally in 1993 with *Political Liberalism* whose Lecture V is made of a slightly modified versions of the 1982 and 1987 papers. The most interesting difference for us between these different versions is the gradual introduction of the concept of 'needs' culminating with Section 4 of Lecture V in 'Political Liberalism' entirely devoted to a discussion of the relation between primary goods and needs. It is very likely that Rawls changed his theory of primary goods after the reading of Scanlon (1975) and Daniels (1981) papers. Indeed, they have been published after the first edition of *A Theory of Justice* but are referred to in all the subsequent formulations of the primary goods theory.
12 Note that Daniels' normal opportunity range is broader than the Rawlsian primary good of opportunity which is restricted to access to jobs and careers.
13 For similar arguments see Boulanger (2006) and Boulanger (2007).

References

Abel, T. and Cockerham, W.C. (1993), Lifestyle or Lebensführung? Critical Remarks on the Mistranslation of Weber's 'Class, Status, Party', *The Sociological Quarterly*, 34(3): 551–556.

Anand, P. and Van Hees, M. (2006), Capabilities and achievements: An empirical study, *The Journal of Socio-Economics* 35(2): 268–284.

Barry, B. (1999), Sustainability and intergenerational justice, in A. Dobson (ed.), *Fairness and Futurity*, Oxford University Press: Oxford, pp. 93–117.

—— (2005), *Why Social Justice Matters*, Polity Press: Cambridge.

Benton, T. (1999), Sustainable development and accumulation of capital: reconciling the irreconcilable, in A. Dobson (ed.), *Fairness and Futurity*, Oxford University Press: Oxford, pp. 199–229.

Blane, D. (2006), The life course, the social gradient and health, in Marmot and Wilkinson (eds), *Social Determinants of Health*, pp. 54–78.

Boulanger, P.-M. (2006), *Sustainable Development as Practical Intragenerational and Intergenerational Justice: Interpretations, Requirements, and Indicators*, Institut pour un Développement Durable: Ottignies.

—— (2007), What's wrong with consumption for sustainable development: overconsumption, underconsumption, misconsumption? in: E. Zaccaï (ed.), *Sustainable Consumption, Ecology and Fair Trade*, Routledge: Abingdon/New York, pp. 17–33.

Comim, F. (2003), *Capability Dynamics: The Importance of Time to Capability Assessments*, mimeo, St Edmund College: Cambridge, online, available at: http://cfs.unipv.it/sen/papers/Comim.pdf.

Cruz, I. (2011), Human needs frameworks and their contribution as analytical instruments in sustainable development policymaking, Chapter 6, this volume.

Dahrendorf, R. (1979), *Life Chances*, Chicago University Press: Chicago.

Daniels, N. (1981), Health-care needs and distributive justice, *Philosophy and Public Affairs*, 10(2): 146–179.

—— (1985), *Just Health Care*, Cambridge University Press: Cambridge.

—— (1990), Equality of what: welfare, resources, or capabilities? *Philosophy and Phenomenological Research*, 50(suppl.): 273–296.

Elder, G.H. (ed.) (1985), *Life Course Dynamics*, Cornell University Press: Ithaca, NY.

Gasper, D. (2002), Is Sen's capability approach an adequate basis for considering human development? *Review of Political Economy*, 14(4): 435–461.

—— (2004), *The Ethics of Development*, Edinburgh University Press: Edinburgh.

—— (2007), What is the capability approach? Its core, rationale, partners and dangers, *The Journal of Socio-Economics*, 36(3): 335–359.

Gershuny, J. (2001), Social structure and life chances, ISER Working Paper 2001-20, Essex University.

Hirsch, F. (1977), *Social Limits to Growth*, Routledge and Kegan Paul: London.

Marmot, M. (2005), *Status Syndrome*, Bloomsbury: London.

Marmot, M. and Wilkinson R.G. (eds) (2006), *Social Determinants of Health*, Oxford University Press: Oxford.

Marmot, M., Ryff, C.D., Bumpass, L.L., Shippley, M. and Marks, N.F. (1997), Social inequalities in health: next questions and converging evidence, *Social Science and Medicine*, 44(6): 901–910.

Max-Neef, M.A. (1991), *Human Scale Development*, The Apex Press: New York/London.

Leßmann, O. (2011), Sustainability as a challenge to the capability approach, Chapter 3, this volume.

O'Neill, J. (2011), The overshadowing of needs, Chapter 2, this volume.

Rauschmayer, F., Omann, I. and Frühmann, J. (2011), Needs, capabilities and quality of life: refocusing sustainable development, Chapter 1, this volume.

Rawls, J. (1971), *A Theory of Justice*, Oxford University Press: Oxford.

—— (1993), *Political Liberalism*, Columbia University Press: New York.

Roche, J.M. (2006), *Capability and life chances: an assessment of two analytical traditions*, Annual Conference of the Human Development and Capability Association: Groningen, Netherlands, online, available at: www. capabilityapproach.org/pubs/1_2_Roche.pdf.

Scanlon, T.M. (1975), Preference and urgency, *Journal of Philosophy*, 77(19): 655–669.

Sen, A.K. (2000), *The ends and means of sustainability*, keynote address at the international conference on 'Transition to sustainability': Tokyo, online, available at: www.iisd.org/pdf/sen_paper.pdf.

Slater, D. (1997), *Consumer Culture and Modernity*, Polity Press: Malden, MA/London.

Spillemaekers, S., Van Ootegem, L. and Westerhof, G.J. (2011), From individual wellbeing to sustainable development: a path where psychologists and economists meet, Chapter 4, this volume.

Sudgen, R. (1993), Review: 'Welfare, Resources, and Capabilities: A Review of Inequality Reexamined' by Amartya Sen, *Journal of Economic Literature*, 31(4): 1947–1962.

Vallentyne, P. (2005), Debate: Capabilities versus opportunities for well-being, *The Journal of Political Philosophy*, 13(3): 358–371.

Wadsworth, M. and Butterworth, S. (2006), Early life, in Marmot and Wilkinson (eds), *Social Determinants of Health*, pp. 31–54.

WCED (United Nations World Commission on Environment and Development) (1987), *Our Common Future*, Oxford University Press: Oxford.

Wilkinson, R.G. (2006), Ourselves and others – for better or worse: social vulnerability and inequality, in Marmot and Wilkinson (eds), *Social Determinants of Health*, pp. 341–359.

Wolf, C. (2009), International justice, human needs, and climate policy, in A. Gosseries and L.H. Mayer (eds), *Intergenerational Justice*, Oxford University Press: Oxford, pp. 347–377.

Wright, E.O. (1997), *Class Counts*, Cambridge University Press: Cambridge; Maisons des sciences de l'homme: Paris.

Yaqub, S. (2008), Capabilities over the lifecourse: at what ages does poverty damage most, in F. Comim, M. Qizilbach and S. Alkire (eds), *The Capability Approach: Concepts, Measures and Applications*, Cambridge University Press: Cambridge, pp. 437–457.

6 Human needs frameworks and their contribution as analytical instruments in sustainable development policymaking

Ivonne Cruz

Introduction

> We define our needs in ways which effectively exclude others meeting theirs, and in the process increase the long term risk for the sustainability of their livelihoods. Most important however, the process through which we enlarge our choices, and reduce those of others, is largely invisible to us.
>
> (Redclift 1999: 59)

The Brundtland Report (WCED 1987), in its first chapters, described briefly their central tenet: 'the concept of "needs" and the "limitations" on the environment's ability to meet the needs of present and future generations' (WCED 1987: Chapter 2). Brundtland's definition on sustainable development (SD) was groundbreaking a few decades ago, but has been more recently contested due to the fact that, even as their statement purported to promote people's fulfilment of needs and those of future generations, they were somehow unsuccessful in defining why this was fundamental to the process.

The World Commission on Environment and Development (WCED) introduced a new vision to tackle social and environmental policy debates while leaving us just short of understanding how to approach the implementation of sustainable development. Nonetheless, the 1987 report showed the requirement for development processes involving transformation of the economy and society and was efficient in providing facts about the overall planetary distress and its causes. The report did not tackle accurately how to prepare an action plan and/or specific strategies for change. It appears to have overlooked the relevance of doing so according to people's cultural and societal values.

The definition and limits of the concept of SD is not central to this work yet some innovative views to the notion are quoted in the following sections. Relevant, however, to this work are the claims from social and political scientists as to what role some of these views play in sustainability and policymaking processes pointing to the Brundtland report and its failure in not making clear assertions on these matters.

In any case, this chapter will support the original inquiry of Rauschmayer *et al.* (Chapter 1) as to how human needs frameworks provide some light in addressing SD policy. Moreover, it will try to describe a series of characteristics that policymaking processes could incorporate into their practice with the aim of converting singular-target SD policies into holistic and multidimensional[1] ones.

The first section of this chapter will give an overview and characterization of the concepts of sustainable development, *integrated* sustainability and specifically, certain attributes of the Human-scale Development approach (H-sD) as an appropriate framework for well-being evaluation (understood holistically and multidimensionally). The aim is to present the spectrum of these concepts/ approaches, their major assets, and their key elements which make them suitable as a goal (SD), as an assessment framework (*integrated* SD notion) and as an analytical instrument (H-sD methodology).

Section two will further define more concrete and practical aspects of the H-sD methodology including an example of how SD policies could be scrutinized under the analysis of human needs. Emphasis will be given to the incorporation of the dimensions proposed by the H-sD approach as distinctive aspects of people's lives where valuable information could be obtained about their characteristics as a society (*being*), the norms, tools, mechanisms and laws that could emerge from the application of a certain policy/strategy (*having*), the actions (collective and individual) that any strategy may motivate and inspire (*doing*), but also the importance of the settings and milieus (*interacting*) where everything takes place. Furthermore, this will also serve the purpose of including the physical environment as an intrinsic element to 'eudaimonic and hedonic' well-being referred to in Chapters 1 (Rauschmayer *et al.*) and 4 (Spillemaeckers *et al.*).

Finally, if the best development process must be one that enables improvement in people's quality of life allowing countries and cultures to be able to be self-coherent (Max-Neef 1998a), evidence that this is utterly possible should be provided. In search of this coherence and demonstrating the relevance of conducting assessments through human needs frameworks, an example of a methodological application is conducted as a guiding tool for practitioners. The case study uses the 'cash for old bangers' policy suggested in Chapter 1 to illustrate the type of information that could be gathered within multidimensional analyses.

For all the above mentioned, the following pages represent groundwork that could still be challenged and refined in the years to come. The adaptations to the H-sD original methodology have been scarcely tested with real case studies and certainly could gain from further inputs in terms of objective valuations, quantitative indicators, or better ways of how to represent and convey the information gathered, to mention only a few. However, the challenge to include human needs frameworks in the making and consolidating of SD policy will remain a huge endeavour to advocate about for many of us – development practitioners and researchers in the field – for the years to come.

Characterizing sustainable development and human needs for policy purposes

Using the concept of sustainable development as a political end

Although the sustainable development roots have been argued to originate largely from the environmental-economic fields (Lumley and Armstrong 2004; Sutton 2004), the concept of SD itself intrinsically incorporates other aspects questioning justice, inequality, participation, a time frame, and people's aspirations for a better life, to mention only a few. Despite of the latter, cultural, technological and ethical dimensions have been recently introduced as innovative ways to better picture a multidimensional and integrated perception of the notion of SD (Anand and Sen 2000; Antequera *et al.* 2005; Colom 2000; Gallopin 2006; Jiménez Herrero 2000). Moreover, these authors have incorporated new features to measure progress toward the sustainability goal.

Indeed, sustainable development achievement is related to the attainment of goals in various and many aspects of human well-being (WB) and environmental conservation issues as well as to those pertaining to intra- and intergenerational behaviour and solidarity. As suggested by Tàbara (2002), not only seen as a principle but as a political ideology, SD aspires to find coherence and balance between the means and the ends in order for them to coexist through time in freedom, equality and solidarity. However, the debate has been widely extended and the understanding of sustainability at the present time looks more like a metaobjective of a process and not really like a process in itself.[2]

The sustainability notion applied to development issues aimed to look like a simple idea to respond to complex problems. However, the difficulties faced in delivering an integrated, objective and generalized perspective, both in science and political action, have produced great frustrations. Notwithstanding, it has opened the way for new transdisciplinary research under the systems view approach. Jiménez Herrero, for instance, has pointed to the relevance of systems interaction to achieve what he calls *integrated sustainability*. He argues that the comprehensive nature of sustainability becomes more evident where the reference point is the set of existing relations between human and environmental systems. SD should be analysed from an integrative perspective and reinforcing a systemic approach. It operates through a set of relations between systems (natural and socioeconomic), dynamic processes (energy, matter and information) and scales values (ideas, ethics) (Jiménez Herrero 2002). Integrated sustainability is therefore the result of the interplay between economic, social [institutional] and environmental sustainabilities which interact according to a set of values and hierarchies (op. cit.). No partial sustainability is hence possible, since all systems are interdependent. Therefore the holistic achievement of SD is seen as the best possible approach.

The latter recalls some of the work done on SD dimensions, cited above, and also referred to in Chapter 1 of this volume; however, this section will try to expand on how the interpretation on the sustainability principle(s) and/or dimensions has stirred policy processes to specific fields of action. Besides popular approaches to SD,[3] an interesting proposal endorsing the importance on policy issues relates to the understanding of sustainability as: 'Basically social, addressing virtually the entire process by which societies manage their material conditions including their social, economic, political and cultural principles that guide the distribution of environmental resources', suggested by Becker *et al.* (1999: 4). Of course a holistic understanding of SD entails certain challenges. In terms of policy effectiveness for instance, how can SD policies embrace the various processes involved within multiple existing systems? Would it be consequently thoughtless to represent and refer sustainability in a plural form (sustainabilities)? And furthermore: would the latter suggest better possibilities to achieve the SD goal?

Sachs suggests in this regard, that 'sustainability criteria must be met in each relevant dimension of [any] type of development. Social and cultural sustainability, ecological, environmental and territorial sustainabilities, economic sustainability and therefore political and institutional sustainabilities; all understood national and international wise' (Sachs 1999: 31–32). Consequently, if we are keen to achieve SD we must think of how to accomplish the sustainability of all entailed and interacting systems for which we need to complete a series of targets at economic, politic, social, cultural and environmental levels, where certainly multiple context dependent outcomes will emerge (Cruz 2007).

Sustainable development realization (throughout its best-known dimensions: economic, natural, social and sometimes institutional) ought to reveal the interaction of their multiple systems. Stahel *et al.* (2005) expand on this idea stating that development does not follow any linear course but involves a network of interlinked dynamics which find their purpose as they interact. Well-being will materialize as a result of the satisfaction of fundamental human needs and the generation of growing levels of self-reliance; and in the construction of the organic articulations of people with nature and technology, of global processes with local activity, of the personal with the social, of planning with autonomy, and of civil society with the state (Max-Neef 1992b: 197).

In practice, including the variety of dimensions that certainly interact with the SD processes is always difficult to represent. In this regard, further questions could emerge: how does policymaking integrate multiple dimensions and their interaction? How does this interaction of variables regarding human, economic, social, cultural, ethical and environmental aspects of life contribute to SD and WB? Or in other words, how could all these dimensions amalgamate and interact positively to enhance the sustainabilities of all systems to attain global SD?

Perhaps in this assumption, we can consider that for each dimension a particular 'strategy(s)'[4] should be put into practice. But indeed, SD policies will only remain coherent with people's values as their needs are realized through those strategies/satisfiers over time and life-changing experiences. The multiple sustainabilities will therefore remain subject to the outcomes and interactions between need fulfilment and the type of satisfiers endorsed to achieve 'integrality' and holism throughout the process (understood as defined above by Jiménez Herrero).

Human needs, satisfiers/strategies and their importance as analytical instruments

Why is it relevant that human needs play a central role in valuating SD achievement? The Human-scale Development theory (H-sD) represents a theory of human needs for development. It has been used for a few decades as a unique assessment framework responding to three fundamental questions alluding to development achievement in holistic terms (economic, social, environmental and institutional): (1) How can we determine whether one development process is better than another? (2) What determines people's quality of life? (3) What are fundamental human needs, and/or who decides what they are (Max-Neef 1992a)?

The theory suggests that a good development process will enable improvement in people's quality of life, allowing people and communities to be coherent within themselves (i.e. positively articulating the social system with nature and technology, the global processes with local activity, the personal with the community, the planning with autonomy, and the public with the state). Chapter 1 of this book (Rauschmayer *et al.*) has depicted some of the most important attributes of this theory and additionally this chapter will support the suggestion of this theory as an appropriate framework, to guide SD policymaking. The work of various authors stressing the relevance of defining dimensions in terms of how human beings establish their relations with their environments has been cited extensively (see Cruz 2008, 2007). However, for the purpose of recognizing the intrinsic value of needs as analytical instruments (Gasper 1996), Max-Neef's approach is thought-provoking. Human development and human needs realization are likely to assume an *optimum* or a *critical* state depending on how they interact within their economic, spatial, political, cultural and natural environments. As Max-Neef explains, the former (optimum) 'humanizes' as the latter 'alienates': in an optimum state of affairs people are able to achieve a sense of identity and integration; the person feels the consequences of whatever she or he does and decides. Within this breath, development of people is possible and a dynamic equilibrium takes place. People feel responsible for the consequences of their actions within their environment, and this can only happen if this environment remains within a human-scale (Max-Neef 1992a: 132). Under this circumstance, people are able to choose endorsing their individual integrity and to resign to letting others act and decide for them. Well-being is hence manifest, as Rauschmayer *et al.* suggest (Chapter 1), since the person is conscious of the needs that are being fulfilled.

On the other hand, within the critical state, development of objects takes place where consequently people become affected by large-scale strategies and are no longer able to rediscover their own selves. Therefore 'they participate less and less allowing themselves to be led more and more' (Max-Neef 1992a: 133). A well-being analysis becomes difficult to undertake, falling into misinterpretations about how people feel integrated or alienated from their environment and the significant aspects of it (economic, spatial, political, social, cultural and natural). Furthermore, it will be even more difficult to characterize all those elements that change and modify people's behaviour when they respond to emotions, intuitions, reactions and feelings.

The H-sD approach embraces a context-related feature, which is determinant of the types or styles of development that people wish to follow. According to this, what is culturally determined is not the so-called fundamental human needs but the infinite possibilities of satisfying them through multiple and different satisfiers. Satisfiers (or strategies, as referred to in Chapter 1, above), unlike needs, are less static (Max-Neef *et al.* 1986). They are modified by the rhythm of history and are diversified according to different cultures and circumstances. Overall, they define the prevailing mode that a culture or a society ascribes to a need. Satisfiers may include: 'organizational structures, political systems, social practices, subjective conditions, norms, values, spaces, contexts, behaviours and attitudes; all of which are in a permanent state of tension between consolidation and change' (Max-Neef 1992b: 201). People and societies vary in forms of *being, having, doing* and *interacting.* The satisfaction or not of needs will therefore depend on the right combination and articulation of specific satisfiers that people will relate too socially and/or individually (Cruz *et al.* 2009).

Furthermore, satisfiers are not neutral; they present various characteristics and are classified for analytical purposes in five types plus the category of economic goods and/or commodities (Table 6.1):

All in all, what is utterly relevant in characterizing this type of human needs approach is the inherent systemic and interdependent feature it entails for need and satisfier interaction. The theory proposes a space for assessment on relevant aspects of human WB achievement (see next section). It suggests the classification of satis-

Table 6.1 Types of satisfiers according to human-scale development approach

Synergetic satisfiers	Are those satisfiers, which, by the way in which they satisfy a given need, stimulate and contribute to the simultaneous satisfaction of other needs.
Violating or destructive satisfiers	Are those imposed arbitrarily and are likely to prevent a second need being fulfilled.
Singular satisfiers	Are those which aim at the satisfaction of a single need, and are therefore neutral with regard to the satisfaction of other needs.
Pseudo-satisfiers	Are elements which stimulate a false sensation of satisfying a given need.
Inhibiting satisfiers	Are those characterized from oversatisfying a need which might eventually cause difficulty in the satisfaction of other needs.
Economic goods and/or commodities	Are objects related to particular conditions in time and history, but represent only one type of satisfiers among a vast range.

Source: Max-Neef 1990.

fiers/strategies in four different existential dimensions or characteristics which express good examples of the various possibilities of action plans, attributes, environments, spaces, mechanisms and so on, available to a particular society to address any specific policy. The outcomes are therefore expressed in terms of human needs realization along the four existential aspects of human WB and denoting qualitative indicators of attainment. This framework for analysis is hence an accurate structure to shape SD policy as it will stir actions to take place within the different aspects relevant to people's values (cultural attributes, laws, mechanisms, tools according to their political or traditional systems, collective actions and the spaces where they interrelate, including the environment). But it also helps to bridge the gap between isolated policies as it encompasses and promotes holism and 'integrality'.

In an effort to prove the latter, the following section will describe some methodological inputs developed on the basis of the H-sD theory to demonstrate how this approach could be useful in advancing SD policymaking through human needs valuation and stressing on the afore mentioned attributes.

Pursuing the ideal of 'integrated ecological humanism'. The relevance of the existential dimensions (being, having, doing and interacting) in needs and satisfiers interaction

In the search for a new type of development, Max-Neef claims that development should be based on what he calls an *integrated ecological humanism:*

> Ecological, based on the conviction that human beings – in order to realize themselves – must maintain a relationship of interdependence and not of competition with nature and the rest of mankind fostering analogies for social order. But also humanistic, as ecological balance must be also subject to human knowledge, judgment and will in terms of conscious political action.
>
> (Max-Neef 1992a: 54)

Within the human-scale perception, the actualization of needs is not only a goal, but the motor of development itself. A need implies either deprivation and/or potential – depending on the extent that needs motivate people (strongly or weakly), the perception of unmet needs motivates and mobilizes people, utterly becoming a resource. In other words, the lack of something might be motor to achieve the fulfilment of the need motivating the person as a key actor in the process. Therefore instead of being satisfied or met, 'needs are to be lived, achieved, or realized from the outset and throughout the entire process of development' (Max-Neef 1992b: 213). For example, the need to participate is the potential for participation; the need for affection is the potential for affection, and so on (ibid.). What becomes utterly meaningful is the freedom of that person to define her satisfiers in order to realize her needs, in achieving a better life which that person and her community values (Cruz 2008). Consequently, needs are never seen as passive instruments but the opposite.

Within the H-sD theory, Max-Neef and colleagues designed a matrix, which was originally intended for development diagnosis, planning and evaluation purposes; therefore, using the matrix as an analytical tool serves the purpose of this chapter and hence this book. This methodology has been used in a variety of ways, stimulating research in the development and environmental fields by putting into practice a vast range of modifications and applications in the last few years (e.g. Carstens 2009; Cruz 2008; Cuthill 2003; Jolibert forthcoming).

The author's contributions were mostly oriented to advance human WB assessments beyond traditional indicators. The way it has been depicted in previous publications (e.g. Cruz 2008) might be restricted to the human development policy field. However, this section will try to illustrate some of the key aspects that could be extrapolated from these exercises in order to be used for SD policy appraisals, where the aim is to provide information about different development realities and strategies within a humanistic and systemic framework, and where outcomes could be translated into holistic and multidimensional policies.

This extension of the original H-sD methodology consists basically on the elaboration of a 'Situational Matrix' alongside a 'Propositional Matrix'.[5] These are extensions from the original methodology that suggests building a negative matrix and a matrix of utopia with quite different purposes. The Situational Matrix is created by interrelating human needs and satisfiers in a given state of affairs or situation. It shows the combination of circumstances at a given moment, indicating most significant constraints or opportunities faced by the interested community. It highlights positive and negative aspects of a given social model revealing difficulties, underestimation of crucial aspects for WB, problematic conditions, potentials, attributes and overestimated characteristics intrinsic to that particular society's reality. It will be some sort of a Polaroid picture showing social, environmental, economic and political features the way they are revealed. The matrix provides information about specific development patterns and strategies that either enhance or repress people's well-being potential but also attributes and positive initiatives within the four existential dimensions of being, having, doing and interacting (Cruz *et al.* 2009). The example of 'cash for old bangers' described in Chapter 1 (Rauschmayer *et al.*) will be partially analysed in Figure 6.1 giving an illustration of the application of the matrices, but by filling out the boxes for just one of the needs involved.

The situational matrix provides information as to how this policy is underestimating the need of 'protection' within its four existential dimensions mentioned earlier. The policy itself looks as if it represented a singular target and somehow pseudo-satisfies in the short term a political goal to garner a greater number of votes. It represents a populist approach to environmental protection (in this case of air quality) when the transaction represents, first, an economic incentive but by no means acknowledges the value of clean air in terms of health, a lower carbon footprint, an important ecosystem service and so forth in the long term. Overall, the policy makes no allusion to key issues for policy success such as social cohesion and longer term environmental education, to mention just a couple. Trading a car for money will indeed fall short in educating people about carbon emissions and the value of clean air as an ecosystem service, for example. In any case, the

Needs according to existential characteristics ········ axiological characteristics	BEING (Personal/ collective attributes) 25%	HAVING (Institutions, norms, mechanisms, tools) 25%	DOING (Personal/ collective actions) 25%	INTER-ACTING (Spaces and environments) 25%
NEED FOR **PROTECTION**				
Examples of the type of information used to fill in the boxes: Global need fulfilment: % Average need fulfilment: %	Elements/ attributes that threatened the realization of the need (e.g. subsidies have a tendency to undermine autonomy in the long run) (← –)	Lack of mecha-nisms, tools, institutions which can support the realization of the need (e.g. temporary policy, hiding electoral goals. Lack of non-monetary long term environmental incentives) (← –)	Values being threatened at individual of collective level (e.g. carpooling, walking, using public transportation are being underestimated and exchanged for a monetary incentive) (← →)	Lack of spaces for interaction, environment deterioration (physical and environmental) (e.g. the urban space is the only one being taken into consideration) (← →)

Figure 6.1 Situational matrix (source: Cruz 2008: 168–169).

Technical notes
- First and overall, matrices are ideally built under participatory processes within specific cultural and social contexts.
- The smaller boxes inside each column indicate the proportion of fulfilment of the need. See Table 6.4 for reference. However, the use of indicators could facilitate the exercise if developed in the future.
- Note each column (being having, doing, and interacting) has equal value representing 25 per cent of a total 100 per cent.
- Arrows like (← –) (+→) and (←→) could be also marked down within each box, indicating negative, positive and unintelligible trends, respectively. This symbol represents a trend in the future. It is valuable information in the sense it provides a tendency for change and amelioration or else, for worsening of the present situation.
- Regardless of the low fulfilment of the need in some dimensions, the trend could nevertheless be positive (+→). The trends are marked down with available information about the specific policy where facts confirm that changing patterns are emerging as a result of a national policy, the signing of an agreement, the acceptance of a new law, institutions being created, etc. These will all represent different types of satisfiers available to switch trends (positive and negatively) as well as long-term policy outcomes.

national and global trends may stir the policy to better outcomes. If there were any existing national, regional or international programme advocating for educa-tion and implementation of mechanisms for ecosystem services valuation, the trend might change in the future, converting this initiative as positive in the sense it supports a larger effort for change. For example, the Corporate Ecosystem Services Review (ESR) is a new methodology for corporate managers. It has been applied in various countries in Europe to develop strategies for managing business risks and opportunities arising from their company's dependence and impact on ecosystems (World Resource Institute n.d.). An initiative like this will probably shift the trend of the policy to more sustainable outcomes in the long run.

Subsequently, the 'Propositional Matrix' is put together (Figure 6.2). It will make reference to the propositional characters of the suggested satisfiers/

Needs according to existential characteristics -------- axiological characteristics	BEING (Personal/ collective attributes) 25%	HAVING (Institutions, norms, mechanisms, tools) 25%	DOING (Personal/ collective actions) 25%	INTERACTING (Spaces and environments) 25%
PROTECTION *Examples of the type of information used to fill in the boxes:* Average fulfilment: %	*Elements describing satisfiers in terms of individual or collective attributes* (e.g. autonomous self-defining community, strong environmental values, etc.)	*Recent implementation of mechanisms, tools, policies that enhance the realization of the need* (e.g. increase of tax exception benefit packages, increase of efficient public transportation, enchancement of a better clean air act, etc.)	*Proposals to enhance collective or individual protection actions* (e.g. community planning, advocating and companying to extend pedestrian zones and car pooling initiatives, etc.)	*Proposal to create certain spaces to potentiate the fulfilment of the need* (e.g. air quality in urban space will improve, also social cohesion will take place in common spaces, etc.)
	Singular	Synergetic	Synergetic	Synergetic

Figure 6.2 Propositional matrix (source: Cruz *et al.* 2009).

Technical notes
- First and overall, matrices are ideally built under participatory processes within specific cultural and social contexts.
- Satisfiers defined underneath the tables represent attributes, laws, mechanisms, actions and environments proposed by the community resembling better strategies to solve development constraint(s). This example uses hypothetical facts, making reference to the circumstances and information provided in Chapter 1.
- Characterization of satisfiers is described in the second row of boxes (these are classified according the Human-scale Development description).

strategies. A propositional attitude means that there is a relational mental state connecting a person to a proposition, like believing, desiring or hoping, which implies intentionality. The matrix is filled out describing one or more constructive and/or propositional satisfiers identified in the SD development policy or plan being evaluated. Depending on the contribution of the identified satisfiers to the holistic performance of the policy, these satisfiers will obtain a certain value responding to their contribution in realizing a given need along the four existential dimensions. Thereby, information on the 'potential achievement' of different proposed satisfiers can be obtained, helping to better establish an effective and holistic SD strategy. The satisfiers are eventually classified as singular, synergetic, destructive, inhibiting or as pseudo-satisfiers (Table 6.1), according to the way in which they fulfil the human needs in the matrix (Cruz *et al.* 2009).

By making superficial assumptions about German values regarding environmental issues, some of the possible propositional satisfiers have been described in the matrix above (Figure 6.2). It should be noticed that some of the proposals for actions (collective and individual), mechanisms and so forth imply the recognition

Assesment value	Trend			Weights
	(−) Negative		(+) Positive	according to need fulfilment
Positive				6/6 = 100%
Medium with high positive trend				5/6 = ~75%
Medium with low positive trend				4/6 = ~65%
Medium				3/6 = ~50%
Negative with high medium trend				2/6 = ~25%
Negative with low medium trend				1/6 = ~15%
Negative				0%

Figure 6.3 Possible trends and weighting values (source: Cruz 2008: 151).

Note
Weights will be calculated according to the situation expressed by the information given in terms of need fulfilment as (positive, negative or neutral). The figure shows approximate values of 75, 65, 50, 25, 15 or 0% out of a 100%. The higher percentage of fulfilment a given policy is able to achieve, the better it will perform in terms of human needs realization. However, for simplification purposes of this exercise no values will be added to the tables. It should be thus considered that numerical values are useful to draft graphical interpretations and information regarding needs fulfilment in percentage estimates.

of societal ideals that perhaps will catalyze change and will push forward any SD policy. The goal of this process is to opt for the largest number of synergetic satisfiers but still, singular ones will sometimes be acceptable. The attachment of people's values to some of these initiatives/strategies is undeniable as citizens have been, and will remain an active part in designing the strategy throughout the process for change. Therefore, alienation will rarely take place and contrarily, a humanizing course of action will emerge as a result.

The search for coherence: how is SD policy tackling multidimensionality?

The logic of the politics of human needs (therefore capabilities, quality of life and life choices (Chapters 3–5) should be defined under cultural-related contexts where insights, hierarchies and priorities attached to any particular idea of development will materialize (Cruz 2007). This is, according to Stahel *et al.* (2005), an ethical, aesthetic and political exercise previous to portray any development model that any society is willing to pursue now and in the future. To Stahel: 'ethical' means that each social group should define what is valuable to achieve and what is not; 'aesthetical' considers that SD is seeking WB and not only issues about living and surviving. The latter also entails a 'political exercise', since the real power for decision making relies on the different ways in which strategies (satisfiers) are articulated within the existential dimensions, herewith translating people's true capacity to influence decisions and to participate in shaping them (op. cit.: 78).

The distinction between needs, satisfiers and commodities (mentioned as part of the H-sD approach) will prevent sustainable development and well-being analyses to fall under further misinterpretations. Being aware of their differences and how they interrelate with one another becomes useful in policy analysis. It is important to identify how often satisfiers have been used to describe basic needs and the confusion it has created in terms of development goals and ends. A good example could be once more the Brundtland report. It referred to 'essential needs' things such as food, clothing, shelter, jobs, water, energy and sanitation (WECD 1987) strictly representing 'basic physical needs' (Chapter 1). Nonetheless, these are clear examples of 'singular satisfiers' to realize the needs of subsistence, protection, identity and freedom. But overall, these satisfiers will not succeed in the overall fulfilment of the human needs system as a whole because they can only tackle one or two existential dimensions (i.e. *being* and *having*) for the case given. The analysis will utterly be incomplete, as has been suggested above. WB is not attained when partial sustainabilities are claimed as having being achieved. Interdependency of systems and/or dimensions, interaction and complementariness must be the imperative such as in the realization of the system of human needs.

Classifying and identifying satisfiers by the way they affect the four different existential dimensions of WB becomes a valuable attribute of the H-sD theory. It certainly helps to emphasize how certain social and cultural settings, as well as development patterns, enhance or inhibit personal and collective freedom, auton-omy and WB. It helps to highlight how people realize their needs in terms of themselves and their own rationality (*Eigenwelt*) with respect to others and the community (*Mitwelt*) and respecting their environment (*Umwelt*) (Max-Neef *et al.* 1986: 21).

Indeed, the uses of these types of appraisals appear complicated and challeng-ing to apply. As we search for coherence within academia, policymaking will still be seeking practicality. Notwithstanding, the results and outcomes are by no means futile when considering, for instance, that a continuous deprivation above a certain threshold of at least one of the established needs will cause the com-plete collapse in the long run of the whole system affecting, consequently, human life. For this reason, equilibrium and correspondence should prevail among needs and satisfiers in order to avoid the depletion of the whole system of needs. This could become a preliminary answer to some of the questions raised in Chapter 1 aiming to consider need realization intergenerationally. The depri-vation of various needs in the system for a long time will resume in the collapse of the system of needs, maybe not in the present but in future generations. Favouring singular and/or destructive satisfiers/ strategies will blurrily attempt to achieve human and environmental WB but in the long run; different types of *poverties*[6] will emerge as a result of the fractional strategies and satisfiers that we as a society and individuals have prioritized through a particular policy.

Therefore, we cannot question the urgent need for political spaces fitted to encourage WB and *integrated sustainability* (cf. section 'Using the concept of sustainable development as a political end'), where opportunity spaces for the expansion of people's choices/capabilities (Sen 1999) and human needs fulfil-ment become tangible. These spaces will certainly materialize the link between an improved government and the consolidation of its participatory, social and political systems' sustainability responding to people's own cultural understand-ings and aspirations. As a result, policy changes will take place. Whether these political changes are aimed at promoting human WB and the realization of human needs systemically will be up to us to decide. If SD policy only embodies a set of destructive and/or pseudo-satisfiers (strategies) emphasizing punctual and specific dimensions or crucial aspects of human WB, then changes toward SD will therefore represent fragmentation and long-term alienation and/or the revelation of poverties. This will certainly have an effect in the future as it will picture the results of fractional WB achieved by present generations.

Conclusion

This chapter aims to highlight the importance and value of incorporating 'inte-grality' and multidimensionality aspects into SD policy enhancement. The aim is also to demonstrate that frameworks like the H-sD approach could contribute to a large extent to this goal.

It has been analysed that sustainability, as a principle, represents a set of human-attributed goals and functions, required to address multidimensionality (i.e. considering all relevant aspects for human WB attainment through the being, having, doing and interacting spheres). In this regard, constructing, advancing or achieving SD implies finding different ways (strategies/satisfiers) to express human flourishing as a universal need or goal. According to Stahel *et al.* (2005: 83), 'development is changing continuously in time and space' and the interaction of dimensions in the process becomes inherently relevant as to what type of outcomes it may reveal.

Literature and history had showed that development is more about people than about objects (Max-Neef 1998b; UNDP 1990–2010) and people's participation in decision making has become more important than ever. People should empower policymaking processes since it involves a responsibility exercise. It will hence allow communities to evaluate certain strategies and discriminate, reject and/or promote others.

This chapter defined central aspects of the H-sD approach and demonstrated how further adaptations to the proposed methodology can conduct satisfier or strategies assessments in SD policymaking. It therefore advocated for the use of these human needs approaches and frameworks to enhance WB achievement and take account of all those significant aspects of people's values in the process.

The example on 'cash for old bangers' provided in Section II may encourage extended discussions, particularly on the subjectivity entailed. Yet, the exercise was here depicted to demonstrate the use of the tool, the type of information that could be obtained from analyses of the kind, but certainly also to stimulate further debates concerning its development and amelioration. This is a brief example of the exploratory work that has been developed in the past few years and has indeed revealed some gaps but certainly great potentials too. Overall, the aim of such work is to put forward new ways of how to define and understand SD as a multidimensional ending resulting from the appreciation of all relevant features of WB; representing essential aspects of people's lives. The fact that SD cannot be achieved fractionately, nor WB could be realized partially, brings us back to the original query mentioned in the first section and the importance of achieving sustainabilities of the various systems (human, natural, economic, cultural, etc.). The importance in policy terms will remain in advocating for synergetic strategies and actions tackling people's most intrinsic values, beings, doings and social aspirations now and for the generations to come.

Notes

1 Meaning the set of relations and interactions among different human, environmental systems (Jiménez Herrero 2002). 'Multidimensional' also defined as: having, involving or marked by several dimensions or aspects (Wordnetweb n.d.).
2 See e.g. Rios Osorio *et al.* 2005 and the characterization of the SD debates as conceptual, contextual, disciplinary and geopolitical.
3 For instance (WCED 1987; IUCN-UNEP-WWF 1996).
4 The term strategy is herein used interchangeably with the notion of satisfiers used in the human-scale development approach. Chapter 1 refers to the term comparable to satisfier, meaning according to Max-Neef (1998a) all the things that, by representing

forms of being, having, doing, and interacting contribute to the realization of human needs. They vary according to cultural backgrounds and contexts but also through historical rhythms, and from their variety; different development models and strategies might be pursued. The theory is largely depicted in Chapter 1 and furthermore in the section 'Human needs, satisfiers/strategies and their importance as analytical instruments' in this chapter.

5   An extended description on the application of this methodology is depicted in Cruz *et al.* 2009 and is more specific and detailed in Cruz 2008. Also the author thanks the valuable contributions of Andri Stahel as PhD advisor and Manfred Max-Neef for his insights and inputs to this work.

6   From the H-sD perspective, fundamental human needs exist according to a pre-systemic threshold from where deprivation of any of the listed needs will cause shattering within the whole needs system and thereby impacting overall human well-being (Max-Neef 1998a; Elizalde 2003). Therefore we should rather be talking not of poverty in the singular, but of poverties in the plural. Every person, culture or society may be rich in certain aspects of life, and poor in others, depending on different circumstances and on how their different fundamental human needs are being satisfied (Cruz *et al.* 2009).

References

Anand, S. and Sen, A. (2000), Human development and economic sustainability, *World Development*, 28(12): 2029–2049.

Antequera, J., Gonzalez, E. and Rios, L. (2005), Sostenibilidad y Desarrollo Sostenible: un modelo por construir, in *SOSTENIBLE? What is sustainability? 7, Cátedra UNESCO en Sostenibilidad*, UPC: Terrassa, pp. 93–118.

Becker, E., Jahn, T. and Stiess, I. (1999), Exploring uncommon ground: sustainability and social sciences, in E. Becker and T. Jahn (eds), *Sustainability and the Social Sciences*, UNESCO & ISOE: New York, pp. 1–12.

Carstens, K. (2009), *Non-Governmental Organisations and Local Institutions: Human-Scale Development and Inter-organisational Relationships*, MSc dissertation, Open University: Milton Keynes.

Colom, A. (2000), *Desarrollo Sostenible y educación para el desarrollo*, Octaedro: Barcelona.

Cruz, I. (2007), Sustainability re-examined through the human development perspective, *International Journal of Sustainability, Technology and Humanism: UNESCO Chair in Sustainability*, 2:133–152, Barcelona, online, available at: https://upcommons.upc.edu/revistes/bitstream/2099/4237/1/Cruz.pdf [accessed 8 September 2009].

—— (2008), *Human Development Assessment through the Human-scale Development Approach – Integrating Different Perspectives in the Contribution to a Sustainable Human Development Theory*, CIDH-CRUMA: Madrid.

Cruz, I., Stahel, A. and Max-Neef, M. (2009), Towards a systemic development approach: building on the human-scale development paradigm, *Ecological Economics*, 68(7): 2021–2030.

Cuthill, M. (2003), From here to utopia: running a human-scale development workshop on the gold coast, Australia, *Local Environment*, (8)4: 471–485.

Elizalde, A. (2003), *Desarrollo Humano y ética para la Sostenibilidad*, Universidad Bolivariana y Programa de Naciones Unidas para el Medio Ambiente: Santiago de Chile.

Gallopin, G.C. (2006), *Los indicadores de desarrollo sostenible: aspectos conceptuales y metodológicos*, FODEPAL: Santiago de Chile.

Gasper, D. (1996), Questioning development, in G. Köhler, C. Gore, U.P. Reich and T. Ziesemer (eds), *Needs and Basic Needs*, Metropolis Verlag: Marburg, pp. 71–99.

IUCN, UNEP, WWF (1996), *Principles of a sustainable society, Caring for the Earth: A strategy for sustainable living*, S.C. Rockefeller: San Jose, Costa Rica, Earth Charter Project, Earth Council, pp. 129–31, revised April 1996, online, available at: www.iisd. org/sd/principle.asp?pid=57&display=1 [accessed 20 April 2006].

Jolibert, C. (forthcoming), Need assessment: a tool for environmental conflict resolution in multilevel governance, Paper accepted at the *Environmental Policy and Governance Journal*: award for the best student papers at the ESEE 2009 Conference, 2009: University of Ljubljana, Slovenia.

Jiménez Herrero, L. (2000), *Desarrollo Sostenible*, Pirámide: Madrid.

—— (2002), La sostenibilidad como proceso de equilibrio dinámico y adaptación al cambio, *Información Comercial Española, ICE: Revista de economía, Desarrollo Sostenible*, 800: 65–84, online, available at: http://dialnet.unirioja.es/servlet/ articulo?codigo=263589 [accessed 29 March 2010].

Lumley, S. and Armstrong, P. (2004), Some of the nineteenth century origins of the sustainability concept, *Environment, Development and Sustainability*, (6)3: 367–378.

Max-Neef, M. (1990), A framework for the future: 'human scale economics' – the challenges ahead, in P.Ekins (ed.), *The Living Economy: New Economics in the Making*, Routledge: New York, pp. 43–54.

—— (1992a), *From the Outside Looking In: Experience in Barefoot Economics*, Zed Books: London.

—— (1992b), Development and human needs, in P. Ekins and M. Max-Neef (eds), *Real Life Economics: Understanding Wealth Creation*, Routledge: London, pp. 197–214.

—— (1998a), *El desarrollo a escala humana*, Nordan and Icaria: Barcelona.

—— (1998b), Etica, economía y desarrollo a escala humana, in C. Parker (ed.), *Ética, Democracia y Desarrollo Humano*, LOM and CERC-UAHC: Santiago-Chile, pp. 249–258.

Max-Neef, M., Elizalde, A. and Hopenhyan, M. (1986), Desarrollo a escala humana: una opción para el future, *Development Dialogue* (special edition) Cepaur-Dag Hammar-skjöld Foundation: Uppsala.

Rauschmayer, F., Omann, I. and Frühmann, J. (2011), Needs, capabilities and quality of life: refocusing sustainable development, Chapter 1, this volume.

Redclift, M. (1999), Sustainability and sociology: northern preoccupations, in E. Becker and T. Jahn (eds), *Sustainability and the Social Sciences*, UNESCO & ISOE: New York, pp. 59–79.

Rios Osario, L., Ortiz Lobato, M. and Alvarez Del Castillo, X. (2005), Debates on sustainable development: towards a holistic view of reality, *Environment, Development and Sustainability*, 7(4): 501–518.

Sachs, I. (1999), Social sustainability and whole development: exploring the dimension of sustainable development, in E. Becker and T. Jahn (eds), *Sustainability and the Social Sciences*, UNESCO & ISOE: New York, pp. 25–36.

Sen, A.K. (1999), *Development as Freedom*, Oxford University Press: Oxford.

Spillemaeckers, S. Van Ootegem, L. and Westerhof, G.J. (2011), From individual well-being to sustainable development – A path where psychologists and economists meet, Chapter 4. this volume.

Stahel, A., Cendra, J. and Cano, M. (2005), Desarrollos sostenibles in *SOSTENIBLE? What is sustainability? 7 Cátedra UNESCO en Sostenibilidad*, UPC: Terrassa, pp. 73–92.

Sutton, P. (2004), What is sustainability? *Eingana: The Journal of the Victorian Associ-ation for Environmental Education*, 27(1): 6–9.

Tàbara, J.D. (2002), Sustainability culture, *Papers de Sostenibilitat 2*, Instituto Internac-ional de Gobernabilidad (IIG): Barcelona, pp. 63–85.

UNDP (United Nations Development Programme) (1990), *Human Development Report*, online, available at: http://hdr.undp.org/en/reports/global/hdr1990/ [accessed 15 Sep-tember 2005].

Wordnetweb, (n.d.) www.wordnet.princeton.edu [accessed 17 March 2010].

WCED (United Nations World Commission on Environment and Development) (1987), *Our Common Future*, Oxford University Press: New York, online, available at: www.un-documents.net/wced-ocf.htm [accessed 14 January 2010].

World Resource Institute (n.d.) *Mainstreaming Ecosystem Services Initiative (MESI)*, online, available at: www.wri.org/project/mainstreaming-ecosystem-services [accessed 17 March 2010].

7 A plea for the self-aware sustainability researcher

Learning from business transformation processes for transitions to sustainable development

Felix Rauschmayer, Tell Muenzing and Johannes Frühmann[1]

Ever since the Agenda 21 was agreed at the United Nations Conference on Environment and Development, held in Rio de Janeiro on 14 June 1992, it has been recognised that concrete actions at the local level are vital to implement the concept of sustainable development (SD). This quest has been taken up and local agenda processes have started worldwide. Individuals engaging in the Agenda 21-processes expect regulatory bodies to take up their suggestions for action and even to support them proactively in the shift towards self-responsibility for achieving more intra- and intergenerational equity. Similar shifts can be observed in business (with the discussions on Corporate Social Responsibility and the Triple Bottom Line) and in other parts of civil society that cannot be restricted to local initiatives.

Very often, regulatory bodies' sustainability actions result in measures that try to influence citizen behaviour through regulatory frameworks and information campaigns. In most cases, this remains without much effect, as – and this is our main assumption for which we will argue – the context and the roots of behaviour have not been sufficiently understood and taken into account.

We distinguish between the external context of behaviour such as politics, natural and societal systems, culture; and the internal roots of behaviour, which consist of more than just knowledge, but also include values, priorities and needs as the motivational factors for any behaviour (O'Neill, Chapter 2 above; Wiggins 2005). The discussion on sustainability has always been linked to a systemic view, with the aim to understand, analyse and evaluate all relationships that occur between current actions in one place and effects in other places and/or in other moments of time. It is our impression, though, that the individual factors and their interplay with structural factors have not been taken into account sufficiently by sustainability policies and research (see also Jackson 2004). This chapter aims to strengthen the arguments on why it is important to look at needs when dealing with sustainable development,[2] argued for in Chapter 1 (Rauschmayer *et al.*) – it does so from a more individual-based and transition-driven perspective.

But the final conclusion of this chapter is different: we think that, when tackling the interplay between structural and individual factors in sustainability research, researchers require special skills and capabilities. There are two main reasons for this:

1   Sustainability research is values-related and very often values-driven research. Additionally, researchers usually have a political stance in this field and are herewith part of the system they want to analyse. The distance to the system may be larger with desk studies than with action or other transdisciplinary research (on the latter see Max-Neef 2005; Hirsch Hadorn *et al.* 2006).
2   Related to this is our assumption (also resulting from our own self-inquiry) that at least those researchers working with methods of action research want to meet their own needs such as meaning and contribution through their research. So, they are neither neutral to the object of research nor are research and its results neutral to their good life (in a deeper sense than just as joy coming from any satisfying work).

Those special skills that are required differ from skills that are usually trained in science. They are basically metacommunication skills that enable the actor to better reflect inner processes and communicate more transparently with other actors in the research process. We call them capabilities and not just skills, as they refer to the ability of the researcher to pursue an activity that is essential for their own good life (cf. Leßmann, Chapter 3). These capabilities have to be stronger when engaging in action research[3] than when doing desk research, as in the former type of research inquiry necessarily has to include self-inquiry.

It is not easy to determine mandate, form, methods and impact of experiences in action research aiming at societal transitions to SD, due to the open systems in society. However, an increasing number of consultants are working in the corporate sector for organizations aiming at being more sustainable – in a financial, but also in a societal or ecological meaning. This work is better delimited, tasks are clearer, and tools for business transformation have been developed for a long time – towards sustainability or other goals. We will therefore take an example from the corporate sector to highlight what transformation processes could imply and why this requires different skills than a financial auditing, for example.

Overall, a transition to SD requires fundamental changes in the individual choices made and behaviours displayed. These changes can be achieved by coercion, by incentives or from intrinsic motivation. The precondition for the latter is a higher level of consciousness, in terms of individual awareness and responsibility. This can be achieved through personal growth and mindset shifts that emerge from personal transformation processes. Behavioural transformation then rests on nonreversible shifts in root perspectives that are at the core of individual motivation compared to externally induced behavioural changes. This ultimately makes personal development and growth a precondition for sustainable development. However, this in itself is not sufficient, as experience tells us that only a holistic perspective and whole-system transformation including changes in the external context does not exhaust the individual's motivational forces, but support and sustain the transition at individual and collective level. Thus, research on sustainable development has to take both into account: internal roots of behaviour and structural factors of the external context of transitions.

For research on sustainable development this has particular consequences. Research and science as a *method of inquiry* have served humanity over the last 350 years in advancement of knowledge that has brought about technological leaps on an unprecedented scale, with unprecedented and unpredictable consequences. Sustainable development is inducing a paradigm shift that requires answering systemic and qualitative questions of direction, scale and values (e.g. with regard to growth and halt of degradation; species survival and ecosystem integrity; environmental justice and intra- and intergeneration equity). It also asks for working backwards from a vision of what is desirable and makes a sustainable world. This means that value judgements and individual and collective requirements for wisdom enter the research agenda more urgently than ever. While the insatiable human 'more' has been served well by research's neutral knowledge for 'how to' achieve progress, not necessarily questioning the aim of progress, the 'what' we want to achieve, referring to the substance and goal of development, has been vacant for too long (cf. Cruz, Chapter 6 in this volume). For sustainable development it is time for researchers to engage more effectively with the what. As with psychotherapy and psychoanalysis, research on internal roots of behaviour, and, in our case, of substantial behavioural change is not effective without *including self-inquiry in one's research.* Our plea, therefore, is for a new breed of research and researchers to work on their own self-awareness and role in researching and facilitating the transition process, while at the same time engaging in transdisciplinary research that learns to master the interrelatedness of systems and holistic approaches.

So, this poses new challenges for researchers to the ones already familiar in traditions such as post-normal science (Funtowicz and Ravetz 1993): additionally to their disciplinary research, they are familiar with competences required by inter- and transdisciplinary work (cf. Hirsch Hadorn *et al.* 2006; Max-Neef 2005). In this chapter, we argue that combining transdisciplinary research with inquiry on needs and values as the roots of behaviour stipulates that researchers are also required to train themselves in domains similar to the ones required for the facilitation of open social processes: self-consciousness, humility, radical recognition of own subjectivity, etc. (e.g. Mindell 1995). This training can not be done in the typical scholarly way of learning and researching, but only through permanent self-inquiry and self-realization using processes and approaches such as community-building processes (Peck 1987), non-violent communication (Rosenberg 2001), neuro-linguistic programming (Bandler and Grinder 1975a, 1975b), Trinergy (Braun *et al.* 2005), or meditation (Singer and Ricard 2008; Goleman 1997).

In the following section we take a closer look at roots for individual behaviour and how a shift in root perspectives can transform behaviour from the inside towards more sustainability. The third section frames this dichotomy between internal roots and external context of behaviour systematically: here, we differentiate between the four complementary perspectives of internal vs external and individual vs collective perspectives. The fourth section briefly argues that there are good reasons to believe that there is an evolutionary development of consciousness that supports a transition to sustainability. The fifth section gives an example of how such integral transformation processes can be managed in a business context. Before concluding the chapter, we draft challenges for the researcher on sustainable development resulting from the lessons learned in the business example.

Roots for individual behaviour and the evolution of consciousness

Research aiming at SD transition has mostly looked at the *external context* of behaviour. When studying sustainable consumer behaviour, for example, the discrepancy between people's so-called 'attitudes' or their 'behavioural intentions' and their overt behaviour is often complained about. Turning to transition science and environmental psychology, this discrepancy is explained as follows: individuals are unlikely to change their behaviour (or at least not in critical masses) in the context of an unchanging environment. An example: in a culturally stable environment and with an unchanging infrastructural network (and the services herein) as well as a stable home and workplace, a given individual is most unlikely to change his/her mode of transport. The external context co-determines how self-evident or difficult it seems for an individual to display certain behaviour (Kaufmann-Hayoz *et al.* in press).

However, individual behaviour is just the tip of an iceberg (Figure 7.1). The *internal roots* of behaviour are constituted by knowledge and beliefs on the external and internal world, but also by values and priorities and basic and psychological needs constituting the main motivation for any behaviour. Information campaigns try to influence the 'thinking and feeling' layer, but have difficulties in reaching 'values and priorities'. The most recent example of not addressing directly the internal roots is 'nudging' that uses unconscious internal mechanisms to design choice situations in such a way that we select the 'right' choices (Thaler and Sunstein 2008).

However, the conviction that sustainable development is a good thing to do is placed in this second lowest layer of values and priorities. The deepest layer is reserved for the concept of 'needs' that represent basic motivational factors shared by human beings (like security, subsistence, creation, affection, meaning and contribution – Max-Neef 1991; cf. Rauschmayer *et al.* Chapter 1; O'Neill Chapter 2; Cruz Chapter 6, all in this volume). Needs translate themselves into behaviour by concrete 'strategies' framed and influenced by values and informed by thinking and feeling.[4] Needs and strategies may be identified at any chosen level: society, organizations or individuals. We argue that it is these strategies and resulting patterns of behaviour (and not the underlying needs) that cause the detrimental effects that may be denoted as 'unsustainable'. Instead of trying to directly

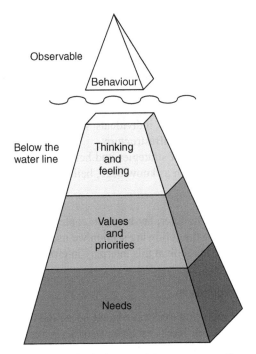

Figure 7.1 The iceberg model: root causes of human behaviour (adapted from Bellin 2010).

change strategies of individuals, e.g. by command and control or economic incentives, new policy mixes for sustainability are more likely to be successful if they explicitly address all layers of the 'iceberg'. The deeper the layer of the iceberg, the more difficult it is to reach it from the outside. Policies (or advertising campaigns) can influence thinking and feeling for a while, whereas values and priorities are rather evolving in a cultural process that expresses itself e.g. by adopting certain lifestyles. Through different modes of governance, policies can nevertheless facilitate or hinder the creative and self-conscious process that allows individuals to express their needs, espouse different values, and access up-to-date knowledge so that their selected strategies are coherent with need, values and thinking (cf. Cruz Chapter 6; Omann and Rauschmayer Chapter 8, both in this book). This means to move from the image of man as a 'passive individual' driven by context and needs, nudged by benevolent or malevolent choice architecture, and governed in a hierarchy by policymakers and their frameworks to the image of an empowered individual with will, choice, and self-responsibility.

Therefore, it becomes important to establish settings where individuals can shift their root perspective and find SD meaningful, something they can powerfully relate to – so that SD becomes part of their consciousness, values and priorities. Such a shift would be similar to the psychological development analysed by Kohlberg (e.g. Kohlberg and Lickona 1976), and interpreted for the development of economic schools of thought by Ingebrigtsen and Jakobson (2009). This shift should enlarge their capability set, i.e. their set of realistic and achievable possibilities to live a better life (cf. Leßmann Chapter 3, above), and finally translate through strategies into a more sustainable behaviour.

   To conclude this section: when looking at the individual behaviour in its context, we look at

- *external context* influencing behaviour of individuals from the outside: external factors may be regulation, rules, infrastructure;
- *individual roots* influencing the choice of strategies and herewith the behaviour of individuals from the inside, such as knowledge, beliefs, values, priorities and needs.

The important part to study lies within the interplay between contextual factors and the roots of individual behaviour. In the following section we use some concepts of Wilber's integral theory (1995) to look at this interplay in more detail.

Introducing Wilber's four perspectives

The dichotomy between individual roots and external context opens the field for a multiple perspective approach. Taking different perspectives is a very common act for human beings and is established in every major language (Wilber 1997): using 'I' as a first person singular pronoun expresses individually subjective content (e.g. I feel excited). Using 'we' as a second person plural pronoun is pointing to an inter-subjective content (e.g. we decided to write this chapter). Using 'it' or 'its' (he/she or they, respectively) as third person pronouns is referring to a look from outside in an objective way (e.g. it is raining). Obviously, humans are using such different perspectives every day, but seldom reflect on it.

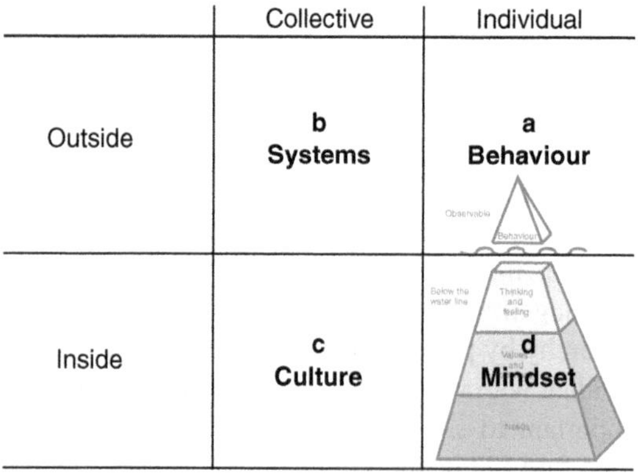

Figure 7.2 Four complementary perspectives on individuals (adapted from Wilber 1995 and Bellin 2010).

Wilber's (1995) four-quadrant model (Figure 7.2) allows reflecting on the use of different perspectives in research and, in our context, to take a more complete look with regard to the transition to SD. The model refines the concept of individuals and their context by using four complementary perspectives which are differentiated between two dimensions: inside/outside and individual/collective. The dimension of inside/outside is based on the dichotomies subjective/ objective: 'inside' refers to introspective and interpretative approaches, e.g. as used in depth psychology or hermeneutics, which necessarily are subjective. 'Outside' points to naturalistic or empirical approaches, e.g. behaviourism, positivism or structural functionalism in system theories.

Each of the four quadrants offers a different view and therefore also different insights on an entity (cf. Figure 7.2 for an overview).

a Quadrant a (outside, individual)

This perspective deals with the behaviour and skills of an individual entity that can be observed and empirically analysed. Wide parts of natural sciences are conducted from this perspective. Looking at human beings, behaviourism is the classical approach for quadrant a. It analyses e.g. habits, routines and rituals of individuals and asks for function, not meaning. The top of the 'iceberg' model (Figure 7.1) is within quadrant a. Discussions in economics that can be situated in this perspective are those around the image of man, such as homo oeconomicus (cf. Söderbaum 2008; Faber *et al.* 2002; Jager *et al.* 2000).

b Quadrant b (outside, collective)

This perspective deals with the systemic embedding of the individual – in natural, social, political, economic or other settings. Main parts of system theory are taking this perspective analysing structural and functional patterns. Beside quadrant a this perspective is the most important in scientific approaches. In economics, general equilibrium theory and econometric approaches are prominent in this perspective. Focusing on SD transition, approaches from quadrant b, such as the resilience approach, give insights on external resources that individuals can access (infrastructure, social networks, institutions, etc.).

c Quadrant c (inside, collective)

This perspective deals with the cultural context of the individual: what is defined as morally right or wrong? What is culturally permitted, accepted, wished for? The main approach to quadrant c is hermeneutics – the art of interpretation. Understanding is derived from an intersubjective dialogue. It is mainly under this perspective that collective values and priorities are developed. In economics, the old institutional school (e.g. Veblen 1899) has been working in this perspective and parts of the discussion on development economics and the management of the commons (Ostrom 1990) also takes into account cultural elements. This 'we' of culture has gained an immense interest and push as part of the 'discursive ethics' debate and wide use of stakeholder engagement to inform internal cultural arrangements with the rise of the civil sustainable development movement.[5]

d Quadrant d (inside, individual)

This perspective deals with the inner experience of individuals. Within science, depth psychology is focused on this domain. Examples of other approaches focusing on this perspective include Existential Analysis (Frankl 1985, 1992), Non-violent Communication (Rosenberg 2001), Neurolinguistic Programming (Bandler and Grinder 1975a, 1975b). Concepts that are used to describe phenomena in quadrant d are thinking, feeling, personal values, needs, world-views, consciousness, convictions, beliefs, etc. We summarize those concepts with 'mindset of an individual' which also represents the part of the 'iceberg' model (Figure 7.1) that is under the water line. Within economics, humanistic economics associated with E.F. Schumacher might come closest to this perspective (Lutz 1992).

By using this four-quadrant model, the concept of individual roots and contextual factors as described in the precedent section becomes more specified, as we notice that the contextual factors, at least in economics, often refer to a systems perspective, leaving out cultural aspects (but see Luks and Siemer 2007, for example). Furthermore, we get a first impression of the interrelations between the four perspectives: e.g. personal values (quadrant d) co-determine the behaviour (quadrant a) as well as economic incentives (quadrant b) and cultural habits (quadrant c). This causation can be complemented by further aspects of this interdependency. Taking multiple perspectives and mapping different perspectives with the quadrant model can serve as a common reference point for theory development and helps framing case studies and pilot projects with a holistic approach (cf. Omann and Rauschmayer, Chapter 8 below, for an integration of Figure 1.1 and the four-quadrants approach). In our view this starting point is (i) open enough to allow a deeper set of leading questions to emerge during an initial phase of common thinking and (ii) concrete enough to serve as a first framework for the development of a common approach and terminology within trans- and interdisciplinary research teams.

Development of consciousness[6]

From our point of view, current approaches analysing and enabling transition towards sustainable paths are mainly conducted within quadrant b – often focusing on policies or trying a systemic look (e.g. Ostrom 2009). Approaches of quadrants a and c are used to some extent, but the subjectivity of individuals (quadrant d) is not sufficiently taken into account. As the roots of human behaviour (emotions, values, needs) are within the domains of quadrant d, main factors and the opportunity to tap into individuals' energy for the transition to SD are ignored. It is here that accountability and responsibility for sustainability can be anchored.

There is a vast literature in development psychology on the development of consciousness for children and juveniles; one of the most known scientists, also relating to the needs approach, is Abraham Maslow who proposed a hierarchy of needs and of values related to the development of consciousness (1987). Building on his and Grave's research on the psychology of human beings as an unfolding, emergent, oscillating, spiralling process (Graves 1974) as well as Kohlberg's research on children's development (1976), authors such as Wilber (2000), Barrett (1998) or Beck and Cowan (1996) propose that Maslow's last stage of development, i.e. 'self-actualization', can be further differentiated and that development can be observed and supported not only in individuals, but also in organizations and societies.

In this chapter, we cannot go into a detailed argument about the conditions and hinderings of such development, about the cultural contingency, or the possibility of generalizing stages of developments that are not necessarily shared by the majority of the population. We will rather assume that there is a development in one's consciousness that integrates and transcends stages which – from the outside – can be interpreted as being decreasingly egocentric (cf. Ingebrigtsen and Jakobsen 2009 for an analysis of economic images of man in this respect). Development in this sense means, inter alia, the inclusion of beings and concerns from an increasingly widening sphere: from oneself and one's survival, to a close group (family) and the relations herein, to the mastery over one's environment through consciously chosen cooperation. In the next stages, the consideration widens even more until it englobes intergenerational aspects; the style of consideration changes from self-centered cooperation to an apparently selfless contribution to all. It is important to note that the development does not mean to leave former stages behind, but to include them in a way that they still are available. For example, in a sudden situation of survival, the focus of acting will rather be on the first stage of consciousness development than on the latter: without caring for one's survival, one will not be able to contribute to others in a durable way.

Expanding on Maslow's needs model, Barrett (1998) developed a model that certainly is not the most fine-grained (cf. Wilber 2000 for an overview), but rather geared towards its use in corporate transformation. Barrett represents the development mentioned above as a shift from self-interest (levels 1–3 in Table 7.1) towards contributing to the common good (levels 5–7). This shift is reflected in the call for social business (Yunus 2008) that brings together financial stability and contribution to a common good. The integration of self-interest and contribution to common goods is also necessary for other kinds of organizations: many NGOs, which focus on their contribution on the common good, are worn out due to the missing self-interest of their activists. The Barrett model (1998) allows measuring and creating value 'maps' that categorize the full range of values across seven levels (Table 7.1). Seeing and understanding which levels are well represented and which reflect potentially limiting values provides corporate

Table 7.1 Seven levels of corporate sustainability (adapted from Barrett 1998, 2007).

Level	Main issue	Related values	Kind of sustainability
7	Service	Compassion, forgiveness, humility and ease with uncertainty	Societal sustainability – societal responsibility, ecology
6	Making a difference	Environmental stewardship, customer collaboration, employee fulfilment and mentoring	Community sustainability – environmental sustainability
5	Internal cohesion	Enthusiasm, fairness, trust and integrity	Cultural sustainability – shared vision and values, strong culture
4	Transformation	Courage, innovation, teamwork and accountability	Structural sustainability – continuous renewal, copyrights, patents, R&D
3	Self-esteem	Results orientation, efficiency, productivity and quality	Organizational sustainability – good practice, organizational effectiveness
2	Relationship	Conflict resolution, employee recognition, customer satisfaction and open communication	Social sustainability – friendship, tradition, ritual
1	Survival	Profit, financial stability, self-discipline and employee safety	Financial sustainability – economic viability, profit

leaders, but also analysts and policymakers, with a deeper understanding of what motivates people in engaging in – or refraining from – key behaviours that drive personal and organizational sustainability.

Linking the discussion of consciousness development to the 'iceberg' and the four-quadrants model, one can say that changes in quadrant b (e.g. new policies) potentially can co-determine behaviour and influence the 'thinking and feeling' layer (referring to the iceberg model, Figure 7.1). Deeper layers, such as values, priorities or needs, though, cannot directly be influenced through collective strategies coming from the outside. The cultural background (quadrant c) can be influenced by external frame conditions and individual actors, but not determined, as culture is a dynamically evolving process. On the other side, cultural changes, being the expression of the internal life of collectives, have an influence on values, priorities and needs of individuals.

Apart from culturally influencing the mindset, collectives can organize spaces and settings where consciousness development from within the individual can happen. These settings have to open some room for inquiry of oneself and of others going below the question of interests, thinking and feeling. Methods used in such settings frequently make use of thinking and feeling as gateways but ultimately address questions of values, needs and individuals' assumptions about their life and way of being. This necessarily presupposes trust in the facilitator and in the methods used. Consciousness evolution from within the individual will not happen when individuals do not have the impression of being free, as – at least in our Western culture – autonomy is a highly valued need (Inglehart *et al.* 2008) whose violation for some persons calls for defiance. Therefore directivity and single-minded interventions targeted at some clear output are to be used consciously.[7]

Despite the efforts of Inglehart and colleagues (ibid.), research on values with a transformational perspective is not widespread on a societal level. We will therefore use an example from the corporate sector to exemplify our understanding of transitions to SD in the light of what has been said above. The lessons learned from this example will then be contrasted with our reflections on the differences between business and societal applications.

Whole-system transformation in the corporate sector – transition to SD as integral development

In the following we share the insights from ongoing transition work within the corporate sector. The Nedbank example points towards the central strand of this chapter: the benefits of getting much better in involving and activating the deepest layers of the human mindset in the transition to sustainable development.

What we want to highlight for researchers in the following short example is how both: (i) the four quadrants and their interplay, i.e. in this example: the systemic outer conditions, the strategic decisions of a company, the evolution of the consciousness of the leadership, and the evolution of a (collective) corporate culture; and (ii) a successful transformation can be monitored at the level of consciousness as represented by values and priorities just below the water line of behaviour (see quadrant d of Figure 7.2).

Let us take a look at Nedbank, a South African bank that faced a real threat to its continuity of business. Following some acquisitions and bad strategic decisions between 2000 and 2003 the share value and profits of the bank evaporated. At the precarious time when the capital was wiped out and a new integration at Nedbank following some mergers had to be done, the executives had also to do a 180-degree strategy-turn and culture change. As the CEO put it:

> Every bit of the organization had to change and we had to become a universal bank. We had to empower people to be closer to the customer and embed completely new business behaviours and values. We needed strategic and cultural transformation.

What is fascinating in this example is that the need for strategic and cultural renewal is really at the core of the sustainability challenge. So how did the company go about achieving this? Before sketching the process in the Nedbank example, we propose three core principles of transformation:

(1) Organizations do not transform, people do.
(2) Transformation begins with the transformation of the leadership group.

(3) Personal leadership is really what is required.

Based on these principles, the first step is to begin the transformation with the top leadership. In the Nedbank example, Gita Bellin, a pioneer of transformation in organizations, has been called upon to work with the top executives of the bank. A typical start to transformation work begins with a diagnostic phase (e.g. values assessment) which is followed by the initial leadership workshop. The workshop focuses on development of self-awareness and consciousness about underlying mindsets, furthermore the cognitive understanding (e.g. Barrett's values model, Table 7.1) and practical skills that enable participants to foster transformation in the organization (this includes e.g. dialogue or coaching skills). After the initial workshop the next steps are laid out following insights and experiences during the workshop. Usually the communication changes significantly after the workshop and new possibilities open up.

The purpose of the initial workshop with the top executives is to create a powerful field of energy in the organization through an integrated work on IQ, emotional and spiritual intelligence. This field has to be thought of as invisible powers that exert visible influence, such as gravity. It is our experience that journeys of transformation commence with organizational fields founded on profound leadership development experiences.

Nedbank took 200 people from the top management through the same process. It completely changed the way the people interacted with each other and reacted towards the company. They carried the transformation programme then to a further 2,500 people, and ran one- and two-day refreshers every year. In the process, executives experienced for the first time – and understood – how their behaviour impacts on the people around them. Having gone through this experience many executives want to do this with their teams and beyond. In effect, the behaviours of the leadership group did demonstrably change including the way they speak to people, supporting each other all the time and work as a team, and break down the silos.

So what is happening in this organization? As soon as the leadership mindset, values and behaviour change, employees and the whole organization can follow the lead, if they have been given the permission and the space to evolve in the same way. The key to engage a whole organization and to manage the process is an ability to measure the effect of transformation work and the changes in people's perception and experience of the current culture. Nedbank uses a values assessment tool from the Values Centre (cf. Barrett 1998, see Table 7.1) every year to track progress. It allows the organization to align behaviour work with the execution and development of its strategy. It tells Nedbank what is happening in the companies and helps to cascade the culture shift throughout the organization.

In Figure 7.3, we see the evolution of the top 20 values in the current culture of Nedbank year on year from 2005 to 2009. The 'italic font'-values that appear in the earlier years are potentially limiting values denoting the degree of distress in the organization. Through the transformation and cultural work the leadership of the organization could create two major trends: reduce the level of limiting

Rank	2005	2006	2007	2008	2009
1	Cost consciousness	Cost consciousness	Client-driven	Accountability	Accountability
2	Profit	Accountability	Accountability	Client-driven	Client-driven
3	Accountability	Client-driven	Client satisfaction	Client satisfaction	Client satisfaction
4	**Community involvement**	Client satisfaction	Cost consciousness	**Community involvement**	Cost consciousness
5	Client-driven	Results orientation	**Community involvement**	Achievement	**Community involvement**
6	Process-driven	Performance-driven	Performance-driven	Cost consciousness	Achievement
7	*Bureaucracy*	Profit	Profit	**Teamwork**	**Teamwork**
8	Client satisfaction	*Bureaucracy*	Achievement	Performance-driven	**Employee recognition**
9	Client satisfaction	**Teamwork**	Being the best	Being the best	Being the best
10	*Silo mentality*	**Community involvement**	Results orientation	Delivery	Performance-driven
11	Performance-driven	**Employee recognition**	**Teamwork**	**Employee recognition**	Commitment
12	*Hierarchy*	Achievement	Delivery	Results orientation	**Making a difference**
13	*Control*	*Silo mentality*	*Bureaucracy*	Commitment	Delivery
14	Being the best	Process-driven	**Employee recognition**	Profit	Productivity
15	Achievement	Continuous improvement	Continuous improvement	Continuous improvement	**People-centred**
16	*Empire building*	Productivity	Process-driven	**Making a difference**	**Living the values**
17	**Employee recognition**	Being the best	Productivity	Continuous learning	**Leadership development**
18	Continuous improvement	Delivery	*Control*	Productivity	Profit
19	Productivity	*Control*	**Leadership development**	Embracing diversity	**Integrity**
20	*Confusion*	Financial stability	Continuous learning	Process-driven	**Ethics**

Figure 7.3 Nedbank's top 20 cultural values from 2005 to 2009: from limiting ↘ to ↗ potential.

values (bold font) and energy (grey arrows) and increase the emergence of higher-level values and creation of positive energy and tapping into people's potential (black arrows).

It is striking that the downward evolution of bureaucracy and control is soon accompanied with a shift towards team work, employee recognition, leadership development and people-centred. It is a shift from a fear paradigm to a trust paradigm in which collaboration and development prosper. Similarly the full emergence of higher level values, e.g. integrity and ethics, takes a space of five years to blossom fully.

It is also striking that the company could rely on one high level value – community involvement and an image as South Africa's green bank due to longstanding commitments to the environmental work and philanthropy. Making contributions to SD has an effect on people's value systems and what the company stands for despite the economic pressures in the early years. It is a stable source of pride and brand value amidst decline. In our four quadrant scheme (Figure 7.2) it is also important to point out that Nedbank manifested this commitment (quadrant d) to sustainability through memberships (e.g. Dow Jones Sustainability Index membership; WWF conservation partnership; Equator principles) and contributions to its sector sustainability issues (quadrants b and c). Furthermore, the bank announced its intention to become 100 per cent carbon neutral.

The importance of social aspects of SD is highlighted by issues that Nedbank focused on e.g. promotion of diversity in its workforce. This correlates to an improvement in the overall culture and in particular the values of team work, employee recognition, leadership development and living the values. The case provides evidence for how important an understanding of the sustainability challenge for an organization is.

What researchers in SD can learn from business transformations

Based on the example of the last section, we use the experiences from the business sector that mostly uses trained facilitators for transformation processes to learn for transition processes in the civil society sector where often scientists take over such facilitating roles. Whereas there has not been a clear focus in the Nedbank example on SD as it is understood in policy documents (such as the Brundtland report, WCED 1987), there are parallels between the transformation process undertaken in this example and the many transition processes required in our current societies. In what follows, we will highlight some of these parallels, but also some differences. We will talk about institutional change, as institutions in a wider sense include organizations (such as Nedbank), but also routines, practices and the like.

Needs, values and transformation

When analysing an institution from the outside, many desirable behaviour shifts and outcomes can be easily identified. External stakeholders, practitioners or policymakers have developed analytical and interventionist mindsets which analyse situations and trends and get prescriptive about 'what' is required and desirable; only the most effective 'how to' seems to be the question. This applies to sustainability issues as well as for any other value-driven analysis, such as those based on efficiency etc.

The inside perspective of the individual adopting the institution (e.g. being part of the organization or carrying out a special practice) is very different; the normative view from outside is resisted and creates a psychological barrier to transition. The inside perspective may be one of survival, with, for example, an established (corporate) culture and often sector-specific world view permeating the inner logic. Often the aim of the institution is not clear, leaving the question of 'how to' not even come into the open. In corporate culture, the 'what for' question is also typically answered in terms of a business case.

The following points have been crucial for corporate transformation processes such as the one described above:

1   Ultimately, 'what for' is a question of motive, meaning and values. Maslow has found an early answer as to the motivational forces and linked them to the development of the personality which is reminiscent of Carl Jung's approach that humans have a natural desire to evolve to higher level of contribution and consciousness (Maslow 1987). Yet for many reasons, the thinking that the development of our personalities is critical and an underused opportunity for the transition to sustainable development has not entered the mainstream of the sustainability and corporate responsibility movement. The most visible expression of personality and ultimately behaviour for the research and work in transformation are values. Therefore, the work on values and their assessments including a view on which levels of consciousness they relate to has become a cornerstone of individual and corporate transformation (Barrett 1998).

2   Personal transformation work is the synonym for deep personal development (Jung 1983[1961]). It creates a shift in root perspective and releases the energy within a critical mass of individuals for an organization's culture to shift. A key to success is accountability – responsibility for one's life, choices and experience in relationship to the organization and the people in it. Without this accountability the transformation process does not happen (Bellin 2010). Only through this internal mirroring of accountability and responsibility can a whole organization become accountable, responsible and an effective creative force for sustainable development.

3   The demands on, and the challenges for, leadership have grown more complex; and new ways for effective leadership have to be found with repercussion also in 'leadership capability development' (Heifetz 1994). It has long been recognized that sustainability requires the support of the leadership of an organization. The equivalent in the field of transformation is the statement that 'the organization is the shadow of the leader'. Therefore, the first step to development in both examples is the deep personal

development work with the CEO/Chairman and the top leadership. This involves the whole of the top leadership population to be effective.

4   In our work we find that the greatest barrier to change is fear. Fear of change, fear of not reaching the targets, fear of not meeting the internal stakeholder expectations, fear of the shareholder to name but a few. The most effective way of overcoming fear is to work on the formation of relationships and trust and a collective vision of the future, and to work with the collective or group which allows the individual to simultaneously shift his behaviour towards more sustainability in line with a cultural shift of the group.

5   Transformation processes are both internal and external. This also applies for individual, corporate or societal transitions to SD. What comes first is the focus on developing the leaders and realigning the collective leadership group towards the next level of development (see Table 7.1). With a view on the four quadrants this includes also role modelling (new behaviours) and developing skills and capabilities to display these. An alignment of all four quadrants to the same set of values can facilitate such a shift towards a successful transformation. The process creates a sequence of development within and outside of individuals.

Within companies a transformation process requires working with individual leaders, departments and whole businesses to define their priorities and needs through deep structure interviews and an assessment and expression of their values. That is the diagnostic and research part. In their 'current culture' the values and priorities are very different from the aspired state in an expressed 'desired culture'. This gives a set of 'from to' (from current to desired) which are the energetic leverage points for the facilitation of transformation. It is an expression of the collective intelligence of the group that these 'from tos' typically match the next steps of development and the strategic needs of the organization. In terms of sustainable development we can speak of a work on the Value-Values Barrier (Elkington 2001), whereby we must be able to help organizations to shift to higher values in order to take a significant step in the transition and generate sustainable value.

The challenge in practice is three fold: getting to work at the highest level of leadership within the organization; getting to work at the deep needs and consciousness level; and to facilitate a powerful shift in root perspective that allows expanding mindsets, the appearance of higher values and associated shifts in behaviours over time.

Facilitation first aims at increasing mindfulness, authenticity and getting leaders to understand higher levels of values. In a company, a CEO initially might hold higher-level values but these might not be reflected across the whole leadership group. It is then a journey of development for each leader to find his/her personal meaning or aspects of passion for sustainable development across the social and environmental systems. Once the higher values are established within the leadership team the whole of the organization can grow into this new frame and the leaders can engage in top-down and bottom-up processes in their parts of the organizations.

There are some similarities to societal processes, but differences as well. The 'what for' question of the goal of a societal transition process to SD is more difficult to conceive of and to argue for than in a business context. This applies in particular to the intergenerational aspect of SD (cf. Omann and Rauschmayer Chapter 8, below). The democratic constitution of most countries requires leadership of key persons in certain fields. Across society, though, leadership persons might be more difficult to identify and their influence on wider spheres appears much fuzzier than in hierarchical organizations. This is especially true with the increasing shift to participatory, adaptive, and multi-level governance. These societal leaders have not necessarily adapted higher values (according to Barrett's model of different types of values, see Table 7.1) and do not display the power of conviction that the pioneers and leaders within the SD movement or social entrepreneurs have. The fuzziness and, hence, instability of their personal power or influence relations is detrimental to their own security. This easily induces fear which then hinders the initiation of personal, group-specific and community-wide transformation processes. Acknowledging the societal conditions and the cultural, political and economic shifts necessary within these is a first and important step for societal transition processes aimed at altering behaviour.

The journey of transformation and outcomes

Regardless of the starting point of a company in their decision to contribute to sustainable development, the successful rooting of the transformation is at the individual level in the inside/individual quadrant and encompasses all four quadrants for a successful initiative (compare Figure 7.4).

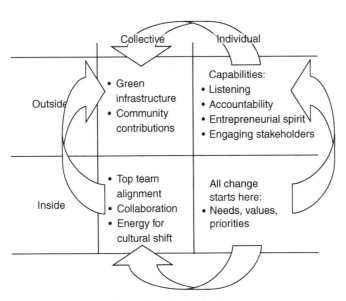

Figure 7.4 Journey of transformation in business.

Within the societal transformation journey, again, things are not as clear-cut as for organizations. Individual changes inside will have impacts on different fields of action within society – through altered individual capabilities and cultural changes. The impacts of these changes will not be limited to one specific field of action, but also to other fields. On the other hand, the resilience of the original system to these changes may be higher than in business organizations due to its non-hierarchical governance.

The skills and capability of the researcher and advisor in the transition

The work that needs to be done and can be done at corporate level is markedly shifting. In the face of extraordinary challenges and complexity, linear thinking is supplemented with systems thinking and new insights into the nature of personal and organizational change. This invitation to experiment to match the new challenges is also given to researchers who are interested in involving themselves in the transition to sustainable development. In their choices and conduct they must be very clear as the job is akin to quantum physics where the researcher determines what the observable is.

Researchers who are able to access and focus on the deeper layer of consciousness can profit to a larger extent from this field of transformation. They do not have to be qualified psychologists[8] but have to have high levels of emotional intelligence and even spiritual intelligence where questions of meaning and purpose are touched, and be able to connect at a profound human level. They need to have deep listening skills and be able to work with empathy. This ability can be described in terms of the development of the transpersonal within the researcher which opens the view on relatedness, energetic states and values (McTaggart 2008; Whitmore 2009). Researchers have the potential to reach that deeper level of individual and organizational truth only if they work on self-development and increase their own self-knowledge and consciousness.

Transformation does not come from intellect. Intellect gets in the way of transformation as it preformats ways of thinking and outcomes. In the transformation process the researching facilitator creates space for thoughts that have not been thought before and that might have been judged unthinkable before. These are true creative acts which are discontinuous with history but commensurate with and grow from the passion, meaning and values of people. They open the gates to the transition to sustainable development.

Conclusion and outlook

The transition begins in the interior world

We conclude by drawing the main lessons of the sections above: the model composed of iceberg, four quadrants and consciousness development; the transformation example from the corporate sector; and the discussion of similarities and differences between transformation experiences in the corporate world and polity.

Being a researcher who wants to engage effectively in transition processes towards SD demands first of all to be aware of the internal perspective of the unit of analysis. As changes in behaviour, culture and systemic outcomes also depend on changes in the interior world (which we call transformation of mindset and consciousness development when talking of individuals), such transformations should not only be allowed, but encouraged and facilitated.

Become a self-aware researcher

Discoveries and shifts in the realms of needs and values are more likely to take place when individuals feel free and secure. Therefore, establishing uncoerced and secure settings that allow for trust to grow is a prime task for researchers engaged in the transition towards sustainable development. A necessary precondition to establish such settings is to have experienced self-inquiry into needs and values, and personal growth for yourself – otherwise, as a researcher you will not be able to effectively connect with the object/subject of research and will not build up the required trust.

The researcher is part of the answer

Herewith, we postulate a further shift in the self awareness of researchers, going beyond the shift that has been analysed by mode-2 researchers (Nowotny *et al.* 2003) and postulated by post-normal science (Funtowicz and Ravetz 1993). This shift includes the possibility of an interrelatedness of researcher and research object that goes beneath the thinking-layer (cf. Figure 7.1) – researchers are called to inquire into their own values and needs, and highest purpose and aspirations and to be able to share them, or create this space for personal growth in this transition, in order to make trust and development possible.

The research agenda has to include higher-level values and the processes and conditions under which they emerge out of human needs

We even postulate that such a shift is beneficial for the transition towards SD, not only because SD is in itself an expression of values. The transition towards SD requires an alteration of deeply-rooted behaviours and social systems towards an expression of higher-level consciousness and values. Societies can evolve into a more sustainable direction if research helps us to excel at understanding and facilitating the emergence of higher-level values including accountability and responsibility.

Take an integral and whole system transformation perspective

In this endeavour it is necessary to combine all four perspectives differentiated above. Taking an 'outside in' approach, one can start from the external context and then aim at understanding the interrelations between policies and culture; between behaviours and mindsets. The other way can be called 'inside out' in order to shed light on the interplay between individual and structural factors. Scenario-building exercises might be an appropriate tool to initiate a process enabling actors to raise their awareness about their basic needs and to widen their capability-set to actively apply sustainability-driven strategies to meet their needs.

Thus, researchers following this approach in their transdisciplinary projects can expect results in insights on what it takes to transform the complex challenges and individual blocks with regard to SD into opportunities for personal, organizational and societal development and, at the same time, into an increased ability and greater energy to create responses in the ways in which individuals and collectives can and ultimately aspire to advance towards sustainability. Last, but not least, researchers who develop their consciousness have better chances to live a flourishing life themselves...

Notes

1 We are aware that this chapter sometimes remains vague and that often we stay with intuitions rather than a fully argued line of thought. We hope that this chapter stimulates discussions and replies so that we can rethink the well-foundedness of our ideas. Our chapter has profited from discussions (with Ralph Piotrowski, Anneke von Raggamby, Lisa Bohunowsky, Tom Bauler, Léa Sébastien, and Carolien Hoogland) when submitting the EU research project InContext (currently in negotiation) and from additional input from Ines Omann and Paul-Marie Boulanger, to whom we are grateful.
2 Also in this chapter, we mostly use the Brundtland definition of SD referring to the fulfilment of needs of current and future generations (WCED 1987). The business example, though, relates to other dimensions of sustainability.
3 Action research is a reflective process undertaken by researchers as a part of a 'community of practice' to improve their way of dealing with problems (Burns 2007).
4 In this respect, the direction of the circle arrow in Figure 1.1 is different: in an analytical sense, the selection of strategies out of a set of capabilities can be explained by the degree to which needs are met, combined with the values put on specific needs and strategies, the cognition about one's capability set, and the expected states of well-being due to the realization of strategies.
5 The EU Commission has recently funded several projects that aim at bridging civil society organizations with the research community in the field of sustainable development to foster movements for a transition. For more information see e.g. Civil Society Oganizations platform on SCP (www.scp-dialogue.net), Action Town – Research and Action for SCP (www.action-town.eu), CEECEC – Ecological Economics for and by NGOs (www.ceecec.net).
6 Consciousness in its philosophical meaning can be understood as 'the basic, raw capacity for sentience, feeling, experience, subjectivity, self-agency, intention, or knowing of any kind whatsoever' (de Quincey 2006).
7 Recent experience with socialism apparently has not produced an evolutionary shift towards more socialist values (Arzheimer 2005). However, a risk taken with organizing

open settings with the aim of achieving a more sustainable outcome might result in some strategies that do not appear to be sustainable.

8 This might even be counterproductive, seen the predominantly quantitative training of psychologists that does not inivite for inner transformation processes.

References

Arzheimer, K. (2005), 'Freiheit oder Sozialismus? Gesellschaftliche Wertorientierungen, Staatszielvorstellungen und Ideologien im Ost-West-Vergleich, in O.W. Gabriel, J.W. Falter and H. Rattinger (eds), *Wächst zusammen, was zusammen gehört?* Nomos: Baden-Baden, pp. 285–313.

Bandler, R. and Grinder, J. (1975a), *The Structure of Magic I: A Book About Language and Therapy*, Science & Behavior Books: Palo Alto, CA.

—— (1975b), *The Structure of Magic II: A Book About Communication and Change*, Science & Behavior Books: Palo Alto, CA.

Barrett, R. (1998), *Liberating the Corporate Soul: Building a Visionary Organization*, Butterworth-Heinemann: Boston, MA.

—— (2007), *The Seven Levels of Corporate Sustainability*, online, available at: www. valuescentre.com/docs/Sevenlevelsofcorporatesustainability.pdf [accessed 2 April 2010].

Beck, D.E. and Cowan, C.C. (1996), *Spiral Dynamics: Mastering Values, Leadership and Change*, Blackwell Publishing: Malden/Oxford/Carlton.

Bellin, G. (2010) Transformation Workshop, Facilitator Material, for Performance Consultants International.

Braun, R., Gawlas, H. and Maywald, F. (2005), *Führen ohne Drama*, Linde: Vienna.

Burns, D. (2007), *Systemic Action Research: A Strategy for Whole System Change*, Policy Press: Bristol.

Cruz, I. (2011), Human needs frameworks and their contribution as analytical instruments in sustainable development policymaking, Chapter 6, this volume.

De Quincey, C. (2006), Switched-on consciousness: clarifying what it means, *Journal of Consciousness Studies*, 13(4): 7–12.

Elkington, J. (2001), *The Chrysalis Economy: How Citizen CEOs and Corporations Can Fuse Values and Value Creation*, Wiley: London.

Faber, M., Petersen, T. and Schiller, J. (2002), Homo oeconomicus and homo politicus in ecological economics, *Ecological Economics*, 40(3): 323–333.

Frankl, V. (1985), *Psychotherapy and Existentialism: Selected Papers on Logotherapy*, Simon & Schuster: New York.

—— (1992), *Man's Search for Meaning: An Introduction to Logotherapy*, Simon & Schuster: New York.

Funtowicz, S. and Ravetz, J. (1993), Science for the post-normal age, *Futures*, 25(7): 739–755.

Graves, C. (1974), Human Nature Prepares for a Momentous Leap, *The Futurist*, April: 72–87.

Goleman, D. (ed.) (1997), *Healing Emotions. Conversations with the Dalai Lama on Mindfulness, Emotions and Health*, Shambhala: Boston, MA.

Heifetz, R. (1994), *Leadership Without Easy Answers*, Harvard University Press: Harvard.

Hirsch Hadorn, G., Bradley, D., Pohl, C., Rist, S. and Wiesmann, U. (2006), Implications of transdisciplinarity for sustainability research, *Ecological Economics*, 60(1): 119–128.

Ingebrigtsen, S. and Jakobsen, O. (2009), Moral development of the economic actor, *Ecological Economics*, 68(11): 2777–2784.

Inglehart, R., Foa, R., Peterson, C. and Welzel, C. (2008), Development, freedom, and rising happiness: a global perspective (1981–2007), *Perspectives on Psychological Science*, 3(4): 264–285.

Jackson, T. (2004), Models of Mammon: A Cross-Disciplinary Survey in Pursuit of The 'Sustainable Consumer', Working Paper Series Number 2004/1, Centre for Environmental Strategy, University of Surrey, online, available at: http://portal.surrey.ac.uk/pls/ portal/docs/PAGE/ENG/RESEARCH/CES/CESRESEARCH/ECOLOGICAL-ECONOMICS/PROJECTS/FBN/MODELS.PDF.

Jager, W., Janssen, M.A., De Vries, H.J.M., De Greef, J. and Vlek, C.A.J. (2000), Behaviour in commons dilemmas: homo economicus and homo psychologicus in an ecological-economic model, *Ecological Economics* 35(3): 357–379.

James, T. and Woodsmall, W. (1988), *Time Line Therapy and the Basis of Personality*, Meta Publications: Cupertino, CA.

Jung, C.G. (1983 [1961]), *Memories, Dream, Reflections*, Flamingo: London.

Kaufmann-Hayoz, R., Bruppacher, S., Harms, S. and Thiemann, K. (in press), Einfluss und Beeinflussung externer Bedingungen umweltschützenden Handelns, in K. Lantermann and V. Linneweber (eds), *Enzyklopädie der Umweltpsychologie, Band 2*, Hogrefe: Göttingen.

Kohlberg, L. and Lickona, T. (eds). (1976), *Moral Stages and Moralization: The Cognitive-Developmental Approach*, Rinehart and Winston: Holt, NY.

Leßmann, O. (2011), Sustainability as a challenge to the capability approach, Chapter 3, this volume.

Luks, F. and Siemer, S.H. (2007), Whither sustainable development? A plea for humility, *GAIA – Ecological Perspectives for Science and Society*, 16(3): 187–192.

Lutz, M. (1992), Humanistic economics: history and basic principles, in P. Ekins and M.A. Max-Neef (eds), *Real-Life Economics: Understanding Wealth Creation*, Routledge: London/New York, pp. 90–112.

Maslow, A. (1987), *Motivation and Personality*, third edition, Pearson Longman.

Max-Neef, M.A. (1991), *Human Scale Development: Conception, Application and Further Reflections*, The Apex Press: London/New York.

—— (2005), Foundations of transdisciplinarity, *Ecological Economics* 53(1): 5–16.

McTaggart, L. (2008), *The Field: The Quest for the Secret Force of the Universe*, updated edition, Harper: London.

Mindell, A. (1995), *Sitting in the Fire: Large Group Transformation using Conflict and Diversity*, Lao Tse Press: Portland, OR.

Nowotny, H., Scott, P. and Gibbons, M. (2003), 'Mode 2' revisited: the new production of knowledge, *Minerva*, 41(3): 179–194.

Omann, O. and Rauschmayer, F. (2011), Transition towards sustainable development: which tensions emerge? How do we deal with them? Chapter 8, this volume.

O'Neill, J. (2011), The overshadowing of needs, Chapter 2, this volume.

Ostrom, E. (1990), *Governing the Commons: The Evolution of Institutions for Collective Action*, Cambridge University Press: Cambridge/New York.

—— (2009), A general framework for analyzing sustainability of social-ecological systems, *Science*, 325(5939): 419–422.

Peck, M.S. (1987), *The Different Drum: Community Making and Peace*, Simon & Schuster: New York.

Rauschmayer, F., Omann, I. and Frühmann, J. (2011), Needs, capabilities and quality of life: refocusing sustainable development, Chapter 1, this volume.

Rosenberg, M. (2001), *Nonviolent Communication: A Language of Life*, Puddle Dancer Press: Encinitas, CA.

Singer, W. and Ricard, M. (2008), *Hirnforschung und Meditation: Ein Dialog [Brain Research and Meditation: A Dialogue]*, Unseld: Frankfurt/Main.

Söderbaum, P. (2008), *Understanding Sustainability Economics*, Earthscan: London.

Thaler, R.N. and Sunstein, C.R. (2008), *Nudge: Improving Decisions about Health, Wealth, and Happiness*, Penguin: London.

Veblen, T. (1899), *The Theory of the Leisure Class*, Macmillan: London, online, available at: www.gutenberg.org/etext/833 [accessed 27 April 2010].

WCED (United Nations World Commission on Environment and Development) (1987), *Our Common Future*, online, available at: www.un-documents.net/wced-ocf.htm [accessed 3 April 2010].

Whitmore, J. (2009), *Coaching for Performance: Growing Human Potential and Purpose*, fourth edition, Nicholas Brealey Publishing: London.

Wiggins, D. (2005), An idea we cannot do without: what difference will it make (eg. to moral, political and environmental philosophy) to recognize and put to use a substantial conception of need? in S. Reader (ed.), *The Philosophy of Needs*, Cambridge University Press: Cambridge, pp. 25–50.

Wilber, K. (1995), *Sex, Ecology, Spirituality: The Spirit of Evolution*, Shambhala: Boston, MA.

—— (1997), *The Eye of Spirit. An Integral Vision for a World Gone Slightly Mad*, Shambala: Boston, MA.

—— (2000), *Integral Psychology – Consciousness, Spirit, Psychology, Therapy*, Shambhala: Boston, MA.

Yunus, M. (2008), *Creating a World Without Poverty: Social Business and the Future of Capitalism*, PublicAffairs: New York.

8 Transition towards sustainable development

Which tensions emerge? How do we deal with them?

Ines Omann and Felix Rauschmayer[1]

Our current lifestyles are strongly determined by a quest for increasing welfare expressed through material consumption accompanied by environmental damage and impacts on society.[2] On the societal level, increasing demand for household consumption requires an increasing purchasing power; both factors are connected to increasing economic growth.

And, as mentioned in Chapter 1, above, (Rauschmayer *et al.*), we are (globally and country-wise) not following a sustainable[3] path; the negative effects substantially degrade the quality of life, sometimes below a threshold of a decent life quality (see for instance Jäger 2007; Worldwatch Institute 2010). In particular the crisis of 2008/09 showed us how unsustainable we are: economic crisis, still increasing greenhouse gas concentrations, peak oil and peak everything being closer than we thought, biodiversity loss, inequality between and within countries at new highs, life satisfaction stagnating or even declining (Nef 2009).

If we want to change the current path, which is the assumption underlying this book, then we have to revise the current trends of an ever-increasing material consumption to meet our needs. This requires a change in consciousness and among others a change of lifestyles (cf. Hinterberger *et al.* 2009).

> Preventing the collapse of human civilization requires nothing less than a wholesale transformation of dominant cultural patterns. [...] This transformation would reject consumerism— the cultural orientation that leads people to find meaning, contentment, and acceptance through what they consume—as taboo and establish in its place a new cultural framework centred on sustainability.
>
> (Worldwatch Institute 2010: 3).

In *The Great Transition*, the New Economics Foundation (Nef) explains why a business-as-usual path cannot be followed (Nef 2009: 3): Climate change and inequality will cost the UK trillions of pounds (in the period to 2050 the cumulative cost associated with climate change will range from £1.6 and £2.6 trillion, while the cost of addressing social problems related to inequality will reach £4.5 trillion, op.cit.: 4).

How to support then a transition to sustainable development? Motivated by the wish to answer this question, we had written what is now Chapter 1, even before we had the idea to produce the book you are holding in your hands. With the present chapter we complement this response, as we close a first learning circle by incorporating what we have learned by reading the other chapters and through our work in the meantime.

The starting point of this chapter is the – probably contrafactual – assumption that there is a (political) agreement to aim for a transition towards SD. The aim of this chapter is not to check how valid these political statements are, but rather to look at innovative and promising ways on how to implement such transition. We look at this transition from a Western, respectively industrial countries' perspective. This means that our capabilities, or possibilities of changing our life courses, are larger than those of inhabitants of poor countries (Boulanger Chapter 5, above).

A transition can be defined as a gradual, continuous process of structural change within a society or culture. Yet not every country follows the same demographic transition curve: there are large differences in the scale of change and the period over which it occurs. Nor is the transition process deterministic: it will adapt to, learn from and anticipate new situations. Transitions involve a range of possible development paths, whose direction, scale and speed government policy can influence, but never entirely control (Rotmans *et al.* 2001: 16).

Such a process can be described by various phases (see, for the Dutch school of transition management, Loorbach and Rotmans 2006). In the light of this chapter we want to see transition as a pathway and fundamental societal change (which can be gradual and smooth but accompanied by quick turns as well) that leads into a world that is definitely different from the existing paradigm (growth-related, as described above) to one with different values, culture and behaviour. According to Rotmans and colleagues, such a transition process would take about one generation (Rotmans *et al.* 2001).

The aims of this chapter are (1) to show tensions that might arise from pursuing a sustainable lifestyle because of needs or values conflicts; and (2) to follow the arguments of Chapter 7 (Rauschmayer *et al.*): a transition towards SD requires that actors start by looking into their inner side, reflecting upon one's values, feelings, world views and being open and prepared to develop. A motivation for the transition mentioned is given in the next section, based on the authors' personal values. Then we differentiate between three forms of tensions we see arising when pursuing sustainable lifestyles and include examples of them. In the last section before the outlook, one process to deal with those tensions is presented that includes inside and outside as well as collective and individual perspectives.

Motivation for a transition

Why do we want to transition towards sustainable development? This question is easy to answer as far as our current generation is concerned. Arguments can be:

everybody wants health, a clean environment, resources to produce and consume, and therefore a certain state of ecosystems. All mentally sane persons care for at least some other currently living human beings and for some of those members of the subsequent generation that we already know or even do not know (Howarth 2007). However, these arguments are not sufficient to justify a generalizable demand of or wish for sustainable development in the long term. Why should one care for future generations beyond the generations of their children and grandchildren?

For many it is morally intuitive that it is a good thing to care for future generations. It is impossible, though, to derive a reason for this intuition from descriptive sciences alone – natural sciences give important answers in the questions on how to develop (or how not to develop), once the questions of values have been clarified. Mythical reasons to give the next generations what we have got from 'god' have been sufficient in former times, but are not sufficient for legitimizing public policy in democratic and secular states (see for instance Wilber 1997, 1981; Beck and Cowan 1996; McIntosh 2007). Some have tried to find a rational, universally acceptable reasoning for why everyone should care for future generations. Empirically, it seems difficult to grant moral value to people that live in a distant cultural world – and this difficulty increases with the perceived distance between the valuing and the valued person (Nida-Rümelin 1997). Even though the morally accepted distance between both has widened in human history (abolition of slavery, human rights, women's rights, …), most members of current societies are still far away from granting the same value to all currently living people (intragenerational equity) and still further away from granting the same value to members of future generations. As had been shown by Parfit (1983, 1990), it is far from easy to give good reasons why we should grant rights to people whose existence depends on our decisions (but see O'Neill, Chapter 2, on this).

Another, a more personal, way to answer the question why we should adopt sustainable development is to explore the roots of individual behaviour, i.e. to look into the feelings and thinking, values, and needs inside oneself (Figure 7.1), which means to inquire and become aware of them (i.e. into the mindset quadrant d of Figure 7.2: inside, individual; for more explanation see Rauschmayer *et al.* Chapter 7, above). The following paragraphs show our own introspection and/or intersubjective dialogue (Buber 1995 [1923]).

Our own motivation

Why do we – the authors – want a sustainable development, i.e. meeting the needs of the current and the future generations?

Ines Omann:
I have been raised in a typical middle-class household in the Austrian countryside, amidst a big family with four sisters and brothers and lots of cousins. This has coined me strongly and makes me value highly a family with strong

internal relations. However, I faced situations in my family that were unfair in my eyes, either against me or against others (the 'behaviour'-layer in the iceberg model, see Figure 7.1 and Rauschmayer *et al.*, Chapter 7, above). These situations left me disappointed, sad and even angry ('feelings'); these feelings made me aware of the importance given to fairness and justice, first with regard to me, but then expanding the focus to others ('values and priorities'). Those others were first sisters and brothers, friends, schoolmates, but soon the whole world. Thus I would say the aim of pursuing justice is an important source of my engagement for sustainable development. Needs that I value highly are freedom, affection, leisure, personal development and transcendence, as well as protection (of nature and of others). I want to live a life that enables me to meet these needs, and I want everybody else to have the right to live according to their needs and values too. In Rauschmayer *et al.*, Chapter 1, where we present our framework, you can see that the flow of life is represented as a circle. This circle is ever ongoing, however, to my understanding and experience, not on the same level. This means that the strategies to meet a certain need change, my feelings that result are not the same during time, neither is the well-being I can experience. There I find meaning in my personal and in the more global human development. Engaging myself for the possibility of further human development on this earth beyond the next two or three generations contributes to my meaning of life.

This wish to move towards sustainable development made me choose my profession as well as edit this book and write this chapter, which deals with the tensions we all face when we decide to support a transition towards SD not only with our job decision but also and above all with the lifestyles we select.

Felix Rauschmayer:
When I see that our current socio-economic development (1) causes suffering as well as endangers and annihilates the life of many individuals of many species; (2) is not able to decrease (or at least not significantly) the number of those currently suffering; and (3) does not clearly increase the capability set of poor people and of future generations, I feel disappointed, helpless, angry and frustrated. I highly value the idea of not causing unnecessary harm to any other living being, and the importance of this not causing harm increases with the ability to suffer. Even though I do not know how future people will be living, I am convinced that they will have the same needs as I have.

Being a rather well-off member of a rich society, I am not afraid for my own well-being due to our currently unsustainable development. I am even not afraid for my own children, despite global warming and all the biological and social processes that this will sharpen and cause. Caring for other sentient beings – alive or not – is a way of expressing my needs for protection and affection. I translate this caring into an engagement for sustainable development in the scientific and political realm as well as in my personal way of living. These are major domains for further strategies to realize these needs as well as my needs of identity, creation, participation, freedom and transcendence.

Comparison between the two authors

For both of us the primary motivation to edit this book and write this chapter first comes from our scientific engagement for SD. We see the current situation as not sustainable, which leads to feelings such as anger, sadness and frustration. Needs are not met – some of ours and, depending on whom we are talking about, some or nearly all of other living or unborn people. In addition, we see the danger that the future generations will not be able to meet their needs.

Felix Rauschmayer values very highly the life of others and not harming them; caring for others as well as engaging for SD (scientifically, politically and in his own lifestyle) are strategies to meet his needs for protection, affection, identity, creation, participation and freedom. Valuing justice and fairness highly motivates Ines Omann to engage for SD (scientifically and in her own lifestyle) and helps meeting the needs for freedom, affection, personal growth and transcendence, protection of nature and others.

Comparing our statements (which we wrote independently from each other), we see that the motivations are very close (nearly same needs, feelings). Differences lie mainly in the values, which arise from our culture and socialisation, where the latter has been quite different between us. We both investigated our mindsets, i.e. our inside perspectives on us as individuals. This perspective is complementary to outside perspectives on individuals (behaviour) and collectives (systems) as well as inside perspectives on collectives (culture) (see Figure 8.1).

As you may have seen in our small statements above, starting with reflecting on the inside means to start with (1) becoming aware of and (2) questioning and changing own values and preferences – this eventually leads to changing existing lifestyles. Lifestyles also change, of course, due to external changes, particularly if these are rather culture-related than mere systemic changes in the natural or institutional environment. As most attention has been given to systemic changes, less to cultural and very little to intra-individual processes, we argue that acknowledging and integrating this last perspective into sustainability

	Collective	Individual
Outside	**b** **Systems**	**a** **Behaviour**
Inside	**c** **Culture**	**d** **Mindset**

Figure 8.1 Four complementary perspectives on individuals (adapted from Wilber 1995).

science and politics can lead to more durable achievements in transition processes.

But 'inside' changes cannot be imposed, but only influenced from the government or the ruling class – German twentieth century history gives examples for this.[4] Weaver and Jordan (2008) argue that supportive constituencies are needed for policymakers to be able to take the risk of starting fundamental changes. This citizens' support can only arise out of certain values, feelings and beliefs (quadrant d), or, as Robinson *et al.* (2006) call it, from new approaches for engaging different groups in public policymaking in sustainability issues.

Coming back to the main theme of this chapter, the tensions we face when pursuing a transition towards SD, we shortly explain here what we mean by tensions, before elaborating on them in the next section. The lifestyle a person chooses is reflected in the selected strategies to meet one's needs. Everybody has already experienced value conflicts when taking a decision in the form of a dilemma or a tension. Sustainable development can be seen as a value (Rauschmayer *et al.* Chapter 1 in this volume) or as a set of values. No matter how we see it, a lifestyle according to these values will most probably lead to conflicts and tensions. By choosing a certain strategy we can meet one need and harm another for instance (cf. Cruz Chapter 6, above, on the different categories of satisfiers). For example, the strategy of using public transport instead of a private car protects subsistence and allows participation in a certain social group as well as creating a new lifestyle; at the same time, it could inhibit feeling free and endangers one's identity. We differentiate between three forms of tensions which will be explained in the following section, based on our framework (see Figure 1.1) and on conflict theory.

Tensions emerging in sustainable lifestyles

As stated in Chapter 1, 'the aim of SD is to increase the quality of life for current and future generations, i.e. to generate increasing well-being and more capability space for current and future generations, at least above a certain level' (Rauschmayer *et al.* Chapter 1). This can only be achieved through a globally diminishing consumption of natural resources (the degree of the reduction being much higher in the industrialized countries). In current politics, we see policies aiming at improving the efficiency without really questioning behaviour (such as factor 4, 5 or 10, Weizsäcker *et al.* 1995; Weizsäcker 2009; Schmidt-Bleek 1993) or at changing behaviour without addressing values and needs. Increasing efficiency aims at avoiding conflicts related to values and deeply rooted practices. Policies based on this concept, though, have achieved a reduction in nature consumption in very few cases only; they rather lead, e.g. through the rebound effect, in a continued increase in nature consumption (Binswanger 2001). Efficiency increase therefore has mostly been used for an ever passing increase in hedonic well-being (cf. Figure 1.1) of the powerful (future generations having the least power), but has not really contributed to an increase in their overall quality of life (cf. Rauschmayer *et al.* Chapter 1). Therefore, as in capitalism, we have to face conflicts between powerful and contemporary powerless people. Taking this analogy further: might then the moral concept of SD take the role that the standards of the International Labour Organization (ILO) have in labour-related conflicts, i.e. aiming at guaranteeing minimal rights of the powerless? We all know about the difficulties of enforcing the ILO standards, but the situation is even worse for SD: it is not clear who harmed whom, the currently poor have very little possibility of making themselves heard, SD does not state rights on an individual level, and members of future generations are not existent at the time when the actions are done that will do them harm (if these people ever exist, cf. Parfit 1983). Metastrategies such as efficiency give the impression that conflicts around SD can be avoided; instead of this, we are now looking for ways how to deal with them.

Rijsberman (1999) distinguished the following sources for environmental conflicts: data and facts; values; relations and interests. All three sources are present in conflicts related to SD, but the value dimension is particularly strong. As said in Chapter 1, values give importance to specific needs and strategies, and values differ between the individuals. One can therefore understand conflicts as conflicts between values given to different needs and strategies. To reach a shared understanding of values, though, may be more difficult than trying to agree on strategies to meet needs, as it implies opening oneself up which requires a climate of trust procuring security (see Cruz Chapter 6).

By applying the needs-based concept for SD (Rauschmayer *et al.* Chapter 1) we notice that all actors are confronted with the same problem: to find strategies that help meeting some of their needs without compromising the same or other needs at the same time. This means that all people aim at a better understanding of those factors which enlarge and restrict their capability spaces, i.e. of the relationships between the strategies on the different levels and the needs involved. A better understanding of these factors would also contribute to find proxies for the participation of future generations in our decision processes. The general idea following from our approach is to keep the capability space as open as possible, by leaving or increasing resources and agency for future generations. Here we come again to the problem SD poses to democracy, already addressed in Chapters 1 (Rauschmayer *et al.*) and 3 (Leßmann): when looking at voting behaviour, at least the majority of voters in current democracies have to value SD more than just paying lip-service to it. Only a widespread anchoring of SD legitimates and enables politicians to pursue SD strategies that limit current access to and use of natural resources. And also, of course, the politicians must feel deeply connected to sustainable development. Using the motivational power of adopting lifestyles of SD role models may be an important step towards meeting these democratic conditions of a societal transition towards SD.

The framework presented in Chapter 1 (Figure 1.1) is individualistic in the sense that it assumes that individuals can alter their quality of life by individual decisions, herewith selecting specific strategies from their capability set in order to better meet their needs which impacts on their well-being. We assume that these decisions are difficult in the sense that tensions arise – within the individual and between individuals. Intra-individual tensions are due to several factors such as: ignorance and uncertainty with regard to values, capabilities, strategies, needs, well-being and their respective relationships; values that lead to incompatible prescriptions; and behaviour driven by habits. Intrasocietal tensions are due to competitive use of resources, differences in values leading to different prescriptions with regard to strategies (and also due to envy with regard to differences in well-being). We now take a closer look at tensions that arise due to a mutually exclusive use of natural capital as we judge this the crucial point with regard to the intergenerational aspect of sustainable development, being also of some importance for intragenerational justice.

Taking up the image of the iceberg (Figure 7.1): in a conflict we see clashing behaviour above the waterline, and we can interpret this as strategies clashing with each other. People have different strategies as they have different understandings of facts and/or different values and priorities. On an individual level, going down to the needs layer allows each individual to perceive that there are more strategies available than just the one chosen; one recognizes that other strategies might better meet one's own as well as the needs of the others. This recognition may help to induce a dynamic that resolves conflicts which are on the level of strategies.

On a societal level, thinking and feeling as well as values differ between different actors. Therefore, it is not astonishing that different actors interpret SD differently according to their belief about the importance of specific needs and about the validity of specific relationships between strategies and needs. Commonly, interpretations of economic actors focus more on their need for freedom whereas environmental Civil Society Organizations (CSOs) interpret SD more with regard to protection. At the same time, the economic liberal strategies, which many economists believe strengthen freedom are, rather, according to many CSOs, reducing freedom. Complementing these rather contrasting layers of human conflicts, the concept of abstract and common needs gives some resort for reconciliation. Noting that at the bottom, the two, apparently incompatible icebergs of two 'conflict partners' are constituted by the same layer eases the tensions. This basic layer can also constitute the basis for addressing conflicts with regard to future generations whose values and priorities, thinking and feeling, and, therefore, whose strategies are unknown to us. The conflicts have a fictitious part insofar as the future generations do not yet exist and, in consequence, they are not bearer of interests, values or needs. But as we or self-acclaimed representatives of future generations have value claims relating to our internal representations of future generations, these conflicts become real internal or external conflicts.

In order to get a clearer picture of these conflicts, we now differentiate between intra-individual, intra-societal and intergenerational conflicts. This categorization parallels the moral development sketched above: a growing cultural distance between the valuing and the valued person.

1 Intra-individual tension: a given strategy or set of strategies, that is prescribed or recommended by SD, can be in conflict with other values. The

sustainable strategies help or inhibit the individual to realize certain needs and no synergetic strategy is found (cf. Cruz Chapter 6, above).

2   Intra-societal tension: The needs of any individual or societal group wanting to pursue sustainable strategies in our societies are affected by the needs of other individuals or groups or affect the needs of other individuals or groups, who might choose unsustainable strategies. This tension points to the interdependency of individual behaviour with societal culture and the systemic embedding of behaviour.

3   Intergenerational tension: this tension arises if certain societal strategies support caring for next generations, but inhibit current needs and vice versa.

The differentiation between the three tensions is somewhat artificial, as they are all interlinked. The intergenerational tension, for example, becomes manifest only through intra-individual tensions when the individual has a moral concern with regard to future generations, or through intra-societal tensions when there is a group of people voicing this concern in society. The examples will show the difficulties of this differentiation. Addressing these tensions in the vocabulary of needs is a first step when trying to overcome mere avoidance of conflicts or mere seeking for compromise between interests.

Examples for tensions

1 Intra-individual tension

An Austrian journalist has started an experiment in the beginning of 2010.[5] He is fasting with respect to CO_2 during this year with the aim of reducing his CO_2 emissions by three-quarters. In his blog (Brandner 2010) he describes the change of lifestyle he is undertaking, his activities as well as the concerns and doubts that he is facing throughout this experiment. His blog has stimulated much attention and many reactions. In an interview with one of the authors in March 2010, he talked about his current intra-individual tensions due to his experiment (Brandner 2010).

His biggest cut was to give up his car and not to buy a new one, although he had been wishing for one for a long time. He dreamt of buying a certain model of BMW. He even went some time ago with his son to the BMW museum and exhibition hall in Munich to see the car and to a make a test drive and: he was fascinated. Possessing and driving such a car would be a strategy to meet his needs for leisure, creation and also protection of nature.

*   Leisure: because of the fun and the good feeling he was experiencing when driving it, the smooth movements of the car, the 'perfect' silhouette.
*   Creation: he calls himself a technology freak; he knows a lot about cars and their technical details. This certain model allows him to live his technical creativity, to be part of this innovative technology and to play with it.
*   Protection: the car uses only 4.5 litres of petrol per 100 km with 120 PS.

This means that it is very energy efficient, which would fulfil partly his need to care for nature. But he also knows that cars using 4.5 litres cannot be a general mobility strategy on a global level.

Instead of buying this car, he chose to mainly use his bike, public transport and his feet as strategies for his private mobility in 2010. He admitted that it had been a hard decision accompanied by inner conflicts. What he did was to reflect upon his values, needs and possible strategies (entering his mindset, Figure 8.1). That way he was able to take a decision which was at first glance not leading to well-being. However, his feelings have changed due to changed values and due to changed experiences. He now is aware that his decision allowed him to meet needs which are currently more important to him than those met by owning the BMW. The relevant needs are leisure and protection of nature (which would have also been partly met by having the car) and, in addition, affection and subsistence.

- Leisure: by avoiding useless or unimportant car rides he saves time, which he can use for himself, for his family, to relax. By this strategy, he is decelerating his whole life.
- Protection of the environment: neither having nor using a car saves lots of energy and resources and contributes strongly to his CO_2 reduction (his need for protection is better met by this current strategy than by having a car).
- Subsistence: his physical health has already improved through cycling to work every day; he is investing the saved money in (regional, organic) food, house insulation, fair trade products.
- Affection: avoiding car-rides gave him more time with his family which improved their relationships.

His conclusion is that seeing his decision in the light of what he lost and won, he can definitely say that his quality of life has increased through a different lifestyle with regard to his personal mobility. So, he could nearly completely dissolve his tensions.

2 Intra-societal tension

Continuing with examples in the same field, there are tensions between those people who wish to use CO_2-poor mobility strategies and the general organization of public and working life which is focalized on the use of cars and aeroplanes, on high personal mobility and a globalized economy making it often very difficult to buy local or regional commodities, as many of them are produced with global inputs or by global players (see for the issue of 'glocalisation', Swyngedouw 1997). Additionally, culture, as the expression of socially shared values, puts moral pressure on those who decide not to pursue those strategies which are socially valued.

An example for the cultural pressure is the question on how to bring children to school. The culturally dominating style is the 'taxi-service' given by parents to their children in order to bring them safely to school or other places, herewith increasing not only CO_2 emissions, but also all other traffic-induced nuisances, such as noise, danger, dust etc. One of the authors decided to use a bike trailer for transporting his children to the kindergarten, even though a car was available. The judgement of other parents was 'irresponsible' as they judged this mode of transport too dangerous (accident, exhaust fumes).[6] Their (supposed) expression of their need for protection clashed with the expression of the author who valued not only the needs of his children, but also those of other born and unborn sentient beings.

There are different elements available for resolving these kind of tensions: changes in structure (quadrant b in Figure 8.1), such as better cycle lanes; in culture (quadrant c), such as a higher social value on environmentally friendly behaviour; and in mindset (quadrant d), such as more coherence between one's own needs and values, as well as thinking and feeling. Changes in these elements may facilitate changes in individual behaviour (quadrant a) and herewith ease the tensions.

Changes in culture require a dialogue that goes beyond confronting the strategies. Each layer (of the iceberg, Figure 7.1) descended gives a greater chance of reconciliation. Some tensions are eased by referring to feelings and rational arguments, others only once the respective values are understood. Referring to common needs requires a high degree of revealing oneself, and herewith inner strength or trust in the partner of the dialogue, and – at the same time – offers another possibility for reconciliation (see also the next section on dealing with tensions).

3 *Intergenerational tension*

Restricting the impact on climate change is one of the currently most prominent strategies for intergenerational justice and, herewith, for protection. Even though we do not know who will live, how these persons will live, what values they will have and what strategies they will favour for meeting their needs, it is plainly obvious that climate change will not contribute to increasing the capability set of future generations at large. Adopting this strategy, one of the authors therefore decided to restrict own travel for professional and private reasons. At the same time, this author wants to learn, contribute and gain professional security (all three judged to be increased by frequent travel to conferences), as well as maintain a link to a family member living in another continent, herewith aiming to realize the need for affection.

There are some societal groups arguing for a restriction of air traffic, usually through economic disincentives or, put differently, through the abolishment of fiscal advantages, or through voluntary payments offsetting CO_2 emissions. But these groups do not have much societal impact for the moment, i.e. flying is a culturally widely accepted behaviour. Therefore this intergenerational conflict mostly takes place intra-individually. Tired of the many intra-individual decisions with regard to the mode of transport for longer distances (plane or train), the mentioned author decided to adopt the double rule, (1) to use airplanes only for journeys that take more than 24 hours by train, and (2) to be very restrictive with regard to intercontinental journeys, be it for professional or private reasons. This rule has created tensions with the family member abroad, and is restricting his professional opportunities. Research is increasingly organized on a global level, and limiting oneself to a geographical area is often met with incomprehension. There are requests for personal or professional exchange (motivated by affection and/or learning) that cannot be met due to travel limitations.

There are different leverage points for a transition towards a more intergenerationally just behaviour: mindset, culture and system. As discussed above, a system's change in democratic societies requires a value shift in a large part, if not the majority, of the society. Values are anchored in communities and individuals, and cannot be changed by order, but only through manipulation or autonomous change. As with the last category of tensions, the latter requires again a 'deep' dialogue or monologue.

Particularly in this last tension, but also in the second one (the intra-societal tension), intra-individual tensions are very present. The overall presence is evidently a product of internal value conflicts where the value of SD does conflict with other values (or, more precisely: where strategies prescribed by SD conflict with other values or vice versa). We consider SD as a value, as it confers specific importance to specific needs and strategies (cf. Rauschmayer al. Chapter 1). Therefore, it has a strong prescriptive force for those people who adopt SD. Of course, SD is not the only value an individual adopts. In consequence, actions towards SD may infringe prescriptions stemming from other values. Intra-individual tensions are small where SD prescriptions can easily be accepted or where prescriptions stemming from other values are neutral to SD, e.g. the recycling of bottles when the necessary environment in form of glass recycling facilities has been created. Intra-individual tensions can be large, e.g. in the case of human population management where the individual rights to sexuality, family and autonomy clash with the requirement to reduce the human population on earth, as it is not possible to imagine a high-quality life for even more than the current population size on a long term perspective. Intra-societal tensions often reflect in intra-individual tensions as well, when claims from other people are acknowledged and perceived as legitimate.

The moral challenge of intergenerational justice, inherent in SD, often conflicts with traditional or narrowly self-regarding values: e.g. traditional cultural norms advise us to care for our current family rather than for future generations. There is an additional issue with intergenerational tensions, as briefly mentioned above: whereas the contemporary bearers of moral claims can make themselves heard, the bearers of moral claims in issues of intergenerational justice are not present. In societal terms their claim only exists because of some individuals who adopt them and make them heard. In other words, this intergenerational claim necessarily has an inside component that cannot be explained by an outside perspective alone.

Dealing with the tensions – a suggestion

The last section described reasons for tensions coming from beliefs and value conflicts. Dealing with tensions requires going beyond the tensions to the beliefs and values lying underneath and addressing them. We see a four-step process as an option to deal with the tensions:[7]

1   Recognizing the tension(s).
2   Reflecting upon the iceberg underneath the tensions (values and priorities, needs).
3   Communicating the reflection results to the persons affected from the tension, if possible.
4   Starting a process of creativity to find ways of dealing or even overcoming the tension(s).

Step (1)   Tensions might initially be recognized by an uneasy feeling when choosing a strategy and/or when applying a strategy. Such tensions might, too, be identified on a cognitive level by sharing this uneasy feeling with people standing close to one or with those having chosen the same or a similar strategy. Another possibility of recognizing a tension in one's individual or societal behaviour might be by being opposed in one's strategy by other people, be it through personal confrontation, or through confrontation to ideas laid down in media or even laws. This first recognition therefore already involves the first underwater layer of the iceberg: thinking and feeling.

From the outside, it is not straightforward to know how to strengthen the ability to recognize tensions. Most likely this can be facilitated by close persons (parents make their children aware of possible tensions; among friends) or professionals (coaches, therapists). Authorities can support awareness by informing citizens via media or in education programmes about possible tensions between their strategies and those supporting SD.

Becoming aware of the tension between, for example, car 'taxi services' for children and the need for a safer environment, can thus be the first step, mediated by friends, media or public administration. Recognizing the tensions means to look at the strategies that I selected to meet my needs and to realize that there are conflicts between these strategies and SD. The recognition, hence, leads to an initial reduction of well-being (conflicts usually have a component that impacts negatively on the need for affection).

Step (2)   The next step would be to look underneath the tension that has been recognized emotionally and/or cognitively. What triggers the tension? It might be a mixture of needs and values, belief systems and convictions as well as habits. It is possible that the tension starts to dissolve, just by reassuring oneself that the behaviour is in line with one's convictions, values and needs, or by shifting the behaviour in order to achieve coherence, or by shifting one's values, beliefs etc. As in the first step, no law or regulation can support this inner reflection by individuals. Again, close persons, media, education and professionals for personal development can support this step. If the addressed tension emerges within decision makers who choose strategies on the societal level, then the reflection has to include not only the inside of the decision maker but also the needs, values and belief systems of the persons he or she is representing. That way, mutual understanding can be created which is conducive to acceptance for the decisions from all sides.

This step is of course linked to the whole iceberg below the waterline, as it requires 'diving' exactly down there. And in concordance with the iceberg below the waterline this step addresses the often forgotten inside of the individual.

Let us look at our framework (Figure 1.1): in the first step we addressed mainly the strategies and noticed the reduction of well-being that might emerge due to tensions with pursuing SD. Here we look deeper into our needs and where they come from: culture, values, thinking and beliefs (the box called Culture/ Values). They influence our needs (which needs do I want to meet now and foremost?) and the strategies I eventually choose. Thus, if I want to reduce the conflicts that accompany my behaviour, I can influence and reconsider the culture I live in and my values and maybe change them or decide to change my behaviour. Being able to do so reflects my own autonomy, potentially increases the coherence of what I am and what I do, and herewith raises my well-being. This well-being is connected to meaning of life, as my behavioural change emerges from autonomy and other values. Thus we talk about eudaimonic well-being (Spillemaeckers *et al.* Chapter 4, above). Alternatively, I can also accept the tensions as they are, if I do not want to change, neither the behaviour nor the areas below the waterline; sometimes, self-inquiry or meditation make such tensions vanish.

Step (3)　This is the time when the person who has recognized the tension, reflected on it and its reasons, goes outside and talks to whomever the tension and related strategies might concern – if this person exists (not possible with future generations – here intra-individual or intra-societal communication has to replace this, see below). The decision maker talks to the affected groups, the individual to other individuals or groups. In the case of an intra-individual conflict, the communication can consist of becoming aware of the reflection results or talking with a close person about them. It is important to get into resonance with the person(s) vis-à-vis these tensions and to respond to them in their language. Forms of dialogue which can support this step are, for example, public discourse (Dryzek 1996), social learning (Tàbara and Pahl-Wostl 2007; Siebenhüner 2005; Social Learning Group 2001), or intersubjective dialogues (Buber 1995).

In particular, if this tension emerges between groups, the government can support this step by according their employees (decision makers as well as those that help in preparing the decision) a special education including social competences, the above-mentioned methods and moderation skills. This education is of great importance also to facilitators in sustainability research (Rauschmayer *et al.* Chapter 7).

If the conflict is intergenerational, then a discourse with the affected people cannot be held. For any simulation of an intergenerational dialogue it is important to reach a shared understanding of the elements that future generations will require for a decent or high quality of life: needs, strategies, capabilities and our influence on them through resource use, cultural change, economic development paths, etc. Adopting SD, we all agree that future generations will have needs for subsistence that will require a certain state and management of ecosystems, and that any paths that inhibit these kinds of capabilities is unfair to them. In a multi-criteria analysis, for example (Omann 2004), the value given to the quality of life of future generations can be reflected through the weight of one of the criteria and the uncertainty regarding the impacts of current decisions on the quality of life can be captured by methods such as multicriteria mapping (Stirling 2001).

This third step addresses all parts of the framework that are taken up by Steps 1 and 2 as it opens up those steps to the outside. We therefore have the link to the strategies, SD and well-being, as well as the link to needs, culture and values.

Step (4)   Through the acts of recognizing the tensions, reflecting upon and communicating about them, clarity can arise that there is not only one strategy to fulfil a need, but 'thousands' of them. Due to habits and not reflecting, only one (or few) of them is usually chosen and declared as the beloved one. The first three steps allow us to leave our single-mindedness and see other strategies (i.e. increase our capability-set through awareness-raising) and – which is important for a change of habits – see the drawbacks of our preferred strategy as well as the advantages of other strategies. Maybe they lead to more well-being, maybe they require less effort and through them, we may even realize other needs simultaneously, being less in conflict with other needs and values that are related to SD. Seeing other strategies *and* experiencing them is a process of creativity (by the way, this allows without extra effort the meeting of the need for creation). This creation process can evolve on the individual level or within communities/groups. Governance actors can even initiate such a process through setting stimulating frame conditions (organize participatory events, for instance a wisdom council[8]). Facilitators, who work in the light of quadrant d (see Rauschmayer *et al.* Chapter 7) can support these events and elicit innovative strategies from the participants. Ideally the event is part of a longer (research) process, which includes experimenting with new strategies in a protected frame, herewith including the emergence of a new culture, even though within laboratory conditions. Protection means here that the consequences cannot become too negative (i.e. expensive, harming health, reducing social capital). The experience (with all senses) of new strategies allows the actor a holistic judgement about the impacts of these strategies, whether they meet the needs as hoped for and reduce existing tensions. It also allows a better idea of political changes needed in order to facilitate the take-up of these strategies in real life and by more people than just the participants in the process.

The fourth step would result in a behavioural change (top level of the iceberg model and mindset), ideally assisted through political changes and clarity about resulting changes through the implementation of this strategy (systems). This change results from changed values, beliefs and culture through a better individual and shared awareness of needs. That way chances increase that the transition is persistent. Thus, this step links to capabilities, strategies, resources and well-being in a direct way and to SD indirectly.

Conclusion and outlook

Compared to Chapter 1 (Rauschmayer *et al.*), this chapter is moving out of the outside view on the individual that explains how individual decisions are made and how they relate to sustainable development and quality of life. The first chapter did not really touch upon intra-individual or collective processes. In the chapter at hand, intra-individual processes were illustrated by our (the authors') motivations that show that our work is related to our understanding of meaning of life. This chapter took up the main issues of the framework proposed in Chapter 1 (Figure 1.1), but put them in an enlarged context, mainly drawing on the inside perspectives; the link to the collective perspective has only been sketched. Understanding how one is contributing to something larger than one's own hedonic well-being (this wider perspective is called 'agency' by Sen, see Leßmann Chapter 3, or 'eudaimonic well-being' in psychological literature, see Spille-maeckers *et al.* Chapter 4, both above) is related to meaning and renders the flow of life possible, i.e. the spiralling of Figure 1.1. Relating the individual to the collective perspective was not only done through describing the motivation, but also by distinguishing three different tensions (intra-individual, intra-societal and intergenerational); examples were given. The interweaving of these tensions re-enforced the conviction that sustainability research and practice has to better include intra-individual perspectives when aiming for sustainable development.

Needs-based policy processes (O'Neill, Chapter 2, where he opts for a needs-based approach in sustainability) provide a means of addressing SD in a more encompassing way than processes that structure knowledge according to substitutability or a segregation into three or more dimensions; they thus offer a promising approach for realizing SD as a set of values.

Taking into account the whole framework (Figure 1.1) and what has been said right above, there is not one perfect leverage point for starting a transition, but different ones which can be seen as a set. It consists of increasing the capability space including the freedom to choose, of stimulating creativity to find other strategies to meet the needs (if the common strategies are unsustainable, i.e. do not permit all living and not yet living persons to meet their needs decently) and of setting the framework that citizens, facilitators and decision makers are motivated to look below the top iceberg level (Figure 7.1) and the individual inside level, i.e. to needs, values, beliefs and emotions. That way the pursuit of SD can be combined with high quality of life. Needs fulfilment leads to higher well-being, which is a constitutive part of quality of life (see Spillemaeckers *et al.* Chapter 4, above).[9]

SD policies can and should support low material or immaterial strategies to meet needs and make material-intense strategies less appealing or even forbid them as, apparently, increase in income which is linked to increased material use does not increase the perceived quality of life for most inhabitants of rich countries (see for instance Layard 2005; Jackson 2009). Policies focusing on more effective strategies to increase quality of life would also increase SD by freeing resources for poor people. Furthermore, there is the high risk that without restrictions on material use, more and more people will not have the resources necessary for realizing their needs.

But a high quality of life is not per se compatible with SD, as shown above in this chapter when we described the tensions. We have shown a four-step process to deal with these tensions. And we have named a couple of possible leverage points for environmental governance. Bringing the four-step process and the leverage points together means starting each intervention by reflecting about possible tensions that could arise, looking to their reasons below the waterline, hence to address emotions, values, beliefs and – very importantly – the needs that people aim to meet.

Methods that could be used for such processes include, for example, needs-based multicriteria analysis (Cruz *et al.* 2009; Rauschmayer 2005), participatory scenario workshops, wisdom councils (Rough 2002), systemic constellations (Sparrer 2007), dialogue, sociocratic moderation and other types of process work (Mindell 1995). What these have in common is a commitment on the part of SD scholars as process managers to explicitly incorporate (the expression of) emotions and values.

We do not assume that the four-step process and the suggested methods can be immediately used on a large scale. First, methods have to be tested and adapted to the context (e.g. governance level, economic or cultural development, issue at hand), and the organizational conditions to be established (e.g. trained facilitators). Second, we do not assume that the majority of the world's inhabitants are yet open and prepared for such processes. However, transition starts with processes and actors in niches (Loorbach and Rotmans 2006). We believe that there is a substantial amount of such niche actors either already reflecting on their lives and work in an integrative manner or open to start such processes – if supported through governance. Much has to be better understood and, foremost, to be done in order to support such a shift towards SD. We see the main challenges in the practical implementation of our suggestion, see the climate of mistrust, competition and impression of scarcity (and therefore of fear) in society at large and in polity in particular. Therefore we cannot yet show that this process can be translated onto a generic level. This is one of the big future challenges we want to address in our work.

We are sceptical as to whether our attempts to move towards SD are sufficient; at the same time, engaging ourselves in this attempt is – as we see it – a better strategy to meet our needs than to resign, to become cynical or to go into hedonic well-being only.

Notes

1 We are grateful to comments from Tom Bauler, Johannes Frühmann and Lisa Bohunovsky on earlier versions of this text.
2 We use too many of our resources, which is shown by the 'overshooting day' or 'ecological debt day', as it is also called, which comes earlier every year or by the ecolo-

gical footprint, which is on average above the sustainable threshold and way above it for industrialized countries; for instance the average footprint of an Austrian citizen is 4.9 ha; the sustainable figure would be 1.8 ha per capita (see WWF 2006).

3 We follow here the Brundtland definition of sustainable development, which says that a development is sustainable if it allows current and future generations to meet their needs.

4 The German socialist regime apparently has not produced a shift towards more socialist values (Arzheimer 2005); it is our impression that the fascist regime was more successful here, as it succeeded better in adopting existing and creating new encompassing cultural movements, herewith inducing a shift in the inside collective perspective.

5 A similar project has existed in Belgium since 2008: see http://lowimpactman. wordpress.com.

6 This judgement also had an intra-individual dimension, as the author also wanted to meet his need for protection by offering a safe mode of transport for his children.

7 We are aware that it is not possible to impose such a process for all conflicts and tensions arising in decision making in the light of SD. It requires certain preparedness, openness and experiences of actors. In this chapter we can only state our ideas but not give solutions for how to bring them into practice. But we hope that – based on experiences won from current and future research projects – we can gain more insight on the practical implementation of our ideas.

8 The Wisdom Council Process is a new way to transform the collective decision-making process of large systems. It facilitates people to become more informed, competent, creative and collaborative and to come together in one whole-system conversation where the most important issues are resolved. The point of the Wisdom Council Process is to generate a creative, system-wide conversation that reaches specific conclusions, the will to implement them, and builds the spirit of community. The goal is to have everyone talking in a thoughtful, creative, heartfelt way about the big issues and to cooperate for consensus views to emerge (from www.wisedemocracy.org/break through/WisdomCouncil.html and www.tobe.net/ wisdom_council/wc.html [accessed 3 April 2010]); Rough 2002.

9 The overall objective of SD is to secure and increase the resources and capabilities necessary for increasing the quality of life for all people as a precondition for needs fulfilment and for individual well-being (European Council 2006). We do not see quality of life as a precondition for needs fulfilment and well-being, but as a resultant of sufficient capabilities leading through needs fulfilment to a high state of well-being.

References

Arzheimer, K. (2005), 'Freiheit oder Sozialismus?' Gesellschaftliche Wertorientierungen, Staatszielvorstellungen und Ideologien im Ost-West-Vergleich, in O.W. Gabriel, J.W. Falter and H. Rattinger (eds), *Wächst zusammen, was zusammen gehört?* Nomos: Baden-Baden, pp. 285–313.

Beck, D.E. and Cowan, C.C. (1996), *Spiral Dynamics: Mastering Values, Leadership and Change*, Blackwell Publishing: Malden/Oxford/Carlton.

Binswanger, M. (2001), Technological progress and sustainable development: what about the rebound effect? *Ecological Economics*, 36(1): 119–132.

Boulanger, P.-M. (2011), The life-chances concept: a sociological perspective in equity and sustainable development, Chapter 5, this volume.

Brandner, E. (2010), Personal interview; online, available at: www.nachrichten.at/ oberoesterreich/klima [accessed 1 April 2010]

Buber, M. (1995[1923]) *Ich und Du*, Reclam: Stuttgart.

Cruz, I., Stahel, A. and Max-Neef, M.A. (2009), Towards a systemic development approach: building on the human-scale development paradigm, *Ecological Economics* 68(7): 2021–2030.

Cruz, I. (2011), Human needs frameworks and their contribution as analytical instruments in sutainable development policymaking, Chapter 6, this volume.

Dryzek, J.S. (1996), Strategies of ecological democratization, in W.M. Lafferty and J. Meadowcroft (eds), *Democracy and the Environment: Problems and Prospects*, Edward Elgar: Aldershot, pp. 108–123.

European Council (2006), *Renewed EU Sustainable Development Strategy*, 10917/06: Brussels.

Hinterberger, F., Hutterer, H., Omann, I. and Freytag E. (eds.) (2009), *Welches Wachstum ist nachhaltig? Ein Argumentarium*, Mandelbaum: Vienna.

Howarth, R.B. (2007), Towards an operational sustainability criterion *Ecological Economics* 63(4): 656–663.

Jackson, T. (2009), *Prosperity Without Growth: Economics for a Finite Planet*, Earthscan: London.

Jäger, J. (2007),*Was verträgt unsere Erde noch? Wege in die Nachhaltigkeit*, Fischer: Frankfurt/Main.

Layard, R. (2005), *Happiness: Lessons from a New Science*, Penguin: London.

Leßmann, O. (2010), Sustainability as a challenge to the capability approach, Chapter 3, this volume.

Loorbach, D. and Rotmans, J. (2006), Managing transitions for sustainable development, in X. Olshoorn and A.J. Wieczorek (eds), *Understanding Industrial Transformation: Views from Different Disciplines*, Springer: Dordrecht, pp. 187–206.

McIntosh, S. (2007), *Integral Consciousness and the Future of Evolution: How the Integral Worldview Is Transforming Politics, Culture, and Spirituality*, Paragon House: New York.

Mindell, A. (1995), *Sitting in the Fire: Large Group Transformation using Conflict and Diversity*, Lao Tse Press: Portland, OR.

Nef (New Economics Foundation) (2009), *The Great Transition*, New Economics Foundation, London.

Nida-Rümelin, J. (1997), Praktische Kohärenz, *Zeitschrift für philosophische Forschung*, 51(2): 175–192.

Omann, I. (2004), *Multi-Criteria Decision Aid as an Approach for Sustainable Development Analysis and Implementation*, PhD thesis, University of Graz, online, available at: http://seri.at/wp-content/uploads/2010/05/Omann_2004_SustainableDevelopment-and-MCDA_PhD.pdf.

O'Neill, J. (2011), The overshadowing of needs, Chapter 2, this volume.

Parfit, D. (1983), Energy policy and the further future: the identity problem, in D. MacLean and P.G. Brown (eds), *Energy and the Future*, Rowman and Littlefield: Totowa, NJ, pp. 166–179.

—— (1990), Personal identity and the separateness of persons, in J. Glover (ed.), *Utilitarianism and Its Critics*, Macmillan: New York, pp. 93–102.

Rauschmayer, F. (2005), Linking emotions to needs. A comment to Fred Wenstøp's article 'Mindsets, rationality and emotion in multi-criteria decision analysis', *Journal of Multi-Criteria Decision Analysis*, 13: 187–190.

Rauschmayer, F., Muenzing, T. and Frühmann, J. (2011), A plea for the self-aware sustainability researcher: learning from business transformation processes for transitions to sustainable development, Chapter 7, this volume.

Rauschmayer, F., Omann, I. and Frühmann, J. (2011), Needs, capabilities and quality of life: refocusing sustainable development, Chapter 1, this volume.

Rijsberman, F. (1999), *Conflict Management and Consensus Building for Integrated Coastal Management in Latin America and the Caribbean*, Inter-American Development Bank: Delft.

Robinson, J., Carmichael, J., Van Wynsberghe, R., Tansey, J., Journeay, M. and Rogersk, L. (2006), Sustainability as a problem of design: interactive science in the Georgia Basin, *The Integrated Assessment Journal Bridging Sciences and Policy*, 6(4): 165–192.

Rotmans, J., Kemp, R. and Van Asselt, M. (2001), More evolution than revolution: transition management in public foreign policy, *Foresight*, 3(1): 15–31.

Rough, J. (2002), *Society's Breakthrough! Releasing Essential Wisdom and Virtue in All the People*, AuthorHouse: Bloomington, IN.

Schmidt-Bleek, F. (1993), *Wieviel Umwelt braucht der Mensch? MIPS – Das Maß für ökol*, Wirtschaften: Birkhäuser.

Siebenhüner, B. (2005), Can assessments learn, and if so how? A study of the IPCC, in A.E. Farrell and J. Jäger (eds), *Assessments of Regional and Global Environmental Risks*, Resources for the Future: Washington DC, pp. 166–186.

Social Learning Group (2001), *Learning to Manage Global Environmental Risks*, MIT Press: Cambridge, MA.

Sparrer, I. (2007), *Miracle, Solution and System – Solution-Focused Systemic Structural Constellations for Therapy and Organisational Change*, SolutionsBooks: Cheltenham.

Spillemaeckers, S., Van Ootegem, L. and Westerhof, G.J. (2011), From individual well-being to sustainable development: a path where psychologists and economists meet, Chapter 4, this volume.

Stirling, A. (2001), A novel approach to the appraisal of technological risk: a multicriteria mapping study of a genetically modified crop, *Environment and Planning C-Government and Policy*, 19(4): 529–555.

Swyngedouw, E. (1997), Neither global nor local: 'glocalization' and the politics of scale, in K.R. Cox (ed.), *Spaces of Globalization: Reasserting the Power of the Local*, Guilford Press: New York/London.

Tàbara, J.D. and Pahl-Wostl, C. (2007), Sustainability learning in natural resource use and management, *Ecology and Society*, 12(2): Article 3, online, available at: www.ecologyandsociety.org/vol12/iss2/art3/.

Weaver, P. and Jordan, A. (2008), What roles are there for sustainability assessment in the policy process? *International Journal of Sustainable Development*, 3(1–2): 9–32.

Weizsäcker, E.U. von, Lovins, A. and Lovins, H. (1995), *Faktor vier: Doppelter Wohlstand – halbierter Verbrauch: Der neue Bericht an den Club of Rome*, Droemer Knaur: München.

Weizsaecker, E.U. von, Hargroves, K., Smith, M.H., Desha, C. and Sasinopoulos, P. (2009), *Factor Five. Transforming the Global Economy through 80% Improvements in Resource Productivity*, Earthscan: London.

Wilber, K. (1981), *Up from Eden*, Shambhala: Boston, MA.

—— (1995), *Sex, Ecology, Spirituality: The Spirit of Evolution*, Shambhala: Boston, MA.

—— (1997), *The Eye of Spirit. An Integral Vision for a World Gone Slightly Mad*, Shambala: Boston, MA.

Worldwatch Institute (2010), *State of the World 2010 Transforming Cultures from Consumerism to Sustainability*, Earthscan: London.

WWF (2006), *Living Planet Report 2006*, online, available at: http://assets.panda.org/downloads/living_planet_report.pdf.

Index

For Product Safety Concerns and Information please contact our
EU representative GPSR@taylorandfrancis.com Taylor & Francis
Verlag GmbH, Kaufingerstraße 24, 80331 München, Germany